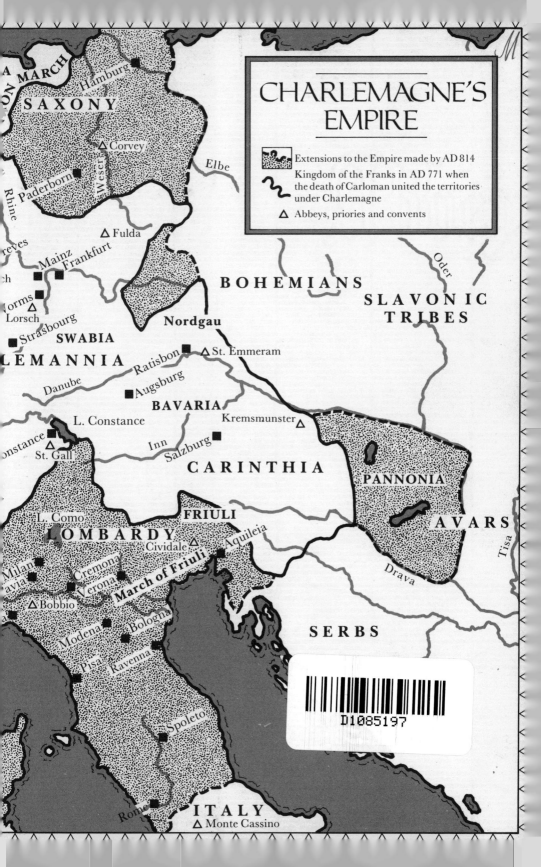

THE EMPEROR:
Charlemagne

THE EMPEROR:
Charlemagne

by
Russell Chamberlin

Franklin Watts
New York
1986

B
Charlemagne

Charlemagne, 742–814
Holy Roman Empire — History

Contents

Illustrations

Acknowledgements

The author is indebted to Messrs Constable and Co. for permission to quote from Helen Waddell's translation of the *Medieval Latin Lyrics*: to Lufthansa and DER for generously providing facilities for a visit to Aachen; and to Dr Ludwig Falkenstein of the University of Aachen for an Aachener's view of their great fellow-citizen. The Cultural Attaché of the Embassy of the Federal Republic of Germany provided invaluable information on the Karlpreis.

Dirge for the Dead of the Battle of Fontenoy,
fought between the grandsons of Charlemagne on
25 June 841, so beginning the break-up of the Empire

When the dawn at early morning drove the sullen night away
Treachery of Saturn was it, not the holy Sabbath day
Over peace of brothers broken, joys the Fiend in devilry

Cry of war is here and yonder, fierce the fighting that outbroke
Brother brings to death his brother, this man slays his sister's son
Son against his father fighting, ancient kindnesses fordone.

Never was there wilder slaughter, never in the field of Mars
Law of Christ is broken, broken, Christian blood is shed like rain
And the throat of Cerberus belling maketh glad the hosts of hell.

Fontenoy they call it, once a springing well and little farm
There where now is blood and slaughter and the ruin of the Franks
Shuddering the fields and copses, shuddering the very swamp

Yea, I Angilbertus saw it, the whole deed of horror done
I that make a rhyme upon it, there was fighting with the rest,
And alone am left surviving of that foremost battle line

I looked back upon the valley and the summit of the hill
When Lothair strong king and valiant, scattered them before his
    sword
Drove them flying on before him to the crossing of the ford.

Yea, but whether they were men of Charles or men of Louis there,
Now the fields are bleached to whiteness with the white shrouds of the
    slain
Even as they bleach in autumn with the coming of the gulls

Be no glory of that battle, never let that fight be sung
From his rising in the morning to the setting of the sun
South and North, bewail them who in that ill chance to death were
    done

Cursed be the day that saw it, in the circuit of the year
Count it not, let it be razed from the memory of men
Never shine the sun upon it, nor its twilight break in dawn

Angilbert, fl.841
Translated from the Latin by Helen Waddell

Introduction

A geographical globe shows a truth about Europe which is not immediately evident upon a map: Europe is not even a continent but merely a peninsula of a continent. It would have been reasonable to expect that this small, densely populated finger of land would long ago have become one nation. The fact that it has not done so is, in part, its strength: the conflict and tension between the European 'nations' created the European dynamic that allowed it to influence an entire planet.

That is on the credit side. But, on the debit side, is the awful series of wars that, century after century, have torn the peninsula apart. Italians against Italians; Spanish against Belgians; Dutch against English; British against Germans; Germans against French . . . the Hundred Years War; the Thirty Years War; the Napoleonic Wars; World War I; World War II; followed by organized terrorism as isolated ethnic pockets strive, too, for national status. Only now, after the blood-letting of World War II showed just where that path was leading, has Europe attempted to return to the path abandoned 1100 years ago at the Battle of Fontenoy and try, at least, to make one state or one nation again out of the peninsula. The glib, standard gibe that the Holy Roman Empire whose foundations were laid by Charlemagne was never holy, Roman or an empire is true enough but, like all glib gibes, misses the essential point: for over a thousand years Europeans thought it ought to exist, or actually acted as though it existed even while they knew they were falling short of the great ideal. The ideal flourishes again, if only fraily. On each Ascension Day, in Charlemagne's own beloved city of Aachen and in the actual remains of his great palace, a ceremony is held which symbolizes this ideal: the citizens of Aachen bestow the Charlemagne Prize (Karlspreis) upon the statesman – of whatever nationality – who has done most to forward the cause of Nation Europe.

This, the ideal of European unity, is the underlying theme of the present book. We can see now that Charlemagne was not the last of the Romans, as he has been romantically and misguidedly cast, but the first of the Europeans unconsciously foreshadowing the twentieth-century attempt. He did not hesitate to use the awesome magic of the name of Rome for his own purposes, but it was in order to protect a new and untried structure and not to prop up an old and tottering building. Most outward signs of what he created disappeared within a generation of his death, for he was over a millennium too early. But the dynamic continued, subtly guiding the aspirations of untold generations. And how his fellow Europeans regarded his reign is shown by the fact that, within a generation, they looked back upon the Carolingian empire as to a Golden Age and promoted its creator to rank with the legendary heroes of Europe along with Siegfried and Achilles and Arthur and Merlin.

Few subjects in European history have been so relentlessly dissected over the past few decades as the Carolingian achievement. Inevitably, the pendulum has tended to swing the other way and after centuries of literal adulation Charlemagne has emerged as a man feeling his way in an unprecedented situation, and not a species of demi-god imposing order. Some scholars, indeed, would deny that he achieved anything of lasting significance. Yet, like some great chord of music whose last echoes remain only just within the range of sound, the echo of what he created continues. It is summed up coolly, cautiously, by the British scholar D. A. Bullough in an essay assessing Charlemagne's achievements in the light of recent scholarship. While arguing that the Carolingian influence can easily be traced in art and literature, 'It is more difficult to recognise it in the concepts and values – until recently tacitly accepted rather than defined – which have given a unity to the variegated political and cultural experiences of post-Carolingian Europe and offer a hope (although a diminishing one) for a continuing, distinctively European, solution to the human predicament' ('Europae Pater: Charlemagne and his achievement in the light of recent scholarship', *English Historical Review*, LXXXV, 1970).

PART I · *The Cauldron of Europe*

It is the duty of a patriot to prefer and promote the exclusive interest and glory of his native country: but a philosopher may be permitted to enlarge his views and to consider Europe as one great Republic.

Edward Gibbon, *Decline and Fall of the Roman Empire*

I The Kingdom of the Franks

They come into our vision from out of the total darkness beyond the Rhine and the Danube to be illuminated fitfully but brilliantly by the light of civilization. A handsome, large-boned, fair-skinned people addicted to rich, vivid colours, the men clean-shaven with close-cut hair, the women and tribal chiefs wearing their hair long, for no woman fought in battle and no enemy would ever have the leisure to grasp a chief's hair while his companions lived. Originally they were loosely grouped round a war-band leader. This association, though loosely structured, was a mutual bond of such strength that it could be dissolved only by death. Tacitus brought his lucid Latin mind to bear upon this aspect of their nature and he, citizen of a state whose head was worshipped or murdered according to political need, was interested and amused by – and, it would seem, a touch envious of – that system which he called a *comitatus*, the group of men round a single strong man, each sworn to defend the other till death. Unlike their fellow Teutons they were no horsemen; in defeat in battle they had no means of flight, if they considered flight, and it was perhaps that stark necessity which created the bond between them. And, unlike their fellow Teutons again, unlike the Vandals and the Goths and the Ostrogoths and the Herulians and the Gepids, they would retain their name throughout history, passing it down through the centuries only slightly changed. In course of time it would pass into most European languages as an adjective and synonym for all that was free and manly and open and 'frank'. So powerful was their influence that, outside Europe, the Islamic enemies of Europe would call all the inhabitants of that turbulent peninsula 'Franks'.

The Franks began crossing the Rhine, settling in the Rhineland and in what is now Holland and Belgium, from the mid-third century onwards. And they crossed, and settled, by invitation, for the vast structure of the Roman Empire was still intact with the great city at its heart and the undefeated army throwing a bronze wall around it from Scotland to Persia. But the structure was already creaking under its own weight and the presence of those little bands of Frankish soldiers, hired to defend what the citizens of Rome could not themselves bother to defend, was an indication of things to come. In the past Rome had used barbarian mercenaries with great skill, using them first as auxiliaries and then, with judicious gifts of land, turning them into good citizens. The value of a mercenary lay precisely in the fact that he had no roots and to ensure that its auxiliaries did not become dangerously attached to any one part of the empire, the army moved them around in an endless game of chess – Iberians to Britain, Pannonians to Gaul, Teutons to Persia. But gradually, as the years became decades and the decades centuries, that wholesome restlessness slowed down and became, at last, stasis. The barbarians began to make themselves at home; the Franks began to root themselves in northern Gaul.

One of the great romantic myths of history portrays the 'Fall of the Roman Empire' as a species of Hollywood scenario in which shaggy, skin-clad 'barbarians' hurl themselves upon elegant, cultured 'Romans', raping, murdering, destroying what they could not eat, wear or carry off. The 'barbarians' were inferior in culture, not in intelligence: they could, and did, respond to the majesty of the empire. For a people without records, that empire must have seemed, quite literally, eternal: an almost supernatural structure around which the world always had and would revolve. The outward evidences of that structure were impressive enough: the broad, handsome roads down which an army could march hour after hour without varying its pace; the aqueducts and pipes which brought water to the people, instead of obliging the people to seek water; the bridges which effortlessly spanned great rivers or awesome chasms; the buildings of brick and stone and marble which brought together tens of thousands of humans in one area. All this would have had its effect upon a people whose world was bounded by the endless forests, whose roads were the rough narrow paths through those forests, whose tribal groups would be numbered in hundreds rather than thousands. But they were also intelligent enough to realize that none of this outward show was accidental or the result of magic, that behind it was a hugely complex human system. The Visigothic chieftain Arhalhauf spoke for most of his fellow barbarians when he summed the matter up thus, towards the end of the fourth century:

It was at first my wish to destroy the Roman name, and erect in its place a Gothic empire, taking to myself the place and powers of Caesar Augustus. But when experience taught me that the untamable barbarism of the Goths would not suffer them to live beneath the sway of law, and that the abolition of the institutions on which the State rested would involve the ruin of the State itself, I chose the glory of renewing and maintaining by Gothic strength the fame of Rome, desiring to go down to posterity as the restorer of that Roman power which it was beyond my power to destroy.

The Franks, indeed, enter history fighting side by side with the Roman army in one of its last great battles, that of Châlons which first checked, then held and finally turned back one of the most truly destructive of barbarian invasions, that of the Huns under Attila. The leader, or captain or chief, of the Frankish host was a man called Merovech. We know nothing whatsoever about him before, during or after the battle. We know only his sex, his race and his name, but he must have done something extraordinary to have attracted the attention of his fellow Franks for his name, transformed into Meroving was to become, quite literally, sacred – the name of the dynasty of kings who ruled the Franks for over two centuries, until thrust aside by the father and the uncle of Charlemagne.

Merovech may have belonged almost wholly to legend but his son, Childeric, belonged entirely to history for his tomb was discovered, accidentally, at Tournai in what is now France in 1653. And its contents established, at once and for ever, that these Merovingians were no muscular savages but, by AD 482 – the year of Childeric's death – were members of a civilization. So rich indeed were the contents of that tomb that most were stolen when thieves raided the Imperial Art Gallery in Paris in 1853. But they had been recorded, both pictorially and literally, and from the descriptions and the remaining artefacts it is possible to piece together something of the life-style of a fifth-century Frank. And what emerges, immediately, is that Childeric regarded himself as a direct successor of the Roman masters of Gaul. In addition to the old animal motifs, which had decorated the ornaments of his ancestors, was the balance and symmetry of Rome whether in the form of actual antique gems mounted in relatively crude Frankish settings, or in designs which attempted to copy that fashion, as in his seal ring with a portrait bust and the Latin inscription *Childerici Regis*.

A half-legendary figure, and the occupant of a tomb introduces the Franks; but now the story moves more rapidly into the clear light of history with Childeric's son, known to his contemporaries as

Chlodovech, but to posterity as Clovis.* Born in AD 465 he was sixteen years old when he ascended the still shadowy throne of the Merovings and was barely twenty when he launched himself and his nation upon a whirlwind campaign of conquest. By now, the end of the Roman Empire in the north-west, at least, was plainly in sight. The legions had long since been withdrawn from Britain, the most northerly outpost; even in Italy itself expeditionary forces sent by the emperor from the safety of Constantinople inflicted only temporary reverses on the waves of newcomers all anxious to feast on the lush land. In Gaul, the great structure was plainly collapsing leaving Clovis with two choices: he could either ally himself with the power which had made his nation and his family great, loyally defending it to the last, or he could turn upon it and rend it in a general free-for-all, grabbing what he could in the process. And being the kind of man he was, he turned upon it and rended it, now allying himself with neighbouring tribes in a concerted attack upon the remains of Rome, now betraying the alliance as expediency dictated, never giving quarter, never showing mercy. He killed all possible rivals to his leadership, no matter how close their relationship; he killed all those who fell into his hands through the chance of war and who might later pose a threat. He had one objective, and one only: to push out from those cold, flat lands and marshes of the north down towards the rich lands of the south, to the valleys of the Seine and the Loire and even the fabled lands beyond, Provence the lush daughter of Rome.

But Clovis was no mere thick-necked killer. At the very outset of the Frankish dominance of the west he encountered, recognized and did his brilliant best to solve one overriding problem: communication and control. Later, after the reign of Charlemagne, that problem would become virtually insuperable as the network of roads and posting towns collapsed. Thereafter, as communication deteriorated it became impossible to impose any form of overall control. In Clovis's day, still enough of the infrastructure survived to be adapted, if crudely adapted, to his needs. But he had to take one simple, irrevocable step. He became a Christian. To be exact, he became a Christian professing the faith according to the Orthodox Catholic Church.

In any discussion of the life-style of the so-called 'Dark Ages' it is essential to try and establish what the word 'religion' meant to the

---

*A final metamorphosis of the name into 'Louis' provided probably the longest run of monarchic titles from Louis I to Louis XVIII, kings of France.

inhabitants of those ages and what it means to us. For we are using the same word to describe two quite different human phenomena. The twentieth century is far more in tune with Classical Rome, or even with Classical Greece, in regarding religion as being, privately, a matter of a personal moral code and, publicly, a matter of ceremonial designed to display communal unity. The long-drawn-out battle between Church and State has ended not so much with the defeat of the Church, as of the Church drawing aside from the mêlée of daily politics. The position of the Vatican, a religious island in a secular sea, symbolizes the whole. In only a few countries can the ancient, dangerous synthesis be seen at work: in Northern Ireland, in Poland, perhaps; in some Islamic countries – Iran, certainly, Saudi Arabia perhaps, and Pakistan – none of them very happy examples of the effect.

The separation of Church and State is a new phenomenon. From the triumph of Christianity in the fourth and fifth centuries, to the triumph of Puritanism in the seventeenth century, the interacting ferment was at work. Governments of whatever race, and of whatever cast of thought, were perfectly prepared to behead, impale, burn and, in general, slaughter hecatombs of their subjects in defence of some subtle interpretation of theology, while those subjects were as fully prepared to bring about the agonizing deaths of their fellow citizens, overturn their governments and plunge their country into anarchy in order to see the triumph of their particular interpretation. The final break between the eastern and western Roman empires indeed was on a point of religious practice, the worship of images. It is difficult to account both for the speed of establishment of this trend of thought, following so swiftly on the vast tolerance of the Roman Empire, and for the universality of its spread among people for whose immediate forebears religion was a set of practices rather than beliefs.

So it was likely that the pagan Clovis would, either for political or personal purposes, make a religious decision. But, again, he had two choices of the form of Christian worship he could adopt. That practice of Christianity that was later known as Roman Catholicism – a form of worship adopted by the bishop of Rome and his flock – was by no means dominant at the time that Clovis made his decision. Challenging it was the form of Christian belief known as Arianism from Arius, the Alexandrian theologian who tossed it into the already seething pool of Christian controversy in the early fourth century. With dangerous logic he argued that, if Christ had been begotten, there must have been a time when he did not exist; therefore he could not be regarded as eternal;

therefore he could not be consubstantial (of the same substance) as the Father. The belief was condemned at the Council of Nicaea in AD 325 when the Nicene Crede made its appearance. Nevertheless, Arianism spread throughout Christianity – and spread not only among the poor and ignorant, but among the rich and powerful. It appeared at the Byzantine court; it appeared among the Visigothic conquerors of Spain and the Lombard conquerors of Italy; it appeared among the Burgundians and the Ostrogoths. But it did not appear in Gaul. This great fragment of the Roman Empire clung still to the Roman beliefs. Clovis adopted that belief and instantaneously ensured the support of all its holders in the area most vital to him.

It was not only the theological or spiritual attributes of Christianity that made Clovis's baptism a fulcrum of European history: the Christian Church could offer such a man as him a truly priceless gift – the gift of order. Another of the great myths of history, akin to that myth of the barbarians destroying Rome, is the myth of Christianity eroding the very basis of the Roman world, substituting its pale, life-denying creed for the robust certainties of Rome. The English-speaking world is particularly susceptible to this myth for it is enshrined and promoted by one of its most brilliant historians and most polished writers, Edward Gibbon. And Gibbon hid a hatred of Christianity behind a veil woven of wit and irony and logic and sheer beauty of language. Later he was to describe how, on an October evening in Rome in 1764 he, a young man of twenty-seven, 'was moving amidst the ruins of the Capitol while the bare-footed friars were singing vespers in the temple of Jupiter' and had that moment of vision which was to lead to the writing of his enormous work. No reader can mistake his meaning: the ruins of the Capitol and the presence of the friars were related, the one causing the condition of the other. Gibbon set the trend for the subtle denigration of Christianity, encapsulated at last by the lush nineteenth-century poet Swinburne, 'Thou hast conquered, O pale Galilean: the world is grown grey from thy breath'.

Whereas, of course, long before Christianity emerged as an alternative, the great institutions of Rome were already showing signs of stress. And when they tottered and fell, they left a space – but it was a clearly defined space, waiting for an occupant, and that occupant was the nascent Church. In Rome itself, the once humble bishop of Rome would not only occupy the place of the emperor but take some of his titles, the potent *Pontifex Maximus* among them. In the provinces, those 'dioceses' which had been the unit of civil administration, each under its *propraetor*, easily and naturally fitted themselves around the newly-created bishops. The dynamic of the empire continued, if in modified form and for a different end, and he who could link himself with that framework had created an immensely efficient tool of monarchy.

And more. Not only had he ensured political success in his own time, but immortality and justification after his death, for from the first the Church had recognized the enormous power of the written word and after the secular and pagan historians and chroniclers and poets of pagan Rome had gone to their grave, the totality of learning was in the hands of the clergy. Seventy years after Clovis, there appeared the Gallo-Roman historian, Gregory, Bishop of Tours, and it was largely through Gregory that posterity learned of the exploits of Clovis. His lethal proclivities now appear as God-given, for following the custom of medieval clerics Gregory automatically classified the spilling of pagan, or heretical, blood as a pious action. It is he who tells the story of the chalice of Soissons which all but guarantees Clovis a place in heaven. After the capture of Soissons, a valuable chalice was taken as loot. Clovis, according to Gregory, wanted to return it to the Church but a Frankish soldier insisted on following custom and split the chalice in two with an axe 'Half for each'. Even a king could not gainsay custom and Clovis, perforce, submitted. But as soon as the opportunity presented itself, Clovis split the soldier's skull, crying 'Thus didst thou treat the chalice of Soissons'.

However suspect Clovis's religious conversion might be, there is no doubting whatsoever that he, too, regarded himself as a successor of the Roman masters of Gaul. No matter that the emperor was now a Greek in Byzantium, or that the empire as a going structure was palpably at an end, as Clovis's own successes showed, still he demanded those outward symbols which were the sign of legitimacy. Reverently, almost humbly, this formidable Frank who now ruled over most of what had been Gaul petitioned the emperor for the office and symbols of consul. And the Emperor Anastasius, marvelling perhaps at the gullibility of the Frank, was graciously pleased to give that which he had no means of withholding. Dressed in the richly embroidered robes of a consul, Clovis rode through the city of Tours while the people, says Gregory, proclaimed him as Augustus.

Clovis was the true founder not only of the Merovingians, but of the first state to root itself permanently in the rich tilth of the empire. Others had attempted and seemed, indeed, destined to a far more brilliant future than this Gallo-Frankish hybrid: the Ostrogoths and Lombards in Italy, the Vandals in North Africa, Visigoths in the Iberian peninsula, all had a head start on the Franks. But each, in time, disappeared, victims of the same Mediterranean restlessness that had allowed them to establish themselves in the first place. Clovis, by contrast, was carving out his kingdom far from the established places of power, still maintaining his links with his Germanic origins with all its freshness and vigour.

But Clovis, King of the Franks, was also a man of his time and his race and no Frank had yet fully grasped the idea of territorial power. Even Charlemagne, in the fullness of time, would style himself King of the Franks and not 'King of Francia', Roman Emperor and not 'Emperor of Rome'. The kingdom which Clovis had so vigorously acquired was an idea rather than a place, a personal estate to be disposed of as he, personally, thought fit rather than a state to be handed over to a chosen successor. He was merely following Frankish custom when, at his death at the age of forty-five in 511, he divided the kingdom between his four sons. This action triggered off nearly two centuries of bloodshed as the inheritors fought among themselves for dominance. Three centuries later his descendant Charlemagne would blindly follow the same custom, in turn triggering off endless bloodshed from the same cause.

Clovis's kingdom was immense in extent, a testimony to the extraordinary energy and administrative genius of the man. In modern terms he had conquered all of France, all of the Low Countries, all of Switzerland, most of Germany as far as the Elbe (with the exception of a Saxon enclave around modern Hanover which would give Charlemagne a lifetime's problem). He had added Burgundy and Bavaria and most of Aquitaine – all quite distinct entities – to what was now known as Francia or Frankland, the name 'Gaul' already receding into history. He had no one capital but moved his court, as need required, from Metz to Orleans, from Paris to Cologne or Soissons.

Each of these conquered territories had customs and laws of its own so that the 'kingdom' was at best a loose federation having in common only the last dilution of Roman law. The confusion was further compounded by the ancient tribal division of the Franks themselves. They fell into two main groups or tribes: the Salians, originally occupying north-east France and the Low Countries, and the Ripuarians, occupying the Rhine and Moselle valleys. In due course the homeland of the Salians became known as Neustria (the 'New Lands') and of the Ripuarians as Austrasia (the East Lands—part of the name survives as 'Austria'). In addition to the ordinary stresses and rivalries set up between the various groups was the rivalry between Austrasia, which tended to regard itself as the archetypal Frankish homeland, and Neustria, the more Romanized portion of the 'kingdom'.

Genius might have allowed Clovis to rule this remarkable hetero-geneous kingdom of his – but it was a genius which did not disdain to draw upon the moribund empire for its techniques. The mighty ghost of Rome still haunted its Germanic usurpers. Memory of that vast marble complex on the Palatine Hill, the very seat of the emperors, continued in the name 'palatium': the court of Clovis and his successors might be as restlessly peripatetic as that of any nomad, but it was known as a 'palace'. The officials in the provinces to whom he confided local control were known as *comites* – counts. And the trusted counsellors whom he sent out to oversee the work of these men were the *missi dominici* – the Messengers of the Lord.

The system worked because the relatively unsophisticated Franks took only what they wanted, or could understand, from a system that had become too complex for its own good. It worked for nearly two centuries and, coming at last into the hands of Charlemagne, proved flexible and strong enough to be the basis of a continent-wide empire. Indeed, it was strong enough and flexible enough to work despite the 'sacred kings' at its centre.

It is a truism that it is the victors who write history and it was obviously to the advantage of Carolingian apologists to blacken the character of the Merovingian kings. On their behalf, too, the Merovingians could argue that, in the absence of the custom of primogeniture, they were cursed with that need to divide inheritance with all its concomitant hatreds. Clovis himself had not hesitated to eliminate all possible rivals to the crown and, with that precedent it was, perhaps, understandable that his four sons should follow the same system. Admittedly, they took it to extremes: when one brother died the others, instead of hastening to the succour of his widow and orphans, slaughtered them – one brother, Chlothar, personally cutting the throats of the children.

But even when all these allowances are made, there does seem to have been something approaching madness on the part of the Merovingians, in all the males and some of the females. The English historian, J. A. Symonds, in trying to define the characteristics of Renaissance tyrants, coined the word *haematomania* – blood madness – to account for the delight some of them seemed to experience in the actual physical spilling of blood and the inflicting of extreme agony when a simple execution would, politically, suffice. Such a term would well apply to Chlothar, the final survivor: when his son rebelled against him, he was not content simply with executing him but confined the young man, his wife and small children in a hut, set fire to it and watched and listened while they burned to death. Chlothar's successor, Chilperic, earned the title of 'Nero and Herod of his time' from Gregory of Tours, and indeed his reign in Neustria resembled the rule of the emperors in Rome at Rome's most decadent. The hideous punishment of gouging out the eyes, introduced from the Byzantine court, was inflicted for minor breaches of the law. He strangled his wife Galswintha in order to marry his mistress, thus launching a murderous family feud, for his brother Sigebert, king of the Austrasians, was married to Galswintha's sister Brunhildis. Sigebert was murdered by Chlothar's mistress. Brunhildis, maddened now with hatred and grief, took up the feud in her turn. Chlothar was murdered, leaving a baby son. Brunhildis now ruled as queen in Austrasia, another Boadicea, it seems, fierce, utterly ruthless, using assassination as readily as any of her male relatives and rivals until even the Austrasians had had enough and tied her, living, to a ferocious wild horse . . . So the *haematomania* of the Merovingians was transmitted from generation to generation, ending only when the will to live itself petered out and the dynasty mewled itself into extinction, helped there by the rising Carolingians.

However, blood madness did not necessarily exclude culture. Even Chilperic could have held up his head in any Renaissance court: he was a poet and musician of some distinction; he reformed the German alphabet and went some considerable way in reducing the draconic effect of the tribal Salic law upon women. This we know of him, even though much of it comes to us through chroniclers hostile to him and his house. The few fragments of Merovingian sculpture that survive show a level of culture that would not be surpassed for five centuries. But only in our own time has an objective picture of the level of Merovingian culture – the culture into which Charlemagne was born – become possible.

On the night of 31 May/1 June 1942 the city of Cologne became the target for the first massed air raid. During the six or seven hours between sunset and sunrise of that clear summer night, a thousand heavy aircraft of the Royal Air Force unloaded their tonnage of bombs in wave after wave. Over the following two years, aircraft of the RAF and USAAF took it in turns, by day and by night, to pound the city. Even as late as 1950, Cologne resembled nothing so much as a vast rubbish dump composed of brick rubble and burnt timber – with one extraordinary survival: the cathedral.

Cologne, under its name of Colonia Agrippina, was the furthest city of the Roman north-west, washed by the Rhine, looking east towards the trackless forests and swamps whence came the Germanic tribes. The cathedral is built well within the old Roman circumvallation and, though its spires were not completed until the nineteenth century, its foundations are rooted in Carolingian and Merovingian churches. Miraculously, it survived the bombing, but so shaken that one of the first tasks of the reviving city was to look to the great building. In restoring the foundations, excavations were made deeper than ever before. In 1959 one of these excavations, beneath the choir, encountered two richly furnished graves. One was that of a child – a little boy about six years old; the other that of a woman. A coin found in the woman's grave placed her death as taking place some time after 526 – at about the time that Chlothar succeeded to the throne. Neither grave bore any identification but, apart from the richness of their contents the fact that they were buried here, in what would have been even in the sixth century Cologne's major church, argues that they were members of the royal house. Despite the fact that t'.ese were Christian burials, the mourners followed the pagan custom of burying grave goods with them for use in the next world. The little boy had a beautifully-made child's helmet, as well as a set of adult battle-gear: sword, spears, battle-axe, bow and arrows, shield. He had no ornaments except a gold ring and what was presumed to be a sceptre. The woman, by contrast, had been buried with a quantity of exquisite jewellery as well as such domestic goods as bronze bowls, glass vessels and a silver-mounted drinking horn.

These were the first major Merovingian graves discovered since that of Childeric in 1653. But, almost immediately, another grave was discovered which was not only even richer, but illustrated the extent of the Merovingian kingdom, for this grave was found in the crypt of the abbey church of St Denis in Paris. And, unlike the Cologne burial, this was precisely identifiable for on the finger of its occupant, a female in her early forties, was a gold ring bearing the words ARNEGUNDIS REGINE. There is only one Queen Arnegunde in European history, and that was the wife of Chlothar. The body was in a well-made limestone coffin, lying on a bright red blanket, dressed in a linen undergarment with a tunic of violet silk and a veil of red satin. Even without the profusion of jewellery, this burial would have pointed not only to the fact that the occupant was of a high class, but came from a rich society. The silk that caressed her body had travelled thousands of miles to this northern city from the Far East; the satin probably came from Italy; the jewellery, by contrast, was local. Not only was it beautifully made, evidence of a highly sophisticated industry, but the artists had confidently used Germanic forms, whereas these had been banished completely from the jewellery found in Childeric's tomb. In the ninety-odd years that had elapsed between Childeric's death in 482, and Arnegunde's death in 570, the Merovings had passed from an almost slavish imitation of Roman forms and Roman customs to the confident development of their own. The Franks had come of age.

But the 'sacred kings' themselves were in decline. The ferocious energy which had propelled Clovis from the status of a tribal chief to that of king, the energy which had enabled his sons and grandsons to consolidate his gains, even if they fought mercilessly among themselves had, by the 650s, wholly dwindled away. The 'sacred kings' were now effete, pleasure-loving young men, who found early graves – not, as their immediate forebears did, through violent death whether in battle or at the hands of a fratricide, but simply worn out through excesses. What those 'excesses' were we can only guess. The chroniclers hint at the usual causes, an excess of wine and sexual exertion, and their age at death would seem to indicate some such cause of unrestricted self-indulgence. A graph would show a spectacular decline in ages from that of Clovis, who died at the reasonable age of forty-five, to Clovis II, dead at the age of twenty-four in 656; Chlothar III, dead in 660 aged eighteen; Childeric II, dead at the age of twenty in 673. The last kings, before the Carolingians finally thrust them aside, died in their teens.

Einhard, Charlemagne's personal friend and meticulous biographer, provides the most vivid and (allowing for the fact that he is writing nearly a century after the deposition of the last Merovingian) the most authoritative account of these last wretched years of the Merovingian dynasty:

> The King, contented with the mere royal title, with long hair and flowing beard, used to sit upon the throne and act the part of ruler, listening to ambassadors, whencesoever they came, and giving them at their departure, as though of his own power, answers which he had been instructed or commanded to give. But this was the only function that he performed, for besides the empty royal title and the precarious life income which the Mayor

of the Palace allowed him at his pleasure, he had nothing of his own except one estate with a very small revenue on which he had his house, and from which he drew the few servants who performed such services as were necessary and made him a show of deference. Wherever he had to go he travelled in a wagon, drawn in rustic style, and driven by a cowherd. In this fashion he used to go to the palace and the general meetings of the people: in this fashion he returned home.

Einhard's contempt leads him into some historical inaccuracies. The wagon 'drawn in rustic style by a pair of oxen' was a ceremonial honour of the early Franks; passing into Italy, indeed, it became the *carrocio*, the ox-drawn cart which carried a city's shrine and banner into battle during the long-drawn-out wars between the city states. The 'long hair and flowing beard', too, were not badges of decadence as he seems to imply but were the outward signs of royalty, a survival from the primitive days when the chiefs wore their hair long to distinguish themselves in battle. But his contempt was shared by others, becoming ever more scathing as the centuries passed, until at last a French historian coined for these last Merovingians the lapidic phrase *rois fainéants* and, as the 'do-nothing' kings, they are lodged finally in European history.

Looking back at those kings, eighteenth- and nineteenth-century historians found themselves wholly at a loss to account for their continued parasitic existence. Indeed, when an energetic would-be rival, a man called Grimoald (of that Carolingian house which would eventually succeed them) attempted to usurp the wholly useless Dagobert III, the Franks actually rose in rage and killed him. The great nineteenth-century historian of Italy's invaders, Thomas Hodgkin, summed up the opinion of his colleagues, marvelling at the fact that the Franks seemingly willingly continued to nourish these drones at the expense of the kingdom's welfare. 'Immersed in his swinish pleasures, with his constitution ruined by his early excesses, what could the sickly youth, the Childebert or Chlothair of the day, do to overtake the mass of business which the administration of the realm, with its highly centralised mechanism, imposed upon him.' And seeking parallels in his own day for this extraordinary state of affairs, Hodgkin could find only the Mikado of Japan whose Shogun ruled in his name, 'while depriving him of every shred of actual power [furnishing] the closest parallels in all history to the relation of the Frankish *major domus* to the Merovingian king'.

The twentieth century, with its powerless constitutional monarchs, has perhaps a clearer idea of the role of the supposed *rois fainéants* than nineteenth-century historians with their robust, clear-cut view of the role of the monarch in society. Einhard's description of the king delivering speeches to ambassadors 'which he had been instructed or commanded to give' exactly corresponds to the Speech from the Throne which the British monarch delivers on the opening of Parliament, a speech whose every word has been written by the elected government but is delivered by the monarch as though it were a personal command to that government. And there is no indication that an attempt to remove that monarch would meet anything but the most profound and active resentment from the monarch's supposed subjects. British customs are, perhaps, extreme in this matter but similar factors are operating among the surviving monarchies of Europe and, in one case – that of Spain – the *rois fainéant* has actually been brought back after a generation in exile. If some of the oldest, most stable nations in twentieth-century, technological, egalitarian Europe still regard themselves as pyramid-shaped, with a monarch essential to complete the structure, how much more so would the Kingdom of the Franks, emerging out of the chaos of the collapsed empire, seeking a role in a bewildering new world.

Einhard was the first to notice, and record, the development of a phenomenon produced by that vacuum at the centre of power: the emergence of an official called the Mayor of the Palace. 'The wealth and power of the kingdom was in the hands of the Praefects of the Court, who were called Mayors of the Palace, and exercised entire sovereignty, looking after the administration of the kingdom and all that had to be arranged at home or abroad.' He is a familiar figure in history, this *éminence grise*, this shadowy man behind the gorgeous trappings of power whose hands are firmly upon the actual levers of power: Cardinal Richelieu to Louis XIII, the Grand Vizier to the Sultan of Turkey and, in our own time, Martin Bormann to Adolph Hitler are among the best known. But such shadowy men prefer to remain in the background either because they lack the leader's charisma, as with Bormann, or because the front man is indeed little more than a puppet, as with Louis XIII. What is unusual in the case of the Mayors of the Palace is that they gradually emerge in the foreground, not only openly and contemptuously pulling the strings but, in the fullness of time, discarding the puppet altogether, taking on its title and trappings while retaining still their own true power.

It is curious, and perhaps indicative of the fusion of Latin elements into Merovingian culture, that this essentially Germanic office should be known only by a Latin name, the *major domus*. Each palace of the kings had its mayor; originally, indeed, each king would probably have had several mayors, one for each of his estates and probably even for different functions within the household. But gradually, one powerful man emerged as mayor in each palace and as the Frankish kingdom polarized into two parts, west and east, so the natures of the mayors also changed. The mayors of Neustria tended to side with the king against the nobles, the mayors of Austrasia followed the reverse. Because of the tendency to drift from east to west (an Austrasian king inheriting from a Neustrian would usually take up residence in Paris or Soissons) the Austrasian mayors not only grew ever more powerful in the absence of their titular lord, but gradually made their office hereditary. Judging by the comments of unsophisticated contemporary chroniclers they were usually vigorous, competent, quite unscrupulous and decidedly unpopular. A certain Protadius is described as being 'a man of great cleverness and energy in all that he undertook, but fierce was his injustice to private persons. Straining too far the rights of the treasury, he strove to fill it and to enrich himself by ingenious attacks on private property'. But the Franks were still Franks, not so far removed from primitive origins when social injustice was rapidly resolved by a sword-cut. Despite the attempt of his master to save him, Protadius paid the penalty of overweening pride in a virile society. His successor was Claudius, 'a Roman by descent, a prudent man, a pleasant story-teller . . . Taking warning by the example of those who had gone before him, he bore himself gently and patiently in his high office, but this only hindrance had he, that he was burdened with too great fatness of body'.

But a corpulent, easy-going mayor was an anomaly. Survival in such an office with the necessity, on the one hand, of abstracting legal power from the source of legality and, on the other, of keeping at bay, or placating, or suppressing a formidable laity demanded an unusual combination of skills – the kind of skills that would inevitably lead to the highest of all offices.

The changeover took over a century, from the murder of Brunhildis in 613 to the crowning of the first mayor in 754. It began bloodily, murderously; it ended smoothly, legalistically, and it demonstrated above all the enormous power of the Church, even a church still grateful for and totally dependent upon the support of the secular arm. The effective instrument of the changeover was Arnulf, Bishop of Metz; so effective that his descendants (he was married and had children before becoming bishop) were known as Arnulfings until the greatest of them,

Charlemagne, obscured the founder's name with his own so that the dynasty was thereafter known as the Carolingian. It is mostly from Carolingian apologists that posterity learns of Arnulf as being an upright, virtuous, learned man – so virtuous, indeed, that in due course he will become a saint of the Christian Church.

He may have been all these things, but, according to the admittedly tortuous and obscure account of events transmitted by the chroniclers, it was he who in concert with a mayor of the palace presided over, or at least acquiesced in, the hideous death of Queen Brunhildis. In order to overthrow the old tigress, they called in Chlothar, King of Neustria who, after her military defeat, indulged his Merovingian *haematomania* to the fullest. The old woman – she must have been in her late sixties – was first publicly humiliated (curiously, by being led through the camp seated on a camel), then tortured for three days and finally murdered by being tied by her hair, one arm and one leg to a wild horse. Her young grandchildren, the last true heirs of Clovis, were also murdered.

Doubtless all this was done at the direct instigation of Chlothar. But, in the long run, it was the dynasty founded by Pippin and Arnulf who benefited, for a son of Arnulf married a daughter of Pippin and their greatgrandson was the father of Charlemagne. But though the new dynasty had grasped the levers of power in Austrasia it was still only as agents of the 'sacred king' no matter how worthless that 'sacred king'. It was Pippin's own son, Grimoald, who made that fatal miscalculation when a boy king 'ruled' in Austrasia. Ritually, Grimoald shaved off the lad's royal locks, sent him into a monastery and proclaimed his own son king. He was a hundred years too early and even the stilted words of the chronicler who recorded the sequel convey something of the indignation of a people robbed of their mystic figurehead. 'The Franks, being very indignant thereat, prepared snares for Grimoald and, taking him prisoner, carried him for condemnation to Clovis II, King of the Franks. In the city of Paris he was confined in a dungeon and bound with torturing chains: and at length, as he was worthy of death for what he had done to his lord, death finished him with mighty torments.'

But the power of the Merovingians had resided in their ability to give rich gifts of land to their more dangerous nobles, easy enough during the great period of expansion and conquest, progressively more difficult as the situation stabilized. When the rivalry between Neustria and Austrasia exploded into open civil war, there was actually no king in

Austrasia. It was an Arnulfing, also known as Pippin who, in 687, crushed the Neustrians and emerged as ruler of the Franks, although a ruler without a crown.

2   The House of the Arnulfing

Some time about the year 680 Pippin II, mayor of the combined palaces of Neustria and Austrasia, was seated in quiet conversation with his wife Plectrudis when an excited messenger came into the room. Seeing that the mayor was not alone, he stopped short in some confusion for he had come to announce the birth of a son to the mayor's mistress. The Franks were, admittedly, decidedly casual about matrimony, practising what appears to the eyes of posterity as a system differing little from polygamy. But the messenger had a lively awareness of the violent temper of Plectrudis and apparently decided to wrap up his bald message. 'Long live the king,' he called out. 'It is a man' (*carl*). Pippin seems to have shared the general opinion of his wife's temper and was little disposed to enter into any detailed discussion about the new-born child whose advent had been so embarrassingly announced. 'A man is it? Then let him be called that.' In that manner, according to Carolingian legend, one of the most famous personal names in European history came into being. The new-born baby was indeed called Carl. Gallicized into Charles and with the suffix of Martel he would in due course become the grandfather of the most famous Charles of all.

The Arnulfings were now quite undisputed rulers of the Franks, at times indeed ruling without even a king on the throne. But it seemed that they were in danger of inheriting the more self-destructive vices of the Merovingians – in particular the arrogance which sprang from undisputed possession of power, and a lethal tendency towards family feud. Pippin had ruled wisely and well, but on his death-bed he decreed that the vital office of mayor should be inherited by his eight-year-old son, his only surviving legitimate son. In other words, he decreed that the reigning eighteen-year-old king should be advised, guided and

ected by a little boy ten years younger than himself. The logical
ın to have been chosen was Charles, now some twenty-four years of
he Franks would have been indifferent to Charles's illegitimacy
ıey would, and did, react strongly to being ruled by a beldame
.gh her small son. But Plectrudis loathed her stepson Charles. In
'etime Pippin had been wholly unable to affect a reconciliation
ın the two and, immediately upon Pippin's death, Plectrudis
Charles into prison.

However, she had reckoned without the Franks. They were no
Romans or Byzantines to accept, docilely, the rule of a woman merely
because she happened to be the widow of their last ruler. The Neustrians led the revolt. In the confusion, and almost certainly aided by his
late father's friends, Charles escaped from prison. The Frankish state
was on the edge of disintegration with Plectrudis and her son shut up in
Cologne, subject peoples rising, a puppet king making his appearance
and the ferocious undefeated Saxons pressing in from the north.
Charles, in a series of well-aimed massive blows which earned him that
soubriquet of the Hammer, reshaped the state, crushing its external
enemies, ensuring the loyalty of the rebellious elements and disposing,
in some manner, of Plectrudis and her son. The re-establishment of the
state alone would have earned him an honourable, if limited, place in
Frankish history but in 731 he emerged on the European stage as the
champion of all Europe and of Christendom. In that year he defeated an
immense Saracen army at Poitiers.

The receding perspective of history casts into permanent form events
which contemporaries might well regard as temporary. Ever since the
Moors were expelled from Spain by Ferdinand and Isabella in 1492,
Islam has been confined to the southern and eastern shores of the
Mediterranean and, with Christianity occupying all the northern lands
this seems an inevitable division. But it was very nearly not so. In the
ten years before his death in 632 the Prophet Muhammad had united all
Arabia under him, turning that fierce, austere people into a burning
brand with a single aim, the spread of Islam throughout the world. By
the end of the century they had fanned out to north-east and north-west:
north-east into Persia, north-west into Spain. Island-hopping to cross
the Mediterranean, they held on to the islands as bases, contributing
to the break-up of the Roman Empire, for the main link between
Constantinople and the western empire was by way of the sea-road
and, as an Arab chronicler wrote exultantly, 'The Christians cannot
sail so much as a plank on the sea now'. Spain was to be the limit of their

permanent advance to the north, but from their advanced bases, the tribesmen launched their devastating attacks deep into the heart of Christendom. Even Rome did not escape: a flotilla of their fast, murderous galleys stormed up the Tiber. The Romans, heirs to the world's greatest military force, cowered behind their walls while African tribesmen ransacked the unprotected basilica of St Peter's, despoiling the very tomb of the apostle in an access of religious hatred.

Islam, in the form of Saracens or Moors, crossed the Straits of Gibraltar in 711 and within months had overthrown the Visigothic Kingdom. They spent some five years securing their base, and made so good a job of it that they would remain in Spain for the next 700 years. Then, in 720, came the advance northwards across the Pyrenees towards the rich lands of southern France which must have seemed paradisial after the austere landscapes of Spain and North Africa. In 725 they reached Autun in the very heart of France, a little more than 150 miles from Paris, destroyed most of the city and carried off immense treasures. Commanded by the resolute, resourceful Saracen Abderrahman, representative in Europe of the Caliph of Baghdad, there seemed no particular reason why their bridgehead should not be consolidated into permanent occupancy. Indeed, had their northward advance been undertaken even five years earlier when the Franks were distracted with internecine fighting they might have succeeded in doing just this, with incalculable effects on the future of Europe. But Charles Martel had succeeded in welding his nation into one, and it was as one great hammer that the Frankish 'host' took to the field. In 731 Saracens and Franks faced each other on the old Roman road from Poitiers to Tours – the road that led eventually to Paris. For seven days the armies watched each other while Abderrahman sought a means of out-flanking the solid wall of the Franks. There was no such means but, unperturbed, with the consciousness of a century's undefeated expansion behind him, the Saracen moved to the attack.

A Spanish chronicler, Isidorus Pacensis, left a contemporary account of the battle. It is better than nothing, but it leaves a lot to be desired, the author being more desirous of extolling the noble Christians than telling us how exactly they fought. 'The men of the North stood as motionless as a wall: they were like a belt of ice frozen together, and not to be dissolved as they slew the Arabs with the sword. The Austrasians, vast of limb and iron of hand, hewed on bravely in the thick of the fight: it was they who found and cut down the Sarcen king.' But what emerges even from this halting account is that the Frankish tactics had not changed in centuries. They still had no horse, they still fought side by side to the death.

The clearest account of Frankish arms and tactics is given by an outsider, the Greek writer Agathias. He is writing long before the time of Charles Martel but the innate conservatism of the Franks, fighting familiar enemies for the most part, would have ensured little change over the years. 'The arms of the Franks are very rude: they wear neither mail shirt not greaves, and their legs are only protected by strips of leather or linen.' He, too, remarks on the odd fact that the Franks had hardly any horsemen while their near relatives, the Batavians, had been among the most famous horsemen in the Roman auxiliaries. 'Their foot-soldiers, however, are bold and well practised in war. They bear swords and shields, but never use the sling or bow. Their missiles are axes and barbed javelins. These last are not very long, they can be used either to cast or stab and the iron of the head runs down so far the stave that very little of the wood remains unprotected.' Agathias was intrigued by the singular use to which these Franks put their short, heavy spears. They were thrown with great force over a short distance. The enemy would catch it on his shield – but then would be unable to release it before the Frank was on him. The weight of the spear would drag the shield down and the Frank would accelerate the process by putting his foot on the shaft, forcing the shield down further and then 'cleaves his uncovered adversary or pierces his breast with a spear'.

A Frankish attack would be preceded by a storm of the throwing axe to which Agathias refers. It could be used in hand-to-hand combat but, like the American tomahawk, was carefully weighted for use as a missile weapon. In throwing, a twist of the wrist would ensure that the heavy, curved blade led edge foremost. If it struck the enemy on head or right arm it would effectively remove him from combat; if it bit into the shield it would hang there, its weight throwing him off balance.

Armies best improve their weapons and tactics either by fighting superior armies, or by being inducted into them. The Franks had been perfectly well acquainted with Roman military skills: they had fought side by side with the Romans and, perforce, adopted many of their weapons. It is curious, therefore, that far from improving upon or even retaining those well-tried skills they should have gradually reverted to their traditional methods. The explanation probably lies in the wide-ranging nature of the Roman Empire, drawing upon raw materials throughout the civilized world, and the relative parochialism of the

Franks, dependent upon what could be found in their own lands. Frankish swords provide a remarkable demonstration of human ingenuity triumphing over poor materials. The core of the sword was made up of strips of case-hardened iron (each of which was made up of thinner strips) welded by hammering one end together when hot. The welded end was placed in a vice, the whole heated again to yellow heat, then twisted tightly together. Three such bars formed the heart of the sword, and a fourth bar was then welded along one side. This, sharpened, formed the cutting edge. The need for this protracted method of construction arose from the paucity of large pieces of iron of the same quality – but the result was a sword of astonishing toughness, sharpness and flexibility.

Cassiodorus, secretary of the great Ostrogothic king Theodoric, provides a clear description of such a sword. He is writing to a chief, conveying Theodoric's thanks for a number of presents, which includes these swords.

> Your Fraternity has chosen for us swords capable of cutting through armour, which I prize more for their iron than for the gold upon them. So resplendent is their polish clarity that they reflect with faithful distinctness the faces of those who look upon them. So evenly do their edges run down to a point that they might be thought not shaped by files but moulded by the furnace. The central part of their blades, cunningly hollowed out, appears to be grained with tiny snakes, and here such varied shadows play that you would believe the shining metal to be interwoven with many colours. The metal is ground down and vigorously burnished by your shining dust until its steely light becomes a mirror for men: the dust is granted you by the natural bounty of your land, so that its possession may bestow singular renown upon you.

The 'shining dust' is probably kieselguhr, occurring naturally and plentifully around the Elbe, and those 'tiny snakes' are the last outward indication of the painstaking welding together of the strips of iron.

The Roman regarded his *spada* simply as an instrument; for the Frank, however, the sword was not simply a token of his manhood but, after the triumph of Christianity, his religion. It was a common practice to include a saint's relics physically in the hilt of the sword whose very shape reminded its owner of the origin of his religion. That veneration was passed on to all the descendants of the Franks so that the Germans and the French and the English all took the sword as the ultimate symbol of courage and of justice. It even had a personal identity and personal name: Charlemagne was supposed to have bestowed the slightly incongruous name of Joyeuse on his great blade and the sword of Roland would enter legend as Durendal.

It is probable that Charles Martel and his immediate band would have been mounted at the battle of Poitiers. But even now the Frank regarded the horse as, essentially, a mode of transport and dismounted in battle. And facing these stolidly standing men were Arab horsemen who had already gained fame for the speed and agility of their mounts, and who measured their success not only by the numbers of enemy killed but by their own deaths, that infallible passport to Paradise. They had met foot-soldiers before and triumphed, scattering them with ease. But there was present here one element they had not before encountered: absolute discipline. Infantry can always hold its own against cavalry provided it stands firm, but this in turn requires absolute control from the centre. Charles Martel provided that control. Hour after hour the Arab horsemen hurled themselves against that unyielding mass; hour after hour they fell back and the Franks remained where they stood, the only movement being forward a few yards to collect the missiles hurled during the last engagement.

The last charge must have taken place some time about sunset. All that night, the Franks stood to and when morning came found that they were masters of the field. The Arabs had not simply retreated, but had fled in disorder leaving their camp untouched. The first Frankish scouts cautiously exploring found themselves gazing in wonderment at what seemed to them fabulous riches. The very tents were made of crimson and yellow and purple silk – the kind of materials kings might wear were here used for so humdrum a purpose. Inside were more riches, not only the Saracens' own property but the booty they had collected during their long march. Martel and his counsellors must have been astonished: why did Abderrahman capitulate so utterly? Hindsight provides a possible explanation: like Napoleon and Hitler the Saracen had found it a simple matter to penetrate deep into a large, disorganized country but thereafter, through its very absence of order, found it impossible to hold down. His line of communication back to Spain was most dangerously extended and, having tested the true mettle of the leader of the Franks, he sensibly decided to withdraw to his secure base. But why leave the tents and the booty? Perhaps they were intended as a lure, for once the compact Frankish formation had been broken up as soldiers scrambled for loot, the victory almost certainly would have been his. But the formation was not broken up until the commander-in-chief gave the order.

Charles Martel lived for nearly ten years after Poitiers but passes almost wholly from our sight even though quite evidently he kept the firmest of grips on the kingdom. It is tantalizing in the extreme to know so little about this man who had a personality so formidable as to impose his will upon an army at its most vulnerable moment, the moment of victory. Judging by a vicious little story put about by clerics he lacked a certain respect for Holy Church. A prelate of St Denis, where Charles was buried, after a vision opened his tomb. There was no human corpse inside – only a black, winged dragon which rushed out and flew away. It would seem that Charles did not hesitate to lay hands on the domains of the Church, a certain way to earn both the pangs of Hell and the obliquy of posterity.

But at about the time of his death there was born to his son Pippin a child – a boy. He, too, was a bastard as had been Charles Martel. He, too, was given the simple, all-embracing name of 'Man' – Carl. Later, after the boy had indeed become a man, and the man become an emperor, those who toyed with the heresy of the transmigration of souls were free to wonder whether the soul of Charles Martel might not, at his death in 742, have entered the body of Charlemagne.

When, some eighty years later, the little clerk Einhard came to write the life of his beloved friend and master, he set himself one overriding limitation: he would not be the mere conveyor of second-hand anecdotes and neither would he twist the truth. If he did not know, he would remain silent. At the very beginning of his biography he naturally touches on the subject of Charles's childhood – but only to say: 'I can find nothing about these matters in writing nor does anyone survive who claims to have personal knowledge about them.' Now this disclaimer and self-imposed limitation bears no kind of sense when applied to the king's early years. If Charlemagne had a fault in Einhard's eyes, it is that he was inclined to be garrulous, touching on every subject under the sun in his curiously high-pitched voice. Master and man were as intimate as it was possible to be, bearing in mind their respective stations. It is altogether inconceivable that during the many, many hours of conversation between the talkative, extrovert Charles and the attentive Einhard, the king never once referred to his childhood, or speculated on the relationship with his father. His mother, Bertha, survived his father by many years, living in the court in that extended family relationship which Charles so loved and cherished, and by inference we can build up a clear enough picture of her and of their relationship. She was evidently a decidedly strong-willed woman, cavalierly arranging a marriage for her twenty-nine-year-old son – already a reigning monarch – as though he had been a teenage girl. Later, he repudiated that marriage and firmly kept his mother out of politics, to her decided irritation. But throughout her life, his relationship with Bertha was one of warm filial respect and affection.

But his father? It is here that Einhard's silence is significant. Even though he honourably refused to record mere hearsay, there is no reason whatsoever why he should not have recorded Charlemagne's opinions of his father – unless Charlemagne specifically charged him with silence in the matter. The inference is that the relationship between father and son was, at best, uneasy – an only too common attitude in the Merovings and their successors. There is, perhaps, a hint to be found in the soubriquet given his father – le Bref. Soubriquets for monarchs are usually manufactured by chroniclers and historians for their own convenience – as often as not after the death of their subject. One cannot imagine Charles the Fat or Ethelred the Unready being so identified in their lifetime. Pepin le Bref is translated as Pippin the Short – but does this mean short in stature, or in temper? It is unlikely that Charles placed much emphasis on his bastardy – virtually a characteristic of his family; he, certainly, had no compunction in producing an unknown number of his own, to the future confusion of European royalty. Einhard did not hesitate to record the fact that Charles and his younger, legitimate, brother Carloman had a very bad relationship with each other. Why then did he avoid any reference to the all-important father/son relationship unless it was so bad that it constituted a scandal at court and Charlemagne, with his lively sense of history, did not want it recorded in permanent form?

In his physical description of the king, Einhard leaves us what is probably the most detailed verbal description of a medieval monarch. There is a curiosity about the supposed portraits of Charles as there is a curiosity about the supposed portraits of Christ. It is altogether remarkable that the face on the Turin Shroud, created in whatever manner before the fifth century AD, should so closely resemble the long-accepted traditional portraits of Christ, even though the face in the Shroud did not become visible until the invention of photography in the nineteenth century. Similarly, although there is no one portrait of Charlemagne of which it can be said that here, without doubt, is the face of the great king, yet all those that survive have a strong family likeness from the admonishing fair-haired gentle giant of the Carinthian manuscripts, created shortly after his death and long forgotten, to the fifteenth-century fresco in the Vatican with its sombre, menacing northern king. It may be that all relate back to an authentic contemporary portrait, now lost, backed up by Einhard's brilliant description.

The portrait conveyed by Einhard is of a man in maturity – probably in his late forties, which would be about the time that Einhard first met him – and already a little corpulent. The most obvious thing about him was his immense height and build. Einhard describes him, oddly enough, as being seven times the length of his own feet. Earlier commentators mistook this for a measurement of seven feet high, making the man almost a monster. Such a measurement did indeed pass into legend: the Charlemagne of the Turin legend is eight feet high and he of the *Song of Roland* is little less. Nineteenth-century antiquarians, with their passion for detail, forced open the emperor's tomb and measuring the bones found that he was six feet three and a half inches in height. Fully dressed and wearing a helmet or crown he would have towered over his subjects, a majestic figure. Another outstanding characteristic was the colour of his hair and beard, yellow-gold in youth, platinum in manhood turning imperceptibly to silver in old age. Here, again, nature had given him an advantage over the mob. The Italians, in particular, accustomed to olive-skinned men of relatively low stature and uniformly black hair, responded to this towering, silver-haired emperor as to a god-like figure. He could be terrifying in rage, Einhard noted, the large 'piercing' eyes almost literally transfixing a delinquent. But his habitual expression was 'brisk and cheerful' – altogether a man who could draw men to him.

Reading back from Einhard's portrait of the mature man, it is possible to get some picture of the youth. He would have been, in the Anglo-Saxon term, a 'strapping young man', dominating his peers by sheer physical strength, outstanding among them by reason of the flowing golden hair that later identified him as of royal stock. Both as a young man and as an adult, he was entirely free of the besetting vice of all northern peoples – the drunkenness which was enshrined by some of them even in their constitutions. The modern civic regalia of English and German towns, unlike their Latin counterparts, invariably include some form of drinking vessel. The emperor Claudius arranged for two young German princes held hostage in Rome to go drinking with German mercenaries in order to ensure that they could keep pace with their thanes on return to their tribes. Einhard went out of his way to emphasize this uncharacteristic departure from a universal custom: 'He had a fierce hatred of drunkenness in any man, and especially in himself or in his friends.' Unless one drank only cold water, it was not possible to avoid either wine or ale but Charlemagne treated them simply as adjuncts to the meal, contenting himself with a cup or two – as did those, who were wise, who shared the table with him.

Einhard remarks upon his passion for roast meat – in effect, a passion for roast game meat – a passion so great that it very probably led to his death for he had contemptuously rejected the regime of boiled meats which his anxious doctors had prescribed. Charlemagne undoubtedly acquired the taste for such a dish as a young man, the normal appetite created by the energy requirements of a body like his, amplified by his equally great delight in hunting. In the Europe of these early centuries the human hunger for protein did not even begin to be satisfied by the meat provided by the delicate, scarce and expensive domestic cattle raised on the small scattered farms. But, by contrast, all the protein that was required was freely available in the vast forests for anyone who had the courage and skill to hunt it down. Hunting, like religion, is one of those concepts which changes with the centuries. In the past distant from Charlemagne – in that past recorded on stone or in paint in Egypt and Babylonia in particular – the king had demonstrated his courage and, hence, his fitness to lead in war by hunting down ferocious but inedible beasts of which the lion was predominant. In the future distant from Charlemagne, the hunt would become purely recreational, with the huntsman either pursuing a fast but totally defenceless creature which relied for survival entirely on that speed and skill, or he would kill large, dangerous creatures safely from a distance with a projectile weapon. In Charlemagne's Europe, the huntsman killed for food, but as a result of direct confrontation which more approximated the confrontation in a Spanish bullfight – with individual man pitted personally against individual animal – than in almost any other hunting since in civilized history.

There were three main sources of protein in the European forests: deer, wild ox and boar; of these, two could be described as 'prey' only in the most technical sense and of those two the wild boar was by far the most dangerous. The ox was immensely powerful and notoriously bad-tempered but slow-witted with it. The boar, though smaller, was far more intelligent, agile and ferocious. A wounded deer sought only to hide: a wounded ox, as often as not, would also seek shelter, lumbering away at a certain point in the combat. But wounds made the boar even more dangerous, a whirling, slashing, raging creature whose tusks could rip a man open like an overripe melon. It required courage and skill and a cold precision of a very high order to kneel waiting to receive the quarter ton of enraged pig, knowing that one had to have not only the strength to hold the lance while the boar impaled itself upon it, but also the knowledge and skill to direct the point of that lance at the only truly vulnerable point, the heart. Hunting was a young man's delight, but it was also one of the most useful training grounds for a future warrior.

Charlemagne would have learned to hunt as soon as he was old enough and strong enough to hold the long, heavy boar spear. He would have learned the arts of warfare not in the gorgeous, wasteful, simulated mock-battles known as tournaments in the later Middle Ages, but in the grim, workman-like setting of the palace yard, giving and receiving blows with some grizzled veteran of his father's war-band; learning how to give that twist to a *francisca* so that the heavy axe flew through the air with the keen cutting edge foremost; learning the best moment to hurl the heavy spear – not too soon so that it gave the enemy a chance to dodge, and certainly not too late so that it allowed the enemy to come to close-quarters while the thrower was still empty-handed. Above all, he learned how to wield the great sword. Outwardly, there was little finesse in its use, for the massive weight of metal dictated its movements so that, for most of the action, it was used virtually like a battle-axe; but there was a skill in recovering it before the swordsman went off balance and, unlike the battle-axe, it could be used in some degree to parry and defend.

The court in which the boy was growing up was no savage chieftain's hut. The Merovingians, for all their deplorable characteristics, had imbued their subjects with a genuine love of culture. The Franks did not leave learning to pale, timid clerks but looked upon the ability to read and write as part of the education of a prince. And here, along with that tantalizing silence about Charlemagne's childhood, posterity encounters in his biography the even more tantalizing reference to his supposed illiteracy.

Discussing Charles's intellectual skills and interests in his maturity – skills which included the much-admired art of rhetoric and the almost magical art of astronomy – Einhard remarks: 'He tried also to learn to write, and for this purpose used to carry with him and keep under the pillow of his couch tablets and writing sheets that he might in his spare moments accustom himself to the formation of letters. But he made little advance in this unseasonable task, which was begun too late in life.'

Einhard's anecdote has given rise to one of the romantic myths of the Carolingian Renaissance: the picture of the great barbarian king, so mighty in war, ruling with an iron hand his great empire – yet carrying a little boy's slate around with him, wistfully, without success, attempting to drink at that well of learning which he, himself, had created. This picture bears no relationship to reality at any single point. Einhard himself says elsewhere that the king was not only fluent in Latin, but knew enough Greek to follow the speeches of Greek ambassadors – a skill denied the scholars of the early Italian Renaissance. It is, perhaps, possible to learn an alien language parrot-fashion, but certainly not possible to learn it fluently either without being able to write, and read, or without living among its practitioners. Charlemagne never ventured into Greek-speaking lands and entered Italy only in his maturity. There is, too, the evidence of the fragments of poetry that have been conclusively attributed to him. In these is very clearly evident his delight in words, his ability to weave them into complex structures, which disposes of the theory that he was dyslexic – unable to recognize the actual shape of words. Einhard was almost certainly referring to his master's inability to write the exquisite script which posterity has called the 'Carolingian minuscule' and which was introduced into the court on his own initiative. The writing he would have learned as a child was the ugly, spiky script in common use not only in Francia but even in sophisticated Italy. By the time the Carolingian minuscule was in general use at his court, he would have been a mature man and would indeed have found difficulty in mastering it. There would, too, be no incentive apart from the pure delight in calligraphy, for a king no more expected to write his orders than he expected to groom his horse. It was a task for specialists. But there seems little doubt that Charles was able to read.

That ability could have brought him little joy in his schooldays for learning was at an absolute nadir throughout Europe. It was a question not of a lack of quantity, but of quality. In some ways, perhaps, it might have been best had book learning been placed in suspension for, in that way, generations of schoolboys would have been spared the arid treadmill of grammar, going round and round again and again the same handful of concepts until all meaning was wrung out of language. The so-called School of Toulouse set the standard. Its practitioners had the impudence to give themselves classical names – Virgil, Cicero, Terence,

Aeneas – creating in effect a mutual admiration circle in which, for instance, they declared loftily, 'He who has not read Cicero has read nothing' – but the Cicero they referred to was the pedant of Toulouse, not the philosopher of Rome. In their endless dissection of language one is irresistibly reminded of kittens tangling a ball of wool. They boasted of their ability to spend fourteen days in a row – not infrequently coming to blows – arguing as to whether *ego* had a vocative case. In the words of a nineteenth-century church historian, Augusta Drane: 'They worked their hardest to involve all Europe in a fog of perplexity.'

The practitioners might be absurd, but the system they served was by no means ignoble, and such a youth as Charles was able to grasp it with sufficient confidence and firmness for the man Charlemagne to build upon. Learning was divided into seven main subjects – the elementary *Trivium* of grammar, rhetoric and dialectic and the advanced *Quadrivium* of music, arithmetic, geometry and astronomy. The subjects had far wider connotation than exist today. Grammar could, indeed, be limited to the arid technicalities of textbooks such as those known as 'Priscian' and 'Donatus'. But it could also include the whole tremendous sweep of Latin literature and the young Charles was singularly fortunate in having, as tutor, Abbot Fulrad of the abbey church of St Denis, a truly pious priest who nevertheless did not regard pagan poetry as a spring of corruption and the work of the devil, as did so many of his more bigoted co-religionists, and who planted in the eager young mind the love of literature which was to have so rich a flowering a generation later. Charles was fortunate, too, in that his study of music was wider and deeper than for most young men of his generation for whom 'music' was little more than the rules of plainsong. He was just fifteen years old when there arrived at his father's palace, as a rich gift from the emperor in Constantinople, the first organ seen in Europe. So unprecedented was the gift that it was recorded in most of the chronicles, the monkish chronicler of St Gall describing it, nearly eighty years later, presumably after seeing and hearing it at first-hand: 'The great chests were made of brass, and bellows of oxhide blew through pipes of brass and the brass was like the roaring of thunder and in sweetness equalled the tinkling of lyre or cymbal.' Here, again quite by chance, was one of the great formative experiences of his life, for later, as king and then as emperor, he took a warm and informed interest in the development of choral singing, backed by that great instrument.

Of the two supposedly mathematical subjects, arithmetic was still caught up in the strait-jacket of Roman numerals, its prime use being to deal with chronological problems relating to the complex Church calendar. But geometry, by contrast, took in virtually all the natural world, including everything from what we, today, would describe as geography to the healing properties of herbs and, by extension, the rules of medicine. And the final subject, astronomy, was Charles's particular favourite, precisely the kind of subject in which his restless, ranging, speculative mind would delight.

The son of a Frankish chieftain was from an early age drawn into his father's adult world. And in the case of the son of Pippin, mayor of the palace of Austrasia, that association was not only the association of the battlefield but of the high and dangerous world of politics. For great events were afoot in Francia after the death of Charles Martel. Following that dangerous Frankish practice he had divided the inheritance between his two legitimate sons. Pippin, then about twenty-seven years of age – a cool, balanced, rather calculating young man he seems from the sparse evidence of the early chronicles – took the traditional heartland of the Frankish realm while his thirty-year-old brother, Carloman, took the western half. In the past this had been a recipe for dissension and, at times, outright civil war but a fortunate sequence of events resolved the current problem: the two brothers had common enemies pressing in on their borders from the Saxons in the north-east to the Aquitanians in the south-west and when a degree of stability was achieved Carloman, ever the more impulsive, generous and religious-minded of the two, to the astonishment of all entered a monastery.

With the accession of Carloman and Pippin in 742 it is possible to detect, even at this distance of time, a quickening of the Frankish pulse, an impression as though the brothers had rolled up their sleeves and set to the refurbishing of the realm. Their father, Charles Martel, had not troubled to place a king on the Merovingian throne for he was unique lord of the land. They decided to do so, probably as a useful means of negating any rivalry that might develop between themselves. Childeric III was to prove the last of the 'sacred kings' and the exact extent of his power is shown by the meek way in which he alludes to his accession, giving thanks to 'the famous man Carloman, Mayor of the Palace, who hath installed us in the throne of this realm'. Carloman, as the elder, would have been the nominal mover of such an action, thus gaining the eighteen-year-old boy's pallid thanks. But it was Carloman's own personal religious motives which led him to commission the Anglo-Saxon missionary, Boniface, to clean up the kingdom of the Franks and, in particular, to direct its swarming clergy again on to the path of virtue.

It is worthwhile pausing here to look at the life of the man, born Wynfrith but now known as Boniface, for he was thrice remarkable. Remarkable in himself, as a character; remarkable in the crucial role he was to play in Frankish and, hence, European, history; remarkable, above all, as an example of the human capacity for adaptation. He was of that race now known as Anglo-Saxon, born in Devon about 675. His not-so-distant forebears were the continental Saxons, those fierce neighbours of the Franks, the last true pagans in Europe, reputed to practise cannibalism, certainly known to practise human sacrifice and whose subjugation was to take Charlemagne thirty bloody years. Yet these same Saxons, having crossed the North Sea to Britain and mingled with Jutes and Angles to form the English nation, in a remarkably short space of time developed a culture so sophisticated as to run the danger of being corrupted. Above all, Anglo-Saxon priests combined the energy of their ferocious forebears with great learning and a deep, inextinguishable love of their religion. They were the Jesuits of their day, burning with zeal, the Church Militant, but gaining converts and maintaining orthodoxy not by axe and rope and fire but by logic and eloquence and, predominantly, a joyous belief in a gospel of salvation.

Anglo-Saxon missionaries became the spear-head of the Roman Church's crusade among the heathen of the north and Boniface towered even among these courageous and learned men. In Rome he was given his nickname, *bonifatius*, as testimony to his eloquence for it means 'good speaker' (not 'good doer' – that aspect of his character was taken for granted), and Pope Zacharias gave him what amounted to a free hand and a roving commission. In Bavaria he threw himself into the task of eliminating the last traces of paganism (or, to be exact, the last official traces, for the old religion would continue underground here, as elsewhere, for centuries). But no longer was horseflesh ritually eaten, or sacrifices offered up for the dead. Charles Martel, who was keenly aware of the value of Christianity as a taming influence, was certainly opportunist, if not cynical, in promoting Boniface's efforts along the periphery of the Frankish realm, in particular in drawing the Rhinelanders into the net of civilized, Frankish, Christianity. And now Martel's son, Carloman, brought the saint into the heart of the matter, turning his formidable attention upon the corruption that existed in the centre of the realm among those supposed to be the wardens and custodians of virtue, the clergy themselves.

In his letter to the Pope, telling him of the commission with which Carloman had charged him, Boniface gives a curiously exact account of the beginning of ecclesiastical decadence, 'ecclesiastical discipline has been trodden underfoot in the Frankish realm for at least sixty or seventy years'. In other words, the decline in the morals of the clergy (and, by extension, among the laity) began at about the time the Merovingian kings lost their grip and became the *rois fainéants*. He then goes on to give a list of crimes among the clergy, in particular the monastic clergy, which was to become wearisomely familiar throughout the Middle Ages and well into the Reformation. He cites the case of bishops 'who are drunkards and criminals, who follow the chase or fight fully armed in battle, shedding with their own hand the blood of Christian or heathen alike'. He found priests with four or five concubines who 'in spite of their lewdness still perform the offices of priest, claiming that they can intercede for the people and offer the holy sacrifice'. The seduction of nuns by the clergy seems to have been particularly prevalent, partly due perhaps to that easy-going Frankish tolerance of sexual irregularity and certainly notorious enough to attract Boniface's fierce indignation. His reforming zeal inevitably aroused equally strong opposition. It was only the fact that he was known to be acting on the direct authority of the pope, and energetically backed by Carloman and his brother, that prevented Boniface and his Anglo-Saxon companions, 'the strangers' as they were contemptuously called, from being hustled out of the kingdom. But he emerged in due course not only as the unofficial patriarch of the north but as archbishop of Mainz – having deposed a predecessor who had obeyed the blood-feud law of the Franks by killing his father's killer.

And how much was Boniface's influence at work in Carloman's decision to retire from the world? This elder of the two all-powerful brothers was the more religious and generous of the two – but also the more impulsive, liable to explode in mindless rages. During a campaign against the neighbouring Alamanni, driven to fury by their endless breaking of treaties, he rounded up hundreds (according to some accounts, thousands) of the tribesmen after promising a safe-conduct and presided over their slaughter. The massacre of Cannstadt evidently deeply disturbed him and, towards the end of the year 747 just five years after he had succeeded to the mayoralty, he laid down his worldy burden and with the prompt agreement of his brother entered a monastery in Italy. He returned again, under very curious circumstances, but that was the effective end of his claim to rule.

In that manner the crisis that lay at the very heart of the Frankish state, the division between two powerful men, was peacefully resolved and Charles's father emerged as sole and supreme ruler. And it was now that Pippin began to consider ideas about the nature of the monarchy. Rome was probably the first to hear of what those ideas might be when Boniface wrote to Pope Zacharias referring to 'certain secrets of my own which Lul the bearer of this letter will communicate viva voce to your Piety' – secrets so important that they could not be entrusted to writing, for that too-precipitate forebear of Pippin's who had tried to grasp the crown of the Merovings had paid for his lack of judgement with his life.

Soon it was common knowledge, according to a Frankish chronicler, that 'In the year 750 of the Lord's Incarnation, Pippin sent ambassadors to Rome to Pope Zacharias, to ask concerning the king of the Franks who were of the royal line and were called kings but had no power in the kingdom save that only charters and privileges were drawn up in their name, but they had absolutely no kingly power, but did whatever the *Major Domus* of the Franks desired.' So the chronicler bumbled on, garrulously describing that final, humiliating role of the 'sacred kings' which Einhard was to paraphrase in a few brisk sentences: 'On the first day of March according to ancient custom gifts were offered to these kings by the people and the king himself sat in the royal seat with the army standing round him and the *Major Domus* in his presence, and he commanded on that day whatever was decreed by the Franks, but on all other days thenceforward he sat quietly at home.' The chronicler never got around to saying what it was that Pippin actually asked of the pope but, quite evidently, it was the simple and obvious question: Who should wear the crown, he who was the puppet, or he who truly ruled? And the pope, influenced by Boniface, came back with the expected answer.

> In the exercise of his apostolic authority he replied to their question that it seemed to him better that the man who held power in the kingdom should be called king and be king, rather than he who falsely bore the name. Therefore the aforesaid Pope commanded the king and the people of the Franks that Pippin who was using royal power should be called king and be settled in the royal seat. Which was therefore done by anointing of the holy archbishop Boniface in the city of Soissons: Pippin is proclaimed king and Childeric, who was falsely called king is tonsured and sent into a monastery.

Thus, bloodlessly, neatly and quite illegally, the dynasty of the 'sacred kings' came to an end and the dynasty of the Carolings began.

Partly through ineptitude, partly though a desire not to give the lie to Pope Zacharias, the chronicler concealed, or misinterpreted a number of issues concerning the deposition of the last of the Merovingians, not least the fact that the unfortunate Childeric was not 'falsely' called king. But the account marks a moment of profound change in European affairs – the moment when an external, priestly authority claimed the power to unmake and to make a king. The Christian religion undoubtedly saved the young ex-king's life. A generation or so earlier a sword thrust would have solved the embarrassment presented by a living ex-king as a possible focal point of dissension. All that happened to Childeric was that his long hair was cut short, thus indicating his loss of royal status, and the crown of his head shaven, indicating his dedication to God. And a man so shaved was, for all legal purposes, as good as dead for he could never again 'enter the world'. It was no bad life that lay ahead of him, for despite Boniface's energetic attempts at reform a monk's life was much what he chose to make of it. But it was the end of the Merovingian dynasty, founded by Clovis two centuries earlier.

Although Soissons was a place of no particular importance now in the Frankish kingdom, Pippin decided that it was there that he would be proclaimed king for it was there that Clovis, first Frankish king, had been 'raised on the shield'. This was a ceremony that admirably illustrated the interlocking nature of Frankish society. About a dozen brawny young men would stand in a rough circle and then, stooping, interlock their round shields of cow-hide and wood to form a platform a foot or so above the ground. The chief would stand upon its wobbling surface as the young men raised him high. It was a simple and obvious ceremony of profound and subtle significance. It showed that the tribe realized that there must be one man above the rest and he had to be raised up so that all could see him. But he was supported by the strong left arms of his fellow Franks. He was not their ruler, but the first among equals: if they withdrew the support of their arms he would fall to the ground. It was the perfect outward symbol of the *comitatus*. Was Pippin himself 'raised on the shield'? The Royal Annals give no indication that this was the case but if he was, it was certainly the last time the Franks elevated one of their number in this fashion.

For immediately afterwards followed that 'anointing' to which the chronicler referred as though it were the central point of the ceremony – as in the fullness of time it would become. The 'anointing' of a king – that is, touching some part of his body with finger or fabric dipped in holy oil – was a ceremony wholly unknown not only to the Franks but to all Europeans. It was a Hebrew ritual, brought for the first time into a European ceremony. It was here administered by a representative of the bishop of Rome and with that bishop's express permission. It turned a palace official into a monarch, and his sons into princes. And there would be a price to pay for it.

3 The Keys of
St Peter

Early in January 754, the fair-haired, handsome, fourteen-year-old
Prince Charles was charged by his father with a mission of ceremonial
delicacy. King Pippin had just returned from a gruelling campaign
against the heathen Saxons and was relaxing in his villa at Thionville
when news arrived that a party of Roman ecclesiastics and their escort
was about a day's march away. The news was certainly not unexpected
for the party had left Rome many weeks before and its mission was of
such urgency that, composed for the most part though it was of elderly,
sedentary men, it had braved the high Alps in the depths of winter.
They had come via the Val d'Aosta, over the snow-covered Mons Jovis,
stumbling at last exhausted into the kindlier lands of Savoy. As their
leader later told Pippin: 'By St Peter's orders my unhappiness was
directed to come to you. We surrendered ourselves body and soul to the
mighty labours attending a journey into so vast and distant a province.
Trusting utterly in your fidelity . . . worn out by the frost and the snow,
by the mighty rivers and most atrocious mountains and divers kinds of
danger.'

Pippin was well aware of the honour done him, for the leader of the
party was Pope Stephen himself and he was accompanied by no less
than two bishops, four presbyters, an archdeacon, two deacons as well
as high officials of the Lateran court. But Pippin had a nice question of
protocol to solve: how to return the honour by honourably receiving the
party in what was now his realm, and yet maintain his own, new status
as lord of that realm. He solved it by sending his eldest son. For the
young man, it must have been a deeply moving and significant occasion;
for the tired old man on a weary horse was the person whom he from his
infancy had been brought up to regard as an all but supernatural person:
Pope Stephen II, Servant of the Servants of God, Vicar of Christ on

Earth, Holder of the Keys of Heaven and Hell whose word could condemn a man to an eternity of suffering, or whose intercession could guarantee him an eternity of bliss.

Charles had met Romans before. Certainly, ever since his father had been elevated to the throne there had been a constant scurry of papal messengers between Rome and whatever villa King Pippin was lodged in at the moment. But this was the first time he had seen high officials of the Church, as well as the highest of all its priests, in a gathering speaking among themselves the language (or, at least, a recognizable variant of that language) which he now associated with all that was powerful and civilized. Their very clothes, when they had divested themselves of the heavy coverings of furs and sheepskins, were with a few variations, the clothes that might have been seen in the streets of Rome at the time of Augustus. The too-complicated toga had long since disappeared but the *pallium*, or mantle, was still in use. So, too, was the *tunica*, though this now had long sleeves for had not St Augustine himself said it was disgraceful for a decent man to possess a *tunica talaris* without sleeves? There was little to distinguish between the dress of clergy and laymen in the party for whom the young Charles was now acting as guide and host, and it was noticeable that they had adopted the sensible hose, one of the few things Romans had taken over from 'barbarians'. Apart from this concession, this group of smooth-shaven, swarthy, black-haired men with liquid gestures and fluent tongue were utterly alien – save in their common faith.

Pippin had arranged for Charles to conduct the party to a meeting place equidistant between Thionville and the great abbey of St Denis which had been set aside for the pope's lodging. The place chosen was another of the royal villas, at Pons Hugonis, and the papal party was still three miles away when the royal party was discerned riding towards them. They met at the third milestone from the villa – and there Pippin dismounted, prostrated himself before the pope and, taking hold of the reins of his palfrey, walked like a humble groom beside him.

Pippin rarely, if ever, did anything without calculation and so presumably he must have had some reason for performing this quite extraordinary act of ritual self-abasement. But it may also be that he was as capable of a generous, unpremeditated response to an emotional event as his brother, or his son. Whatever the reason for the act, it was quite overshadowed by an extraordinary performance by the pope himself in the chapel of the royal villa later that same day, 6 January. It was Epiphany, one of the Church's great feast-days, and Pippin must have been astonished to find Pope Stephen dressed in sack-cloth and with his head liberally garnished with ashes. Throwing himself to the ground, Stephen babbled tearfully of the *nefandissimi Langobardi*, the 'most evil Lombards', the 'stinking Lombards', the Lombards who were the spawn of the devil and who had occupied the territories of Holy Church in Italy and were oppressing widows and orphans – and, incidentally, helping themselves to the Church's rich revenues thereof. 'The blessed Pope with tears besought the most Christian King that by treaties of peace he would arrange the cause of St Peter and the republic of the Romans.' In other words, Pippin was exhorted, in the name of Holy Church and as part payment for that Church's action in seating him on the throne of the Merovings, to mount an invasion of Italy in order to restore 'the lands of St Peter' to St Peter's successor.

Well might Pippin have hesitated to give a reply on the spot. He was well supplied with active enemies to north-east and south-west outside his realm; within, there was the dubious and restless loyalty of his brother-in-law, the Duke of Bavaria, the uncertainty of his relationship with Burgundy and the necessity to consolidate his legal, but painfully new, hold over what had been his brother's half of the kingdom. The last thing he would have relished was to stir up a hornets' nest in Italy by tangling with the formidable Lombards – with whom, as it happened, he was related by marriage for his brother had married a Lombard princess. His wife, Bertha, was on the most cordial terms with the Lombard court at Pavia (and had certain matrimonial ideas in mind for her family), and his thanes certainly had no desire to cross the Alps and fight a crusade for Italian clerics.

Happily for Pippin, the privations of the journey and his own anxieties, together with the rigours of a northern winter, wholly incapacitated the elderly pope. Pippin placed him under the care of Charles's old tutor, Fulrad, and throughout the winter and early spring Stephen was an invalid, at one point his very life being despaired of. During the slow weeks of his convalescence the papal and royal parties hammered out a bargain which would affect the history of Europe until the nineteenth century. In return for that promised military aid, the pope would not only crown Pippin, his two sons and his wife with his own hands but he would give Pippin and his sons the title of Patrician of the Romans.

This was no idle honour and empty title. Over the centuries most of the great offices of the empire had become shadowy or wholly forgotten, consigned into the lumber of history: quaestors and aediles, consuls, senators and the rest either subsumed into the nascent papacy or turned into archaicisms. But he who held the office of Patrician was not only a citizen of the actual city of Rome, as opposed to a citizen of the empire, but head of Rome's nobility – in effect, the secular lord of the ancient city. Even a pope could not, of his own power, give this great dignity: the people of Rome themselves had assented to this glorification of a barbarian, praying that he would defend them in these increasingly perilous times. In accepting the title for himself and his sons – which he promptly did – Pippin had advanced from the status of a palace official to that of king and then to that of Roman aristocrat in just four years.

The quadruple coronation took place in the church of St Denis. The church has long since been engulfed in the sprawl of Paris but at that time stood in open country to the north of the city. Founded by St Genevieve about the year 475 it had fallen under the especial care of the Merovingian kings who steadily beautified and enlarged it and in due course were buried there, beginning that tradition of a royal relationship which would last until the Revolution. In anticipation of his own coronation there Pippin, too, had decreed the enlargement of the church, and this the pope consecrated so that it provided a fitting background for the apotheosis of the new dynasty. Curiously, neither the local chroniclers nor the papal biographers whose task it was to provide a log-book of the activities of the pope, recorded the exact date of this ceremony, but internal evidence suggests it was in early summer, perhaps about June. Charles was fourteen; his little brother Carloman just three years old. Their mother, Bertha, stole the show, the chronicler recording with admiration how she was 'regally dressed in a *cyclas*', a magnificently embroidered robe, close-fitting round the neck and sweeping the ground in that wide circle which gave it its name. Bertha the queen not only had style but a sense of occasion and it is curiously appropriate that she, who so energetically tried to dominate her son in the first years of his reign, should so vividly have emerged from the shadows at this, his first recorded ceremonial appearance. The pope crowned all four, then pronounced anathema on all who 'for all time to come, should presume to elect a king sprung from the loins of any other but of these persons whom the Divine Mercy had deigned to exalt'.

After the coronation came the most difficult task of all – that of persuading Pippin's fellow Franks to take up arms for St Peter. Einhard, Charles's biographer, was able to use both the first-hand testimony of his master and the written evidence of the chronicles when he, recording what happened after the coronation, wrote: 'The war against the Lombards was with great difficulty undertaken by Charles's father on the earnest entreaty of Pope Stephen, because certain of the chief men of the Franks with whom he was wont to take counsel so stoutly resisted his will that they proclaimed with free voices that they would desert the king and return to their own homes.' For all the anointing with oil and the crowning with gold, and the sonorous Latin spoken over him, King Pippin was still little more than the first among equals. His 'subjects', the still free men whose very name was a synonym for independence, would have derided any attempt of his to order them into battle. He had to argue, persuade, entice. And his cause was not helped when, at the great gathering at Quierzy when he was seeking to persuade his fellows to follow him into Italy, his brother Carloman should appear, clad now in monkish robes – not to plead the cause of his spiritual father, the pope, but to urge the Franks to stay at home.

Carloman's retirement from the world had not brought him the peace he had hoped for. His journey to Rome, at the centre of a splendid, indeed, regal entourage, had taken on the appearance of a triumphal tour as he dispensed largesse and the crowds flocked to see this most unusual pilgrim. At Rome he gave rich gifts to the shrine of Peter, including the somewhat incongruous offering of an immense silver bow weighing some seventy pounds. And from Rome, he made his way to Mount Soracte some forty miles north of the city. Even in the twentieth century this extraordinary hill, rearing up suddenly over two thousand feet from the plain, is a haunted and austere spot. Byron caught its shape exactly when he describes how it:

> from out the plain
> Heaves like a long-swept wave about to break
> And on the curl hangs passing.

The legendary pope, Sylvester, who was supposed to have cured the Emperor Constantine of leprosy and so gained freedom for Christianity, had a cell among the gaunt rocks. Here Carloman built his own in imitation of the desert anchorites and lived for some years. But the fame of such a hermit who had given up such great earthly power in pursuit of a heavenly crown, spread throughout a land hungry for the miraculous. His fellow Franks in particular, having visited Rome, would turn aside and climb the steep rocky path to present their respects and gain a blessing and some trinket to take back to their awed families beyond the

Alps. Eventually the press became too much for him and he fled even deeper into seclusion, seeking refuge at Monte Cassino. The abbey, the very mother house of monasticism, the one founded by St Benedict himself in 529 was already more than two hundred years old and it would survive, growing century by century until it resembled a hill-top town, until destroyed by bombardment in World War II. But even behind these great walls, in the rigid routine of labour and prayer that St Benedict had laid down, the world followed the unfortunate monk. According to the abbey's traditions, he did his best to hide his past, humbly accepting the humiliating tasks imposed upon a novice. But his quasi-regal status was discovered and he was drawn into the great matter of the proposed invasion.

Why did he leave the security and relative comfort of Monte Cassino to throw himself again into the worldly affairs he had so dramatically rejected? The papal biographer is quite sure of the reason: 'The most unspeakable Aistulf [King of the Lombards] by his devilish persuasions so wrought upon Carloman the brother of the most pious king Pippin that he drew him forth from the monastery of St Benedict in which he had dwelt devoutly as a monk for a certain space of time and directed his course to the province of Frankland, in order to raise objections and oppose the cause of the redemption of the Holy Church of God.' This may well have been a reason. Monte Cassino was situated in one of the great southern duchies established by the Lombard, and Aistulf may well have put pressure on its abbot to make use of his illustrious and obedient monk. But it is equally as likely that Carloman, after living some years in Italy and actually in a province under the direct dominance of the Lombards, had a rather different view of them than the one which was being presented to his brother Pippin by the pope. He had, after all, been a highly efficient ruler and competent soldier and must have had the gravest doubts about the long-term effects of a Frankish invasion of Italy.

However, his presence at the great gathering of Quierzy proved an embarrassment, not a check. Even as Pippin had to seek counsel of his chieftains before committing the nation to war, so they were still bound to him by the spirit of the *comitatus*; where the war-band leader went, they had to follow or be for ever dishonoured. But, unlike the neighbouring Saxons, they were a legalistic people and both they and their new king Pippin might well have wanted to know on just what grounds Pope Stephen was claiming that the *nefandissimi Langobardi* had robbed St Peter of his property. It would have been at some such stage that

Pope Stephen II produced what is probably the most audacious and certainly the most successful forgery in history, a forgery which was not discovered until the fifteenth century by the Italian scholar Lorenzo Valla, and whose effects were to continue until 1870 when the army of a newly resurgent and unified Italy broke through the walls of Rome and brought to an end the reign of the papal monarch.

In AD 330 Emperor Constantine the Great formally transformed the Middle Eastern city of Byzantium into the new capital of the empire, naming it after himself. There was neither logistic nor legal reason to prevent him transferring sovereignty from Rome to Constantinople. Just a generation earlier the Emperor Diocletian had, after all, made Milan a capital of the empire and now that the centre of gravity had shifted to the eastern Mediterranean it made sense for Constantine to establish his capital there. Wherever the emperor chose to establish himself, there was the seat of empire. The court at Constantinople subtly and inevitably changed over the years: its manners became Asiatic, its language became Greek. But it was still the capital of the Roman Empire, its inhabitants called themselves Roman and though, in the shorthand of history, in due course its ruler would be known as the Byzantine emperor he was the true, legal descendant of the Caesars. In purely legal terms it was the Sack of Constantinople of 1453, when the last Emperor Constantine XI fell beneath the sabres of the Turks, that brought the Roman Empire to an end.

Italy now became merely a province of that empire and to maintain their hold upon it the emperors established a strong bridgehead in Ravenna. The little Italian city blossomed into oriental splendour. The court of the Exarch, as its ruler was called, echoed on a smaller scale the court of the distant emperor. The architecture was transformed into the Byzantine with plentiful use of those richly glowing mosaics that the Byzantines loved. The Exarch was no mere ceremonial office but an active arm of empire, capable of operating what was still the world's most formidable military machine. The emperors may have turned their back on Europe, preferring the pleasures and treasures of the Middle East, but they certainly had no intention of relaxing their hold upon the mother province. In 537, for instance, the Emperor Justinian launched a massive and efficient invasion of Italy during which his great general Belisarius wrested Rome from the grasp of the occupying Goths drawing it again into the ambit of empire.

In transforming Constantinople into the capital of the Roman

Empire, Constantine the Great had overlooked one imponderable but potent fact: Rome was not simply a place, but an idea. A thousand years later the popes encountered the same phenomenon when, preferring the comfort and safety of Avignon to the decrepitude and violence of Rome, they sought to establish the papacy there but were forced, ignominiously, to return to the mother city. Constantine had left a vacuum of power on the banks of the Tiber and the bishop of Rome was there to fill it. The process took centuries. In the beginning, the bishop of Rome was simply another palace official with no greater power than his opposite number, the patriarch of Constantinople, and even until the time of Pippin he acted in the name of the emperor. It was long before his fellow bishops could be prevailed upon to recognize his pre-eminence among themselves and grudgingly acquiesce in his title of 'universal pope'. But to the citizens of the city of Rome he was the sole constant in a shifting, dangerous world, the sole symbol of power. They turned to him naturally, inevitably, and he for his part not only began to wield power, as ruler, but accepted the responsibilities of that power. He became, in a very real sense, the 'relieving officer' of Rome. But he needed funds; funds came only from the land and it was probably as much from this humdrum, but vital, need that some little time before Pope Stephen crossed the Alps to summon King Pippin to the aid of Rome a papal official, probably named Christophorus, neatly transferred the temporal crown from the emperor to the pope.

Christophorus based his work upon the legendary life of St Sylvester, the blameless if mediocre bishop of Rome who ruled over his little flock at the time of Constantine. According to the legend, Constantine was energetically persecuting Christians when he was afflicted with leprosy and, despite the efforts of doctors and magicians, despaired of a cure. Saints Peter and Paul appeared to him in a vision, and told him that St Sylvester could cure him. The old man was brought to the Lateran Palace where the emperor resided, and there told him that baptism alone could cleanse him of the disease.

Constantine agreed to baptism and, as a result, the leprosy immediately vanished. In gratitude he immediately ordained that Christ should be worshipped throughout the empire and that tithes should be instituted for the building of churches. The Lateran Palace was given to Sylvester and his successors for all time; Constantine himself then dug and carried away the first twelve baskets of earth on the Vatican Hill and so began the great basilica of St Peter's.

The legend, though fanciful in its ascription of motives, did not depart widely from known details of fact – the gift of the Lateran Palace, the construction of basilicas, the supreme status accorded to the Christian Church. Christophorus expanded these known elements, skilfully grafting revolutionary theories upon a stock that was both deep-rooted and widespread. He made some blunders that were to arouse the suspicion of scholars centuries later: Constantine was made to refer to himself as conqueror of the Huns fifty years before they appeared in Europe; the bishop of Rome was called 'pope' nearly two centuries before the title was limited to him, and western officials became 'satraps of the empire'. But Christophorus brought his threads together neatly enough before going on to make his forgeries.

The first forgery was a deletion. The legend had stated unequivocally that the emperor retained in his hands all the apparatus of civil government. The phrase disappeared, the document implying that all judges as well as bishops were subject to the bishop of Rome. Then, boldly, Christophorus commenced the actual manufacture of details. To the 'pope' and his successors, Constantine gave the imperial crown together with 'the purple mantle also and the scarlet tunic and all the imperial appurtenances. We bestow upon him also the imperial sceptre, with all the standards and banners and similar ornaments.'

Christophorus was a cleric, anxious to maintain the little privileges and honours of his office, and Constantine was made to grant to the clergy a dignity similar to that which the Senate had enjoyed, 'to ride on white horses adorned with saddle cloth of purest white, wearing white shoes like senators'.

But all this was mere garnishing of the central point – the establishment of the fact that the pope was not merely independent of the emperor but actually his superior. Christophorus made it appear that Sylvester had actually been offered the imperial crown but had declined it as unfitting for the holder of a spiritual office and had accepted, instead, a simple white Phrygian cap, humble forerunner of the great triple tiara. Nevertheless, the fact that he had been offered the imperial crown implied that Constantine – and his successors – afterwards possessed it only on the pope's sufferance.

Christophorus went on to make the point abundantly clear by skilfully twisting the true reason for Constantine's decision to establish his capital in the east – it was not fitting that an earthly emperor should share the same city as the successor of St Peter. And then came the crux of the whole matter, the key phrase which would lead to centuries of bloodshed and corruption. 'Wherefore that the pontifical crown may be maintained in dignity, we hand over and relinquish our palaces, the City of Rome and all the provinces, places and cities of Italy and the regions of the West to the most blessed pontiff and universal pope, Sylvester.'

Despite the astonishing nature of the claim it was accepted wholly if reluctantly even by later opponents of the papacy. Even so great a scholar as Dante Alighieri in the fourteenth century accepted it:

> Ah, Constantine, of how much ill was mother
> Not thy conversion but that marriage dower
> Which the first wealthy father took from thee.

A few years later, in 1350, the chronicler of the city of Piacenza in a noble lamentation summed up the effects of the forgery on ordinary Italians for century after century.

> It is now more than a thousand years since these cities and territories have been given to the priests and ever since then the most violent wars have been waged on their account, and yet the priests neither now possess them in peace, nor will they ever be able to possess them. It were in truth better before the eyes of God and the world that these pastors should entirely renounce the *dominium temporale*: for since Sylvester's time the consequences of the temporal power have been innumerable wars and the overthrow of peoples and cities. Truly we cannot serve God and Mammon at the same time, cannot stand with one foot in Heaven and the other on Earth.

In moving the capital from Rome to Constantinople, Constantine had begun the process of severing Italy from imperial control; in ejecting the Goths from Rome, Constantine's successor Justinian accelerated the process. The kingdom established by the Goths had been virtually a continuance of the old empire in Italy; certainly, the great Gothic king, Theodoric, had been, for all practical purposes, a truly Roman emperor. He had been brought up at the Byzantine court and, at about the time that Clovis had begun to bring north-western Europe under Frankish dominance, Theodoric had set up a brilliant court in Ravenna. Under him was the last flowering of classical Latin literature, under him Italy enjoyed the sunset of empire, the last time she would know unification and order until the late nineteenth century. Then, after Theodoric's death, the Gothic kingdom began to fall apart and Belisarius's brilliant recovery of Rome spelt the beginning of the end.

But it did not spell the beginning of the end of 'barbarian' invasion:

on the contrary, it left the peninsula wide open. And among the newcomers were the Lombards, the *nefandissimi Langobardi*. Initially, they were Arians and this would sufficiently account for papal animosity. But in due course they became good Catholics – so good indeed that Lombards were to be found in high and trusted offices at the papal court. Nevertheless, the popes cherished a deep, passionate and enduring hatred for the Lombards which not only distorted the popes' own judgement, but the picture which posterity has of the people who dominated the Italian peninsula from the ending of the Gothic kingdom to the establishment of Charlemagne's rule. As it happens, Charlemagne himself, in his pursuit of a learning which knew bounds neither of race nor religion, brought to his court the Lombard historian known as Paul the Deacon, and Paul provides posterity with the only 'inside' view of the Lombard people – but unfortunately he failed to bring his history down to his own time, probably out of a sense of conflict of interest between the duty he owed to his own people, and to his patron who had finally destroyed that people's sovereignty. From about 750 onwards, therefore, posterity is dependent largely upon the venomous picture of the Lombards as created by the papal biographers.

The Lombards were part of the great Teutonic peoples, related both to Franks and to Goths. They were perhaps the most consummate horsemen of all those who erupted out of the east. Certainly, no other race had so many laws concerning horses written into the constitution. There was even a crime defined as *meerwhorphin*, the hurling of a man off his horse. Unlike the Huns, who were essentially horse-archers, or the Franks and Goths who regarded their horses as a means of transport, the Lombards perfected that use of cavalry as a battering-ram which found its apogee in the high Middle Ages. Paul tells in awed tones the story of a Lombard horseman who transfixed a Byzantine on his great lance, lifting the wretched man up so that he was wriggling like an insect upon the point of the weapon. They entered Italy not as a collection of war-bands but as a compact, national body moving as one immense group with wives, children and cattle. Yet, curiously, they never evolved a single royal dynasty as did the Franks and Goths, a fact which weakened them greatly as they came into contact and conflict with other, more unified, nations. It was only during the last decades of Lombard rule in Italy that they achieved a single king, ruling from Pavia in what was now known as the plain of Lombardy.

Nevertheless, by the middle of the eighth century they virtually controlled Italy with two great quasi-independent duchies in the south as well as the kingdom in the north. In theory, they too were subject to the rule of Constantinople through the Byzantine Exarch in Ravenna, but in 751 the reigning Lombard king, Aistulf, finally and completely upset the balance of power by attacking and taking Ravenna, bringing to an end all effective Byzantine rule in Italy. And bringing Lombard into direct conflict with Roman or, to be exact, bringing King Aistulf into direct conflict with Pope Stephen. For, dimly, through the ritual execrations of the papal biographers can be detected a note of personal hatred. Stephen, through his chronicler, excelled himself in that invective to which the bishops of Rome had such easy recourse: '*crudelissimus rex*', '*nequissimus*', '*malignus rex*', '*rex impious*' '*atrocissimus Langobardum rex*'. The reason for the hatred was clear enough: Aistulf threatened Stephen on the ground which had been so clearly claimed by the so-called Donation of Constantine. Judging by the claims he made, it is possible that Stephen did not know that the document was a forgery and as such was morally outraged by Aistulf's threats to occupy lands dedicated to St Peter.

> The Exarchate has hitherto belonged to the Roman Empire, though the man who now bears the title of Roman Emperor has proved himself unable to preserve it. But the Roman Empire means the Roman Republic, and the true representative of the City of Rome, if the Emperor abdicates his power, is the bishop of that City. And the bishop of Rome is the successor of St Peter and the Apostle from his high place in heaven watches over his successors. Therefore whosoever interferes with our claim to exercise temporal dominion over Italy incurs the wrath of St Peter and will be shut out by the great Key-bearer from the Kingdom of Heaven.

But it seems that Aistulf, King of the Lombards, cared little for the wrath of the heavenly Key-bearer. He cared even less for the wrath of the earthly emperor, contemptuously ignoring an embassy commanding him to restore Ravenna to the Exarch. Instead, he began a series of lively incursions on what were indubitably papal lands. 'The most atrocious king of the Lombards, persisting in his pernicious design, flamed into vehement fury and roaring like a lion uttered his pestiferous threats against the Romans, vowing that they would all be butchered with one sword unless they would submit themselves to his dominions.' Stephen organized an immense penitential procession through Rome. 'Ashes were sprinkled on the heads of all the people and they walked along with mighty wailings calling on the most merciful Lord God.' The reader might well suppose that Aistulf had embarked on a mission of genocide; he had not, in fact, laid hands on a single Roman and what was at issue here was who would collect the taxes of Rome.

Now Stephen began to look for outside help. In September 753 another embassy arrived from Constantinople but, far from bringing help to the beleaguered pope, it was simply bringing lofty instructions for Pope Stephen to go to King Aistulf and order him to restore the imperial territories in Italy. Stephen's reaction to this preposterous order could only have been a mixture of incredulity and rage. Constantinople was a broken reed: the only possible help could come from the pious and brawny men on the other side of the Alps. A letter to the 'glorious men our sons, all the dukes of the Frankish nation' had brought an invitation to visit Francia. In October Stephen left Rome with his entourage, bound for the north. At the fortieth milestone from Rome there came an encouraging sign – a great globe of fire falling from the heavens south from the regions of Gaul and Lombardy, a sign of great changes coming from the northern lands upon Italy. Pausing for an inconclusive and acrimonious exchange with Aistulf in Pavia, the papal party set off again for the great wall of the Alps, entering it as winter began to close around the high peaks, so desperate now was the pope's need. At the beginning of January they were descending the northern slopes towards their meeting with young Prince Charles.

PART II · *The Road to Rome*

4 The Making of a King

King Pippin led the Frankish host through the Alps in March 755 to begin the war against the Lombards. Twenty years were to pass before his son, Charles – now himself a veteran monarch in his mid-thirties – brought that war to an end and, in so doing, established the basis of the Frankish *imperium* in Italy. But by that irony of archives in which it is the recipient, not the writer, of a letter who usually preserves it, most of the 'inside' information that posterity possesses about this long-drawn-out conflict comes from the papal archives. Three successive popes wrote over a hundred detailed letters to Pippin and to his son and successor Charles, letters exhorting, complaining, congratulating, lamenting, cursing, describing – and all were carefully preserved by Charles himself. In part, the act of preservation arose from that lively sense of history of his; in part, in his own words 'in order that no evidence which would benefit Holy Church might be wanting to my successors'. But it is just as likely, too, that as the pope's claims became ever wider and more ambitious Charles wanted some evidence as to what he had agreed. Their preservation would have done honour to a modern archive system, the copiers displaying an impressive integrity. One of the letters survives only in the form of a brief abstract, to which a note is appended: 'This letter is not copied in the volume because by reason of age it is, in great measure, destroyed.'

By contrast, the replies of Charles and his father are entirely missing, a curious fact when it is considered that their letters were going to a depository permanently situated in the papal palace in Rome.*

*By a further irony of history it may well be that they are currently lying in some long-forgotten repository in modern France, conveyed there during the great looting operation of Italy launched by Bonaparte in 1796; all documents before AD 900 were then removed from the Vatican archives.

Whatever the cause of the lacuna, posterity relies largely on the highly-coloured letters of Pope Stephen and of his successor Adrian, eked out with the still unsophisticated work of the few Frankish chroniclers.

What is clear beyond doubt is that Aistulf collapsed virtually at a touch. The Frankish vanguard was amply sufficient to disperse the Lombards defending the Alpine passes and, after a brief siege of Pavia, Aistulf agreed to all terms, promising 'with mighty and terrible oath' to restore Ravenna and all other territories to the Roman Republic, in other words to Pope Stephen. And having gained Aistulf's signature, Pippin withdrew thankfully to Francia, much to his noblemen's relief. But scarcely had he picked up the threads at home when there came winging over the Alps yet another letter from Stephen, addressed not simply to Pippin but to his son Charles, now a stalwart young Frankish warrior of fourteen. The expected had happened. 'That old enemy of the human race had invaded his [Aistulf's] perfidious heart and he seems to make no account of the promises he gave under oath . . . The very stones themselves would with mighty howlings weep for our tribulations.' Aistulf was indeed intent upon making a thorough nuisance of himself, no longer contenting himself with attacking outlying cities, but launching a vigorous attack upon Rome itself. Or so said the pope. But in the standard catalogue of Lombard crimes that he submitted – crimes which included the burning of churches, the violation of nuns, the beating up of monks and the digging up of bodies – he included, 'The farmhouses on St Peter's property were destroyed by fire: the cattle were driven off, the harvests tramped down and devoured.' Even the unsophisticated Franks must have wondered just what harvests there could have been in the Roman Campagna in the middle of February, the date that the letter was written. But though undoubtedly exaggerated by Stephen's apparently standard hyperbole, there was little doubt that Rome was under real threat from the Lombards. Nevertheless, Pippin and his son, preoccupied with their own domestic struggles, remained reluctant to go yet again a-venturing into Italy. The pope's agitated letters were met with soothing promises but little more. Until there arrived a letter from St Peter himself, a letter which, moreover, was backed up and ratified by the Mother of God.

Writing to his 'adoptive sons' the three Frankish kings – Pippin, Charles and Charles's five-year-old brother Carloman – the 'Apostle' observed:

Our Lady Mary, the ever-Virgin Mother of God, unites her entreaties to ours, protests, admonishes and commands and with all the thrones and dominions and the entire army of the celestial host, as well as the martyrs and confessors of Christ . . . Together we exhort and conjure you to deliver not only the city of Rome entrusted to us by God, but the sheep of the Lord who dwell therein and are troubled, so that my body, and my grave where by God's commands it rests may neither be desecrated by the persecuting Lombards.

And if natural piety did not hasten their steps, the Apostle continued, then an eternity of punishment might change their minds. 'Should you be guilty of delay or evasion, or fail to obey our exhortations in coming to the rescue of this, my city of Rome, you shall be declared to have forfeited the Kingdom of God and eternal life.'

It seems scarcely possible that Pippin, though a 'barbarian' and a deeply pious one, could have taken this letter at its face value. Yet stranger things were accepted as a species of common-place miracle, and certainly the admonishments of the Apostle achieved what the lamentations of the pope had singularly failed to produce. Again, the Frankish host lumbered into action, crossing the Alps as soon as the milder weather of spring opened up the passes. Again Aistulf sued for peace, making his usual large promises. Even more surprisingly, again Pippin accepted those promises, though backing them up by the taking of hostages. But this time fate intervened to ensure that the promises were kept, for Aistulf was thrown from his horse while out hunting and killed. Pope Stephen charitably pronounced his epitaph in a letter to Pippin: 'That follower of the devil, Aistulf, devourer of the blood of Christians, struck by a divine blow has been swallowed up in the infernal whirlpool.'

While Pippin was still in Lombardy, but after he had defeated Aistulf and was contemplating the future disposition of the captured cities, there arrived at his camp two exotically-dressed strangers accompanied by an entourage that indicated their high office. They were emissaries from the Byzantine court who had made the long and dangerous journey with only one purpose in mind. With oriental abandon they threw themselves at the feet of the Frankish king, beseeching him to restore to his imperial majesty those lands and cities which the pestiferous Lombards had stolen from the empire. Here, indeed, was a heady moment for a 'barbarian': to stand, as it were in judgement, over the claims of the Emperor of Rome, now resident in Constantinople, and the bishop of Rome, as to who owned great tracts of the land that had once been mistress of the world. But Pippin, according to the unctuous words of the papal biographer (our only source for what happened next), knew where his duty lay. 'Mild as he was, that worshipper of God declared that on no account whatever should those cities be alienated from the power of the blessed Peter and the jurisdiction of the Roman church, affirming with an oath that for no living man's favour had he given himself once again to the conflict, but solely for love of St Peter and for the pardon of his sins.' He commissioned Fulrad, Charles's old tutor, to turn treaty and promise into fact. The abbot personally entered each of the twenty-three cities that had yielded to the Franks, collecting their great keys, and proceeded with them to Rome where they were laid upon the tomb of the Apostle and accepted, upon his behalf, by the Vicar of Christ, Bishop of Rome, thus immensely enhancing the stature of the papal monarch, who would become one of the most potent figures in European history.

Throughout all these events, destined to have a profound effect upon the career of the future Charlemagne, the present Charles – simply the elder son of his father Pippin – would have been closely involved both on the battlefield and in the council chamber. Had the Frankish end of the correspondence with the Lateran Palace survived, there would have been rich material with which to build up the portrait of the young man as he emerged from boyhood into manhood, for the few, fugitive references in the pope's letters show that he was in the forefront of affairs. The pope is most careful to address him by name in his letters, but exactly how he passed his time from the age of fourteen, to that moment when he acquired the crown of Francia at the age of twenty-nine, is unknown in detail. Warfare would undoubtedly have absorbed most of his energies. There was the unending threat from the ferocious Saxons in the north-east. In the south-west the Saracens were at last driven back behind their mountain redoubt. There was the rumbling discontent in Aquitaine, that beautiful region which had never quite been drawn into the Frankish empire, but was never quite able to remain independent. There was the trouble with Charles's hot-headed young cousin, Tassilo, who became Duke of Bavaria at the age of fifteen. In his overweening pride, Tassilo had committed the ultimate Frankish crime, that of *harisliz* or desertion of his lord in the face of the enemy, abandoning his uncle during the Aquitanian campaign. Pippin had too much on his hands to exact vengeance at the time, leaving it as a dangerous legacy for his son, and one which all but proved fatal.

Off the battlefield, there was much to occupy the young man. The querulous Pope Stephen had died, taking to the grave his endless complaints and demands, but the new Pope Paul, though more fulsome, was scarcely less pressing in his reminders that the Frankish crown owed its very existence to the papacy. Messengers were continually travelling back and forwards between the Alps, bearing letters that inextricably linked together the fate of the papal and Frankish crowns. But the messengers, too, bore gifts – like the table inlaid with precious stones which Pippin presented to the pope and which was received as though it had been the Holy Grail itself, judging by Paul's letter: 'This table we brought in with hymns and spiritual songs to the hall of that chief of Apostles, and laid it on your behalf on the shrine of that doorkeeper of the kingdom of heaven . . . In that same apostolic hall it will remain for ever as a memorial of you, and be sure that you will receive a fitting reward from God and St Peter in the heavenly kingdom.' The pope sends to the Franks books, and a clock 'for use at night'; back across the Alps comes the napkin in which Charles's baby sister Gisila had been christened. Paul seems almost hysterical with delight: 'With great joy and accompanied by a whole cohort of the people, we received this napkin in the chapel where rests the holy body of Petronilla' – particularly appropriate, Paul feels, as Petronilla was, of course, the daughter of St Peter. Behind the lavish compliments was a very real political purpose, orchestrated by a shrewd Latin mind: the acceptance of the napkin turned Paul into Gisila's godfather, making yet another link, yet another potential ground for claiming protection from the most powerful house in the west.

In addition to warfare and diplomacy Charles was involved in the ordinary business of everyday life. It was during this period he made the first of those confusing sexual relationships which was something more than concubinage, something less than marriage, creating tortuous problems for genealogists yet unborn. The Franks called it *Friedelehe*, and it could perhaps be compared with the English system of a common-law wife or husband, a union which was in fact a marriage according to native custom but not as laid down in canonical laws. The girl in question was of good Frankish stock, Himiltrude by name, and she bore Charles a son, a remarkably handsome little boy who was, tragically, deformed. But despite the fact that he was a hunchback, Charles christened him Pippin, following the Frankish custom of giving a future heir his grandfather's name thus signifying, quite unequivocally, his recognition of the child. It was only later, when he had three healthy sons by another woman, that he disinherited Pippin on grounds of his deformity and so turned the boy into a bitter enemy.

Charles himself had been the product of such a union, and this in turn was undoubtedly the cause of the bitterness and tension between himself and his seventeen-year-old brother Carloman when their father died in 768 and they inherited the kingdom. Yet again a Frank followed that dangerous custom, recipe for dissension, of dividing his kingdom between his sons. Carloman, though the younger, regarded himself as the true inheritor, for he had been born in wedlock whereas Pippin and Bertha did not regularize their union until at least seven years after Charles had been born. In addition, the way in which their father had divided the kingdom might have been deliberately designed to exacerbate the bad feeling that notoriously existed between them. Instead of following the Merovingian custom of splitting the kingdom on a line running roughly north and south – which at least had the merit of clarity – Pippin in effect carved out the central portion and gave it to Carloman, leaving Charles with an immensely long strip all along the Atlantic seaboard, and then curving inland far beyond the Rhine, administratively difficult to handle, militarily difficult to defend. Bavaria was not mentioned, a tacit admission of the fact that young Tassilo had virtually got away with murder – for the time being at least – while the turbulent duchy of Aquitaine was split between them both. The division gave Charles the old Roman spa town of Aquis Grana (Aachen), the town which, in later years, he was to make in effect the Rome of the north while Carloman used Soissons as his centre.

Trouble between the brothers broke out almost immediately. Pippin had suppressed, not defeated, the Aquitanians and they seized this opportunity when the Frankish kingdom was in its transition stage to rebel. Charles, who had already campaigned against the Aquitanians, was ready for the rebellion and marched swiftly southward, while Carloman moved westward, the brothers meeting on the northern borders of Aquitaine. And there the quarrel between them flared into the open: quite unforgivably (and foolishly, considering his joint interest) Carloman flounced off, taking his levies with him, leaving Charles to suppress the rebellion on his own. It was a challenge to which he rose magnificently and one which, in the long run, proved of incalculable value to him for it showed his fellow Franks – those fighting men who were not yet 'subjects' except in the most technical of terms – just who was truly ruler and master in the kingdom. His gamble was not as dangerous as it seemed. Unlike Carloman he knew Aquitaine and its people; knew that they were exhausted after nearly nine years' running battle with the Frankish kingdom and he calculated that a short, hard push would send the resistance crumbling. His calculation was accurate, a campaign of two months serving, in effect, to finish off the work of his father. Aquitaine was at last brought firmly into the kingdom, Charles returned a hero, and the petulant Carloman was reduced substantially in stature and reputation.

The personal animosity between the brothers was, if anything, increased by this incident, and symbolized by their almost childish vying for Abbot Fulrad's attention. The ageing abbot of St Denis was a link with the heroic, formative years of their dynasty, their late father's most trusted counsellor, the man who had shaped their own characters, who had the ear of Rome but was also a Frank of the Franks. His abbey was in Carloman's territory and Carloman made haste to confirm it in its privileges; Charles as promptly countered by ceding rich lands to increase the abbey's already impressive wealth. Fulrad balanced between the brothers with some unease, acting at once as a link and a brake but throughout the year 769 the relationship between them approached the point at which their personal entourages fully expected an open break of the kind which had so often characterized the kingdom of the Franks. The matter came to the ears of the pope in distant Rome, alarming him that his natural protectors should be squabbling between themselves instead of concentrating on his enemies. During one of their temporary reconciliations, he hastened to send off yet another letter, congratulating them on their new-found harmony before playing again the same old tune: the Lombards were up to their old tricks; the possessions of St Peter were again at risk; the Frankish kings should turn their attention to more important things like coming again into Italy and raising their strong shields to protect the Apostle's successor. The brothers ignored him, continuing with their bickering. And it was at this stage their formidable mother, Bertha, stepped out of the shadows and firmly took the reins from their hands.

As with her husband Pippin, there are no detailed, personal descriptions of either the Queen Mother's appearance, or her character. Unlike her husband, however, it is possible to deduce at least an outline portrait of her from her actions and the reactions to them. A big, probably a massive, woman with a sense of style in dress that gave her presence; certainly a woman of very strong character, masculine in its direct approach to problems but feminine in its subtlety. Repulsed in a head-on attack, skilfully she could devise an out-flanking movement achieving her end by indirect means; a hard woman, certainly, but also one capable of inspiring genuine affection and respect from those around her, not least from her elder son. During her husband's reign she had, perforce, remained in the background but the course she took as soon as she had the freedom to act, argued that she must have been seething with impatience and disapproval at her husband's almost spaniel-like devotion to Rome.

Bertha had the deep, unthinking piety of her day. But she also had the Teuton's deep, instinctive distrust of the smooth Roman clergy, a reluctance to become caught up in their endless plots and counter-plots. And her distrust of Romans was bolstered by her natural ties with the Lombards, so much closer to her own people in all characteristics. In the time of her husband's uncle, Charles Martel, Franks and Lombards had been firm allies. Her nephew, Tassilo, Duke of Bavaria, was married to a Lombard princess. The Lombard kingdom bordered that of her son, Carloman's. The time had come for Franks and Lombards, fellow Teutons, to enter into a close alliance that would transcend the natural barrier of the Alps. Together, they would hold the balance of power in central Europe – able to hold their own even against the ferocious Saxons, the unwinking enemy – and all this was being imperilled by the family squabbles of her sons.

Bertha spent Easter of 770 at Charles's court at Liège, outlining her plan of action, gaining his permission for a projected journey into Italy. She moved on then to Carloman, repeating her arguments, using the feminine side of her character to smooth the petulant young man's annoyance with his brother. Then on to Bavaria to speak to Tassilo who, with his Lombard wife Liutberga, could be a very useful ally in the mission she had planned. Tassilo's mother, Hiltrud, was a sister of Pippin and the hot-headed young man was therefore bound to the Frankish crown by ties of blood as well as vassalage. Over his head hung the still unexpiated crime of *harisliz*. The new kings of the Franks were as yet of uncertain temper and quality. Altogether, Tassilo had excellent reasons for yielding to the persuasions of his aunt and agreed to make certain overtures to the king of the Lombards. Satisfied, Bertha made her way south, to Rome, to receive the blessings of the pope and listen resignedly to his endless complaints about the evil Lombards. She made soothing promises, presented rich gifts to the tomb of the Apostle and took the road north again to Pavia, the capital of the Lombard kingdom, where waiting for her was Desiderius, successor to Aistulf and destined to be the last king of Lombardy. To Desiderius Bertha unfolded the whole of her plan. She was offering not simply a treaty of alliance, but the strongest of all political bonds, the matrimonial. She was offering her son, Charles, as husband for Desiderius's daughter, Desiderata, and her little twelve-year-old daughter, Gisila, as wife to Desiderius's son Adelchis. In addition, in order to damp the fires that would surely break out in Rome at this news, she asked that Desiderius freely cede over to the pope certain cities that were still a matter of dispute.

Desiderius fairly leaped at the offer. At one stroke he would not only free himself of that Frankish menace which loomed over all Lombard shoulders but tie his family in with the most important family in western Europe. There was one, small, obstruction: was not King Charles already married to the lady Himiltrude? Bertha assured him that that would cause no difficulty; the marriage with Himiltrude had been no real marriage, never having been blessed by Holy Church. Himiltrude would be sent packing, together with her hunchbacked son, leaving the way clear for the progeny of Desiderata – who would be the grandchildren of Desiderius. And so it was arranged. So urgent were Bertha's plans, so vehement her talents of persuasion, that when she left the little Lombard princess accompanied her, enduring the fate of all girls of her class, that of being taken from her home into a strange land, among strange people speaking an alien tongue, and put to bed with one of those strangers. The marriage between Charles, King of the Austrasian Franks, and Desiderata, daughter of Desiderius, King of the Lombards, was duly and promptly solemnized.

If Bertha had thought that the ceding of cities to the pope would have reconciled him to this astonishing volte-face she was, for once, very seriously in error. Pope Stephen III had, through his numerous letters in the past, shown himself a master of invective and dramatization. Now he excelled himself. Even through the barrier interposed by time and an alien, dead language the voice of an almost hysterical rage and hatred and despair comes shrilly and clearly through. There are orthographic indications that the pope departed from custom and himself, personally, penned the missive. Certainly, if it had fallen to any career diplomat at the Lateran Palace some attempt must surely have been made to tone down its shriek of hatred, directed not only against the Lombards but, by implication, against the Franks, the papal shield. The letter was addressed not to Bertha, that impious woman who had abandoned her proper feminine role to meddle in politics, but to the two kings of the Franks:

It has come to my knowledge and fills my heart with dismay that the Lombard king Desiderius seeks to persuade one of you to marry his daughter. The suggestion is truly devilish, and such a union would be no marriage but concubinage. What madness were it if a distinguished scion of the royal house of your glorious Franks, a nation which excels all other nations, should sully himself with a union with the perfidious and foully stinking race of the Lombards, which is never reckoned as belonging among the number of nations and one from which it is certain that all lepers have sprung . . .

On and on goes the diatribe. The entire female sex comes in for attack, beginning with Eve for whose sin all mankind now pays. God, he assures his readers, always punishes, with the most hideous punishment, those who make wanton alliance with a foreign people: 'Who of your house ever condescended to contaminate himself by mixing with the horrid nation of the Lombards.' And, finally, to back up his lecture on hygiene, genealogy, Old Testament Scripture and modern foreign policy, Stephen gave it a supernatural power by laying it on the tomb of St Peter, celebrating mass over it and ending with an anathema which should have chilled the blood of his Frankish readers had they not, perhaps, read such anathemas before:

If anyone dares to act in opposition to our exhortations herein contained let him know that, by the authority of my master the holy Peter, Prince of the Apostles, he is encompassed by the chains of the anathema, excluded from the kingdom of God and condemned to burn in eternal fire with the devil and all the rest of the godless.

Charles might have thought all this a high price for going to bed with a pretty girl from beyond the Alps but, obediently, he obeyed his mother's wishes. Or, rather, part of his mother's wishes. Desiderata was given all the honours of queen of the Franks, but Charles refused to allow his twelve-year-old sister Gisila to undertake her own journey into foreign parts and take a stranger for husband, the first example of his enigmatic desire to keep his close female relatives unwed at home, a desire which was to arouse the deepest suspicions even in so loyal a friend and servant as Einhard. Pope Stephen may well have thought that he had been over-hasty in deploying his supernatural artillery when, within a year of Charles's marriage, he casually dismissed his young bride, sending her back to her father, infuriating Desiderius, standing his mother's policy on its head and causing the first personal rift between them. Years afterwards, Einhard cautiously touched on the matter: 'His mother Bertha lived with him to old age in great honour. He treated her with the utmost reverence so that no quarrel of any kind ever arose between them – except in the matter of the divorce of the daughter of King Desiderius, whom he had married at her bidding.'

The documentation of Charlemagne's life, upon which posterity is dependent to obtain a portrait of the king, varies wildly between meticulous detail during which it is actually possible to trace his thought processes, to great areas of absolute darkness where it is all but impossible even to guess the reason for a particular action. This first year of his reign is perhaps the most mysterious of all. Why did he so passively accept his mother's plans for a bride, plans which not only overturned the policy which his father and he had been following for at least a decade but interfered directly in that sexual life which was of such vast importance to him? He was no green youth but a man of nearly thirty, a veteran of countless battlefields, an experienced observer – and very probably a no less experienced participant – in the jockeying of international politics. And why, having accepted Desiderata (which, incidentally, meant thrusting aside the girl who had been his first love), did he within a matter of months humiliate an innocent and helpless girl, antagonize her powerful father and profoundly irritate his much-loved mother? Einhard retains a diplomatic silence, but his successor, a monk of the monastery of St Gall who wrote a highly romanticized biography some eighty years after Charles's death, is confident that he knew the true reason for Charles's repudiation and its inevitable result. Desiderata 'was an invalid and little likely to give issue to Charles, she was by the counsel of the holiest of the clergy, put aside even as though she were dead. Whereupon her father in wrath, shutting himself up in the walls of Pavia, prepared to give battle to the invincible Charles.'

The Monk of St Gall was certainly wrong when he claims that Charles acted on the counsel of anybody. To the contrary, his repudiation of the young girl created a considerable scandal. His young cousin Adalhard, though only a page in the palace, totally condemned the divorce. It would not only make the king an adulterer, he said, but it would turn into perjurers all those who had sworn fidelity to Desiderata as queen. But the Monk's opinion that it was the girl's physical defect which prompted Charles's action has the ring of truth about it. Charles, in most things so very temperate and balanced, had an all but uncontrollable sexual appetite. There was nothing furtive, or sly, or apologetic about it. One receives the impression, indeed, of an enormous – almost elemental – generative force overflowing conventional channels. Generations yet unborn would proudly lay claim to some title of European royalty on the grounds that they had Carolingian blood in their veins, even though diluted almost to nothing by time and by bastardy. The chroniclers and court poets recorded the names, and gave at least some hint of the identities, of five of his wives and four of his mistresses. But these latter were the important ones, those often seen in and around the court, taking part in its daily life on a regular basis so that they became well known. Their children assumed, in the course of time, dynastic importance as one of the channels of the priceless Carolingian blood. But the identity of the transient sexual companions, those who appeared at camp or even at court to serve a passing need and were later dismissed with a kind word and gift – these are unknown for they excited no particular interest. And their number was probably legion. It is entirely within the bounds of probability that Charles set Desiderata aside, initiating that series of events which, among much else, resulted in the final destruction of the Lombard kingdom, simply because the poor girl was no good in bed. Later, indeed, he gave some evidence of having a bad conscience over the affair, making a money gift to her father ostensibly on behalf of the pope, but coming from his own treasury and quite evidently intended as a peace-offering. Desiderius refused it, and so brought about his own destruction.

Desiderata's bed did not remain long unoccupied. Charles's third wife was a Frankish maiden of high class called Hildegarde. She was only a child barely half his age when he married her, and she died in her mid-twenties. But there was a warm and loving quality about her that comes through even the sparse and stilted Latin of the chroniclers. They had the medieval indifference to psychological portraits, the medieval preference for anecdotes, but even with this limitation posterity can dimly discern a most attractive personality: gentle, charitable, patient, forming the still and constant centre of her great husband's tumultuous life. She gave him the three sons who would inherit the empire he created and the four daughters whom he loved with a passion that some of his closest counsellors uneasily thought indiscreet.

But Hildegarde was not all soft, malleable, retiring femininity. She was a Frank and so expected to take part in public affairs, though like her mother-in-law her contributions were indirect. The Monk of St Gall tells one of his anecdotes which, though evidently well polished, gives some insight into the relationship between husband and wife.

A bishopric had fallen vacant and Charles was interviewing a potential candidate. The young clerk was immensely confident of his ability to fill the demanding role and the king, with a touch of irony, told him to stand behind one of the curtains in the audience chamber 'and mark what kind of help you would receive if you were raised to that honour'. There came then a succession of courtiers, each pleading the cause of their own candidate:

At last Queen Hildegarde came in person to beg the bishopric for a certain clerk of her own. The emperor received her petition very graciously and said that he would not and could not deny her anything but that he thought it a shame to deceive his little chaplain. But still the queen, woman-like, thought that a woman's opinion and wish ought to outweigh the decrees of men and so she concealed the passion that was rising in her heart. She sank her strong voice almost to a whisper and with caressing gestures tried to soften the emperor's unspoken mind. 'My sire and king,' she said. 'What does it matter if that boy lose the bishopric. Nay I beseech you, sweet sire, my glory and refuge, give it to your faithful servant, my clerk.' Then that young man who had heard the petons from behind the curtain close to the king's chair where he had been placed, embraced the king through the curtain and cried, 'Sir king, stand fast and do not let anyone take from you the power that has been given you by God!'

Charles needed no such admonition. Quite clearly there comes the picture of a powerful man's relationship with a loved wife, treating her with both affection and respect – if with a measure of irony – but refusing to allow her to operate outside her own sphere. But as well as holding the love of her husband, Hildegarde was particularly fortunate in possessing the warm friendship of Gisila, his only sister. Gisila does not seem to have pined overmuch about the breaking off of her betrothal to the Lombard prince. She entered a convent, though whether this was at her own request, or on her brother's instructions, is unclear. In either case, it was a way of life that she treasured and one which, in the easy atmosphere of the day, did not prevent her frequent attendance at Charles's court. She shared her brother's ebullience and warmth of character and was immensely popular, not only forming a close attachment with her sister-in-law but with other members of the inner circle as well, some of them of high intellectual attainment. For there was another side to her character, a deeply religious streak which gradually drew her more and more away from the colourful life of the court to the contemplative life of her abbey of Chelles, despite the disappointed protests of the family and friends. These two women, the

Abbess Gisila and Queen Hildegarde, with the Queen Mother Bertha now reconciled to her new daughter-in-law, provided the warm feminine centre of Charles's court in its formative years. In the eyes of Charles's graver counsellors they were, perhaps, just too tolerant of certain of his failings but they gave him the domestic base that he needed as he set foot on the path of European hegemony.

The first problem, the intractable problem, the problem of his brother Carloman, was solved by fate itself. Brooding over his imagined wrongs, egged on by counsellors who seemed to regard their Austrasian cousins with a loathing usually reserved for the infidel, the young man was fully prepared to hurl the kingdom into the horrors of civil war. So says Einhard, and though he was obviously tutored by Charles himself, there is no reason to doubt the king's word as he looked back and mused over his long reign. 'Many partisans of Carloman tried to break their alliance and some even hoped to engage them in war.' Carloman's sudden but natural death solved the problem both for Francia and for Charles, saving the kingdom from civil war and the king, perhaps, from fratricide. Certainly the speed with which he moved to take over key offices argues a considerable degree of preparation. Carloman's widow, under the protection of her late husband's chief counsellor Otker, fled the country, taking her infant sons with her 'for no obvious reason' according to Einhard. The refuge that she – or Otker – chose was a direct challenge and insult to Charles for she made straight for Pavia, home of her brother-in-law's now bitter enemy Desiderius. As events were to show, she did Charles an injustice, but her immediate reaction was understandable for her two little boys legally stood between Charles and a unified kingdom. Yet again an external event saved Charles from the necessity of making a difficult and perhaps unsavoury decision, and he grasped the opportunity to begin the process of welding together the sundered halves of the kingdom. It was no simple task, for Austrasian and Neustrian Franks were far gone in mutual suspicion and dislike. There was, however, one excellent recipe for a ruler who wished to distract the attention of his people from domestic struggles and, at the same time, to give them a common cause and that was to find a common enemy and attack him. An attack on the Lombards was, at this stage, out of the question, so equivocal were the relationships between the races – in particular, between Carloman's Franks and the Lombards. In the north-east, however, there was a very real, very grim, enemy: the Saxon.

Einhard gave a remarkably fair account of the bitter enmity between Franks and Saxons, considering that he was a Frank. While remarking that the Saxons were, admittedly, a monstrous people the fault was on both sides, he thought.

> The Saxons, like most of the races which inhabit Germany, are by nature fierce, devoted to the worship of demons and hostile to our religion, and they think it no dishonour to confound and transgress the laws of God and man. There were reasons, too, which might at any time cause a disturbance of the peace. For our boundaries and theirs touch almost everywhere on the open plain, except where in a few places large forests or ranges of mountains are interposed to separate the territories of the two nations by a definite frontier: so that on both sides murder, robbery, and arson were of constant occurrence.

Although the thought would doubtless not have occurred to Charlemagne, in fact when he was looking eastward across the Rhine to that ancient enemy, he was looking back through time. For the Saxons, in the eighth century, were much as the Franks would have been eight centuries earlier, a fierce, courageous, nomadic people with some very beastly customs, but yet redeemed by an essential belief in the value of the individual. They had no kings but, instead, a number of territorial chiefs. The nation as a whole met in assembly once a year near the river Weser and there the various chiefs chose twelve representatives of the nobles and twelve freemen and serfs who then reviewed the laws, and settled outstanding legal cases. Recognizing the necessity of having a central direction in time of war, a war leader was chosen by lot to lead the army but even his authority lasted only so long as the military necessity. Charlemagne, as a Christian ruler, might be horrified by their anarchy and their paganism; his remote posterity would recognize that they, in their barbarian darkness, had created something of lasting value, foreshadowing the growth of parliamentary democracy.

This first foray of Charlemagne's into Saxon territory was a curtain-raiser, an overture, to thirty years' bloody war but it was, in itself, little more than a skirmish. Unlike the Franks and Lombards who had rapidly taken to urban living, the Saxons still hated and distrusted cities, 'tombs for the living' as they termed them. They developed fortified strong points some of which, in the fullness of time, would indeed turn into full-scale towns but which were now simply places for garrisons. Before Charlemagne's advance, the Saxons simply melted away in that guerrilla tactic so effective against, and so infuriating to, a more sophisticated enemy. But Charles carried out one highly effective action which transformed what was little more than a punitive expedition into what could pass as a holy war. He destroyed the mysterious Irminsul.

Tree-worship was central to Saxon religion. Years before, St Boniface had almost literally taken his life in his hands when, in his direct manner, he had made straight for the great Oak of Geismar in Saxony and, with his own hands, began the work of hewing it down. The worship was attended with horrific sacrificial practices. On the feast of Othin, to whom the tree was dedicated, nine victims, of eight different species including human, were hung in the branches, slowly bleeding to death. It is virtually impossible to establish if the Irminsul was an actual tree, a dead stump, or an immense wooden pillar carved from the bole of a tree, but evidently it stood not only in a sacred grove, but surrounded by some of the rare stone-built buildings of the Saxons. It took the army three days to destroy the idol and raze the buildings around it to the ground and in launching this draconic measure Charlemagne consciously or unconsciously established the theocratic nature of the kingdom he was intent on building. His predecessors, the Romans, had not simply been content to allow barbarians to continue their own curious religious practices, but actually built that freedom into the constitution, strengthening it. Pagan religious practices seeped back from the periphery into the heart of Rome itself, modifying to a dramatic degree the Roman religion so that Isis rubbed shoulders with Minerva, Mithras with Dionysus. The destruction of the Irminsul signalled to the world that there would be only one religion within the Carolingian hegemony. That done, the Frankish host retreated behind the barrier of the Rhine, and Charlemagne settled into his villa at Thionville.

Scarcely had he removed his battle-gear when there was ushered into his presence yet another Roman messenger, carrying yet another complaint from the Roman pope about the devilish Lombards. But this time the complaint had a very personal significance for Charles, *rex francorum*. Desiderius, King of the Lombards, was marching on Rome not simply intent on bullying the pope or laying hands on his revenues, but also to get him to declare that the true King of the Franks was the eldest son of the dead, but legitimate, Carloman, not the living bastard Charles. The King of the Franks prepared once more to descend into Italy.

5 The Golden City

In surveying the dying days of what had once been the great kingdom of the Lombards, Edward Gibbon summed up their ignoble but pitiable condition in one of his lapidary phrases: 'Their minds were not yet humbled to their condition: and instead of affecting the pacific virtues of the feeble, they peevishly harassed the Romans with a repetition of claims, evasions and inroads which they undertook without reflection, and terminated without glory.' Twenty years before, Italy had witnessed the almost comic postures of King Aistulf as he shuttled rapidly from bluster to cringing, pouring out promises of good behaviour while the Frankish king stood grimly over him, capering in disrespect as soon as that king had withdrawn across the Alps. Desiderius seemed intent on following the same pattern: what he did not allow for was that the son was considerably different from the father, that where Pippin had been content to accept promises, Charles would, in the event, accept nothing but total, unconditional and permanent surrender.

Charles actually began the campaign in an oddly conciliatory manner, offering his ex-father-in-law 14,000 *solidi* if he would but surrender the disputed territories back to the Church. There is no obvious reason why Charles should have dug into his own coffers on behalf of the Church instead of getting Pope Hadrian to look into the not unimpressive reserves of the Roman Church. The substantial offer may, perhaps, have been a disguised and generous gesture to atone for the dismissal of Desiderata a little over a year before. Whatever the reason for the offer, her father foolishly refused it and the final attack on the kingdom of the Lombards was set in motion. Charles divided his army into two, sending his uncle, Bernard, down by the great pass now known as the Greater St Bernard, while he himself followed the other route that his father had taken, descending the vast shoulder of Mont Cenis down towards the valley and to Susa. It was a risky thing, this splitting his force, but it was a technique which Charles made all his own and usually with complete success. It worked well upon this occasion. The Lombards fought bravely: they had fortified the valley so well that remains of their walls are still visible 1200 years later. At one stage, indeed, Charles was actually contemplating a retreat back up the mountain when, unaccountably it seemed, panic spread through the Lombard ranks and they scattered. The papal biographers whose accounts are, again, the main source for the battle, naturally attributed the Lombard flight to supernatural intervention, comparing it to the flight of the Syrian host from Samaria as recounted in 2 Kings: 'The Lord had caused the Aramaeans to hear the sound of chariots and horses and a great army . . . so they got up and fled in the dusk.' But the explanation was rather more prosaic. The chariots and horses and sound of a great army the Lombards heard were not produced by heavenly acoustics, but by the very real passage of Bernard's army, swinging round to attack the Lombards on their flank. They broke and ran, the Franks marched on to Pavia and settled down to that most tedious, unpopular and doubtful of military activities, the siege.

A well-founded city like Pavia, adequately supplied with provisions, could hold out indefinitely. Charlemagne had little in his army to equal the great siege weapons of the Romans: he would have to rely on attrition alone. And attrition was as likely to affect the besiegers as the besieged: disease, born of the appalling sanitary conditions created by thousands of men camped under ad hoc conditions, would kill more than would be killed by the missiles of the besieged. In addition, there were the privations to be endured by a static army. An army on the move could reasonably keep itself in food and drink by living off the country through which it passed. Condemned to stay in one place, it stripped the surrounding area like a plague of locusts, and thereafter had to range out further and further to bring in fewer and fewer supplies so that, again, the condition of the besiegers was little better than that of the besieged.

However, Charles was determined that the Lombard problem would be solved once and for all. In October 773 he settled down for a prolonged siege, indicating his intention by sending back to Francia for his young wife, their infant son Charles and the little boy, Pippin. Charles might have put Pippin's mother aside, but the family affection that was so conspicuous an element of his character ensured that the little boy grew up with his half-siblings.

There was also some unfinished business which Charles proceeded to put in hand. At an early stage he had learned that his sister-in-law Gerberga, together with his nephews and Duke Otker, Gerberga's adviser, had left Pavia for Verona. Thither he made his way, leaving the bulk of the army to invest Pavia. The citizens of Verona saw no valid reason why they should endure all the horrors of a siege for a distant and increasingly unpopular king, and for fugitives from Francia, and they made haste to surrender. Gerberga, her children and Otker found themselves summoned before the man whom they had accused of usurping the kingdom. And they vanish from history at that point. Charlemagne may have taken the obvious and most effective way of eliminating a potential centre of dissension but, judging by his tolerance under other circumstances, this seems highly unlikely. According to legend, too, Otker turned up – improbably enough – as one of his Paladins in the *Song of Roland*. The probability is that the two little boys were tonsured, thus effectively and humanely removing them from any possibility of succession, and the belligerent Gerberga ended up in a nunnery. Altogether, Charles might well congratulate himself on a tidy ending of a problem and, with Desiderius safely bottled up in Pavia, on impulse he decided to undertake that which his father, for some reason, had never contemplated – a visit to Rome. Deliberately, he did not inform the pope, his actions thereby taking on virtually the characteristic of a landowner visiting a distant manor. But Rome, too, was the sacred city of Christendom, the longed-for goal of an ever-increasing number of pilgrims from the north. All who could be spared from the siege gladly joined the king as, in bright spring weather he, at the centre of a brilliant company of Frankish dukes, counts, abbots and bishops, accompanied as ever by his wife and children, at last turned his face to the south, travelling down one of the great roads of Rome to the mother city of Europe.

Some time after the Flood, when men again began to move on the face of the earth and grew again in arrogance so that their impiety was confounded at Babel, Noah came to Italy and with his sons Japhet, Jason and Camese built a series of cities upon the seven hills surrounding the Tiber. Jason lived upon the Palatine Hill and, aided by Nimrod or Saturn, built the city of Saturnia upon the Capitoline Hill. Other kings of glorious name, among them Italus and Aeneas, followed the lead of Noah's children and built other cities in the now sanctified area. Then, on 17 April, 433 years after the fall of Troy, Romulus came to surround all these cities with a single wall, making of them one and giving it his name. 'And all the nobles of the Earth together with their wives and children came to live in this new city of Rome.' Thus, in a pilgrims' guidebook called *Graphia aurea urbis Romae (The Description of the Golden City of Rome)* the Romans now viewed their origins, fusing into one picture the strands of Christian and pagan traditions. In it, Virgil and the author of Genesis are accepted as equal authorities, so that Aeneas rubs shoulders with Noah, Saturn with Nimrod, reflecting in literature the fusion of elements which were transforming Rome itself. It would retain its identity as the Eternal City, but its ancient substances were taking on new shape. The vast churches that now rivalled the classic structures had been built from the materials of venerable temples, and the great monuments of the ancient city that survived were transformed either into fortresses for the ceaselessly warring nobles, or into slum tenements for the people.

The peoples of Europe, regarding in wonderment the ancient and imperishable city, wove legends for it that made it a mythological place. They might deplore its tragic fall from greatness, scorn its decadent and violent citizens, but they were touched still by the awe of its mighty past, transforming the reality of its political greatness into magical tales. Thus, centuries later, the Englishman William of Malmesbury would pick up the story of how a certain Lucanius, 'citizen of this place, youthful, rich and of senatorial rank', in a drunken frolic placed his wedding ring on the finger of a statue of Venus and found himself embraced that night by the goddess herself. 'Take me – since you wedded me today.' Lucanius is freed by a Christian priest – but the priest himself employs pagan arts to do so. In a subterranean cavern, golden images of the dead sit motionless before an eternal banquet, and then are stirred to terrible life when an intruder steals an ornament from the table. And even as reality is twisted into fable, so fable appears as reality and Malmesbury soberly records the discovery of the body of the giant Pallas, of whom Turnus sang, still incorrupt so that there was visible 'the gash which Turnus made in the middle of his breast, measuring four and a half feet'.

Lapped though it was by pagan legend, Rome was pre-eminently the Sacred City of Christendom and though the thronging pilgrims might marvel at the body of Pallas, they would turn from it with a shudder and cross themselves (the heroes of the old city being the demons of the new) and seek more holy relics. The Romans made much profit by providing these gullible northerners with fragments of corpses – as Einhard himself was to find to his shame and embarrassment – and though they were of dubious origins they were at least sanctified by the fact that they were purchased in Rome. And when the relics had been purchased and the shrines visited and the offerings of copper or silver made at the tomb of Peter, the pilgrims turned to explore the wondrous city, as pilgrims always had and always would. And it was for these that the *Description of the Golden City* was written – a fantastic mish-mash of legend and garbled history compiled by scribes from oral sources over many generations. Beginning with the foundation of the city by Noah and his sons, it took the pilgrim down to the present, guiding him to the great monuments of the past (though these were but casually referred to compared with the loving detailed itineraries of the catacombs), explaining in confused and inaccurate detail the complex, interlocking machinery of imperial, papal and civic government that ruled Rome. It also provided posterity with one of the few descriptions of the city during the dark centuries.

Outwardly, the city that Charlemagne saw as he approached it in the Easter of 774 differed little from that which had ruled the world five centuries earlier. Its final form had been established when Aurelian built the great enclosing walls in the third century AD. They were Rome's final defence: whatever else was suffered to fall into ruin, the walls were maintained by generation after generation – even in 1870 the army of the newly resurgent kingdom of Italy had to break its way through and overthrow that papal monarchy established by Charlemagne.

The walls gave shape to a city that would otherwise have become a shapeless sprawl. In the first decade of the Christian era, during the years of Augustan splendour, there had been a tremendous upsurge in building, culminating in the reign of Nero when vast structures faced with gleaming marble swallowed whole areas and streets. After the collapse of the empire, the city suffered a succession of devastating sieges and sacks but it was the Romans themselves who dismantled the classic city and that for the most humdrum of reasons – marble, when burned, yields lime which can be used for plaster. In 1883 the Roman archaeologist Rodolfo Lanciani found one of these limekilns. It had been packed with statuary, awaiting the torch, and 'was wholly made up of statues of the Vestales maximae. The statues and fragments had been closely packed together, leaving as few interstices as possible; there were eight nearly perfect statues and we were agreeably surprised to find among the broken ones the lower part of the lovely seated Vesta with footstool which, alas, is now hardly recognisable.' The scores of such kilns in the city were each fed by irreplaceable fragments of past glory. The great blocks of travertine that formed the core of the walls were broken up to make byres and hovels. Those columns that escaped the limekilns, or were not incorporated into new churches, lay where they fell, protected at least by the accumulated rubbish. But Augustan Rome had been built on so colossal a scale that, though it was plundered daily for centuries, the centre of the city survived as an identifiable entity. A contemporary of Nero or Augustus could still have found his way easily enough around the eighth-century city, though he would have been appalled by the filthy condition of the streets themselves. Many were permanently blocked by collapsed buildings: all stank in high summer. The city that had known the splash and play of countless fountains, now endured an endless drought, for the great aqueducts were ruined. The death of imperial Rome could, indeed, be pinpointed to those days of March AD 537 when the besieging Gothic army destroyed the aqueducts. They probably brought about their own destruction, for the vast marsh they thus created bred a pestilence which took them off in thousands. But Rome, too, began to die. Until that date the great aqueducts were delivering a hundred gallons a day for every man, woman and child in the city – a far greater rate than in many a modern city. Almost overnight, a city of nearly a million people became mainly dependent on muddy wells and the unpredictable Tiber. Life began to ebb away from the crest of the favoured hills where were built the palaces and villas of the great. The Aventine and the Capitoline; the Palatine, the Janiculum . . . one by one they became deserted, the people perforce descending back into the marshy, unhealthy plain, in particular to that great horn-shaped area known as the Plain of Mars, while the crests of the hills reverted to bush and heath, the great buildings slowly disappearing under a tide of vegetation.

But the great city had only started its descent into degradation: another three centuries were to pass before it touched bottom with a shrunken population battling with each other – and with wild beasts – among the ruins. In this Easter of 774 it was still a booming, bustling, exciting city, firmly ruled by its bishop and well founded. The new pope, Hadrian I, though disconcerted that the *rex francorum* had not troubled to inform him beforehand of his intention to visit the city, ensured that his reception was with all the ceremony that the clergy and citizens of Rome were capable. For Charles, King of the Franks, was also Patrician, lay lord of the city, and when Hadrian 'falling into an ecstasy of great astonishment' heard that the illustrious guest was barely a day's march from the city, he ordered all the city's magistrates to travel the thirty miles to where their Patrician was waiting on the via Clodia near Lake Bracciano. There they formally presented him with a standard (presumably the great banner of the city with which, nearly thirty years later, he would be depicted – himself as emperor – on the walls of the Lateran). A mile from the city's gate, the royal party was met by the militia and by the schoolboys – the sons of wealthy families who had come to Rome from all over Europe to learn the universal language at its source. The great crosses of the Church were brought out and, at sight of them, the king dismounted and entered the city humbly on foot. He did not, however, penetrate into what used to be the imperial heart of the city but turned aside to enter the house which Fulrad had established on the Vatican Hill outside the city, for he had come to pay homage not to imperial Rome – still nominally under the sceptre of the Byzantine emperor – but to St Peter himself.

The Vatican Hill was still outside the walls of Rome, and would not be enclosed until after the Saracen raid seventy years hence. In the days of imperial Rome it was a desolate area; nevertheless, the increasing population of the city made it of potential value. Part of it became a cemetery and part of it Nero developed as a great pleasure garden where, according to Christian tradition, the apostle Peter was crucified during a night of insane cruelty in AD 64 when the living bodies of Christians were turned into torches. The same tradition held that Peter's body was buried in a shallow grave near the gardens and it was above this humble tomb that Constantine erected his great basilica.

The fourth-century architects were faced with a formidable problem, for the site lay on a slope down which a road ran, flanked by tombs. Work proceeded in haste and, instead of laboriously demolishing the tombs – massive, hut-like structures – the builders merely broke open the roofs, filled the interiors with debris and erected the basilica on top. Thus sealed off, the tombs remained untouched for centuries, providing at last a priceless archaeological record when the search for Peter's tomb began in the mid-twentieth century.

The builders of the basilica began that cannibalizing of material which was to prove far more destructive to Rome than the raids of barbarians. The nearby circus of Nero was an obvious source of material but far more beautiful structures were plundered to build St Peter's. It was a vast but inelegant brick-built structure of ill-assorted materials hastily put together. The great columns that towered in the gloom of the interior were brought from a number of temples: the columns were not only ill-matched but the architects had not even bothered to ensure that any given structure had its correct base and capital. But the ugly, hybrid structure was to endure more than a thousand years before being swept into the lumber of history by the surge of the Renaissance.

In the seventh century the great central door of the basilica was plated with a thousand pounds of massive silver and the shrine of St Peter itself was similarly adorned. This, the most sacred spot of earth in Christendom, now lay far below among the foundations of the basilica, but the architects had carefully allowed physical, if limited, access to it. According to Gregory of Tours, a shaft led down from the high altar to the tomb itself and the faithful could thrust their heads into the shaft to pray, or let down objects to touch the tomb and thereby receive a rare sanctity.

The tomb itself was the object of awe. Pope Gregory the Great described how, when his predecessor wanted to make some alterations to the tomb, 'he received an apparition of considerable horror. I myself in the same way wished to carry out some repairs nearby. As it was necessary to dig to some depth near the tomb the foreman found some bones – which had no connection with the tombs', Gregory hastened to add. Nevertheless, 'he died suddenly with horrifying symptoms'. Other workers involved with alterations to the tomb of St Lawrence all died within ten days, Gregory reported with, it seems, a touch of complacency. 'Those working there saw the martyr's body which, indeed, they did not dare touch' – nevertheless, the awful guardian of the tomb removed them from the world. The shrine and the Vatican itself were run by two separate bodies and they, in their turn, were quite distinct from the papal court itself. The popes kept a house on the Vatican for use during prolonged ceremonies, but the administrative centre of the Church was on the other side of the city, in the Lateran Palace, where indeed it would remain until the palace was burnt down during the absence of the popes in the fourteenth century.

Around the basilica and the shrine of St Peter, on this unattractive hill most of which had been the burial ground for slaves and servants, a royal community had developed, for kings visiting the tomb had no wish to enter Rome itself under the jurisdiction of another monarch, even though he might be thousands of miles distant. The household in which Charles and his entourage established themselves had been built by a Lombard king, after he had abdicated and before he entered a monastery. Aistulf and Desiderius, though dedicated enemies of the pope, were also devoted followers of St Peter and it was here they established themselves when they came to make offerings at the tomb. Nearby was the house of two Anglo-Saxon kings who, with the fervent faith of northerners, had also given up their thrones in order to spend their last years under the shadow of St Peter.

In front of the basilica was a great *atrium* or courtyard, approached by a splendid flight of steps following the contour of the hill. The pope and his court were waiting in a glittering group at the top while Charles began to ascend the steps. Overcome with emotion at actually setting foot on this all but supernatural place, the king sank to his knees and kissed each step before standing upon it. At the top, pope and king met standing upright, as honourable equals. In the years and centuries to come, pope and emperor would seek the one to triumph over the other, to force the other to his knees or even prostrate in total Asiatic submission. But here was a rare moment when equal met equal, as Hadrian I came forward to take the hand of Charles I, leading him on to the basilica and down to the shrine of the apostle.

Hadrian had come to the throne just two years before, in 772: he would remain on the throne for twenty-three years, one of the longest of all papacies and one almost equalling the legendary 'years of St Peter'. And Einhard says that, at his death, Charlemagne wept as for the loss of a beloved brother. During those two decades they argued much, for each was striving to create a virtually unprecedented organization which, operating in the same area as each other, must needs come into conflict. But their fundamental liking and respect for each other enabled king and pope to work in harmony most of the time, unlike the working pattern of their successors. In a large part this harmony was produced by the recognition of inequality, the fact that the pope was dependent upon the king.

Hadrian was the first Roman after a succession of devious Greeks and Sicilians upon the papal throne. He was a member of the Roman nobility and, as a member of the Roman clergy he was, in effect, the leader of a closed corporation within a closed corporation. The Roman clergy emphasized its distinctness, its uniqueness in every possible way. In their dress, in which they clung to privileges supposedly ensured to them by the spurious Donation of Constantine, they imitated the imperial senate using the *mappula* – a white, fringed saddlecloth when mounted (itself a senatorial privilege) – the *campagna*, or flat, black slippers and the *udones* or white stockings. To an outsider, these would seem almost tastelessly trivial privileges but in the highly structured, caste world of Rome they were vital points of difference. The clergy recruited itself from its own ranks, inducting boys at an early age. Indeed, the traditional minor orders known as doorkeeper, lector and exorcist had become meaningless in that they were increasingly bestowed on ever younger children. The candidate was presented personally to the pope by his nearest male relative or guardian and would later be examined for proficiency in reading. Ironically, the Latin spoken and written in Rome was far more corrupt and degraded than that used by the northern 'barbarians' as the ancient language gradually made its transition into Italian. His examination passed, the boy would receive the tonsure. Again, this was a device not simply to set them aside from the laity, as such, but from their own fellow citizens who wore their hair long and so adorned that a Frankish monk noted that they were called 'in admiration or rather derision *hypochoristicos* or pretty things'. The desire of the Roman clergy to emphasize their uniqueness paradoxically included the liturgy. Paradoxically because, while emphasizing the catholic or universal nature of their way of worship, they ensured that the great Roman chant remained unique to Rome. When, in later years, Charlemagne tried to introduce the chant beyond the Alps in order to achieve uniformity he was cheated. The twelve chantors who were sent to teach the barbarians the Roman skill, had been taught a variant of the music.

Hadrian had been brought up by his uncle, the *primicerius* of the notaries, an office so important that its holder deputed for the pope in his absence. Responsible for the documentation of the Church's intentions – in effect, putting into words that which had been inchoate – the office was one of the last bastions of learning in a city where learning was rapidly losing ground to the machinery of politics and militarism. Hadrian evidently benefited from this exposure to scholarship. Certainly the letters of his administration are a considerable improvement on those of his immediate predecessors, both in dignity and style. In place of an almost hysterical style, ranging wildly from a ranting of threats to an obsequious grovelling, is a balanced, cool approach with distant echoes of the great days of Latinity. But Hadrian was also a practical man, taking very seriously his de facto role as Rome's ruler, not only concerned to exact taxes and privileges but also aware of his responsibilities. Energetically he set about rebuilding and restoring, where possible, the city. When the Lombard King Aistulf had besieged the city the Sabbatina aqueduct, one of the last bringing water to the city and actually supplying the Vatican complex, was severed. It is an indication of the supine nature of Hadrian's predecessors that this literal lifeline remained destroyed for twenty years. The papal biographer, turning aside from his usual task of recounting the spiritual and political triumphs of his subject, gave a succinct technical description of the problem. 'There seemed small chance of repairing it for a hundred of the arches, which were extremely high, had fallen to their foundations and lay derelict. But this most blessed and holy bishop Hadrian gathered a crowd of people to restore and rebuild it themselves, and he showed such care and attention to the fabric of the aqueduct that he restored it from its foundations like new.'

Although considerably hampered by lack of preparation, Hadrian had a tight programme for his illustrious guests. Overcome by religious emotion at the tomb of the apostle, Charles humbly begged permission to enter Rome itself in order to worship at the great churches following the *jubilaeum* of pilgrims and to this Hadrian readily agreed. But before Charles and his family were free to do this, there was a number of ceremonial events at which the king's presence was requested – and one without ceremony but of incalculable future significance. Charles and Hadrian had met at the basilica on the Easter Saturday. On the Sunday there was a great presentation of all the Roman magistrates and senior officials to the Patrician, followed by mass at St Maria Maggiore and a great banquet at the Lateran Palace. Monday and Tuesday saw the celebration of more masses at St Peter's and then St Paul's. And on Wednesday there came a crucial business meeting between pope and king when Charles supposedly confirmed the Donation of his father.

Pope Hadrian was a fast worker. If, as his biographer claims, he knew nothing about the coming of Charles to Rome until barely twenty-four hours before, he achieved an impressive level of administrative control not only in setting up the ceremonial events, but also in arranging that business meeting as a result of which he became territorial lord of three-quarters of Italy, the absolute ruler of some 68,000 square miles leaving only Lombardy under the control of the king. Or so, at least, the papal biographer claims. The *Life* of the reigning pope is, again, the only source for this quite remarkable claim, the unknown biographer beginning blandly: 'Now on the fourth day of the week [6 April 774] the aforesaid Pope, with his officers both of Church and State, had an interview with the King in the church of St Peter, when he earnestly besought and with fatherly affection exhorted him to fulfil in every particular the promise which his father, the late King Pippin of holy memory, and Charles himself with all the Frankish nobles made with St

Peter and his vicar Pope Stephen II on the occasion of his journey into Frankland.' The biographer then goes on minutely to detail the astonishing Donation which made the bishop of Rome the biggest single magnate in Italy since the fall of the Roman Empire. 'Then placing it first on the altar of St Peter and afterwards within on the tomb itself, the King and all his nobles promised St Peter and his vicar Hadrian, under the sanction of a terrible oath, that they would maintain his right to all the territories included in the Donation'. In other words Charles, about to take the gamble of establishing himself south of the Alps, is supposed to have deliberately created an enormously powerful neighbour, granting Hadrian dominion over a far larger area even than that to which his father (quite ignorant of Italian topography) had agreed. In the event, Charles paid little attention to his own supposed Donation, nor did Hadrian ever press him on the matter though Hadrian's successors certainly pressed Charles's successors. The king was no oath-breaker, even though he could accept with apparent equanimity such blood-curdling threats of anathema as had been hurled at him on his marriage to Desiderata. Had he been tricked into signing a document he could not read, the wily Romans taking advantage of the untutored barbarian? It seems scarcely likely, for Charles certainly could read and in any case throughout his stay in Rome he was accompanied by advisers as skilled and as learned as the Romans, for 'barbarian' was no longer even a remotely accurate definition of all those who were non-Roman. The probability is that the Donation of Charlemagne comes from the same source as the Donation of Constantine, an ingenious piece of forgery grafted on to a genuine record.

Having completed the ceremonies and the business, the king was free at last to do that for which he had come to Rome – perform a pilgrimage. It is doubtful if he and his entourage bestowed more than a passing glance on the great monuments of antiquity. As a good soldier he would have taken particular notice of the enormous circular tomb of the Emperor Hadrian. It had been turned into a fortress during the Gothic wars and was now the military key to the Vatican and north-eastern Rome but would otherwise have had little significance for a good Christian king. Neither would the great baths of Caracalla or Diocletian, nor the remains of the Golden House of Nero – places, indeed, to shun, being now the haunt of ghosts and demons. The Colosseum was still a place of pleasure, though nowhere near on the scale of the past, with an occasional bullfight or the like in place of the titanic spectacles of the empire. The Pantheon, together with a handful of the pagan temples which had been turned into churches, was in good care; Pope Hadrian had set in motion a comprehensive plan of restoration and refurbishment. But the other monuments of antiquity which had neither military value nor the protection of the church were actively being demolished. Just over a century before, the normal process of decay was accelerated when the Byzantine emperor Constans, still the effective ruler of the city, stripped all the major buildings of their metal parts, to be recast as armaments. The Romans blithely carried on the work of self-destruction, on so great a scale that two professions actually developed to carry out the work, the *Calcarii* (lime-burners) whose stock-in-trade was the marble with which the emperors had covered the brick foundations of their buildings and the *Marmorarii* who saved the priceless coloured marble – but sliced it up to make inlays.

Charles was certainly not indifferent to the great past of Rome; later, he would go to immense trouble to transport antique columns from Ravenna to adorn his new church in Aachen. But Rome was, for him and all like him, Rome of the Martyrs. He would have had access to two guides to the catacombs which give exact and, to posterity, macabre details as to what saint lay where in the bewildering labyrinth south of the city. Even in the 1980s when the niches of the catacombs are empty, the corridors well lighted and carefully limited groups of visitors are shepherded under the watchful gaze of trained guides – even now they strike the most garrulous tourist party with awe as the chill seeps into the very bone, and the site of the endless niches stretching into the darkness gives some indication of the vast numbers for which this was the final home. In the fourth century a young Roman Christian, Eusebius Hieronymous, managed to convey something of the religious awe, mixed with horror, that the places created.

> We went down into the catacombs. These are caves excavated deep in the earth and contain, on either hand, as you enter the bodies of the dead buried in the wall. It is all so dark there: only occasionally is light let in to mitigate the horror of the gloom, and then not so much through a window as through a hole. You take each step with caution, as though surrounded by deep night.

Lying outside the walls of Rome, the catacombs were again and again ransacked by invaders, at first pagans in search of treasures, and then good Christians in search of holy corpses. From the seventh century onwards, the popes began to remove the more vulnerable bodies into the safety of the city, but at the time of Charles's visit to Rome, the catacombs still held almost their full complement. Indeed, it was his own death in 814 which ended their rest, for the breakdown of central authority led to the beginnings of anarchy in which the catacombs were utterly unprotected and the process of emptying them was accelerated. On 20 July 817 alone, 2300 bodies were brought into Rome and by the middle of the century the catacombs were empty, sealed off and totally forgotten until their rediscovery in 1578.

The trade in dead bodies reached a peak during the reign of Charlemagne and his sons, for the Frankish Church, growing ever richer under the Carolingian shield, entered the race for relics which would provide prestige – and fat incomes from pilgrims. Charles's own father had contributed to that insatiable appetite for relics and incidentally was largely responsible for the growth of the odd little cult of St Petronilla. At his request, the body of this supposed daughter of St Peter was moved from its modest shrine on the via Ardea to a tomb on the Vatican Hill, there to become a major saint in the Carolingian pantheon. It was on Petronilla's tomb that Pope Paul laid the baptismal napkin of Charles's sister Gisela, thus tying the family of the Frankish king ever more firmly to the fortunes of Rome.

The royal party was back in Lombardy by the beginning of May 774, Charles taking over the last days of the siege of Pavia. For it was now quite evident that the long-drawn-out affair was coming to a close, the city being in the grip of disease. The end of the 200-year-old kingdom of the Lombards was a sad anticlimax, Desiderius surrendering himself into Charles's hands together with his wife, Ansa, and an unnamed daughter who may have been Charles's repudiated wife. The future of all three was already mapped out, Desiderius being promptly tonsured and placed in a monastery in Francia – where he obtained quite a reputation for piety – while the two women, too, were humanely but permanently put out of the way by being obliged to take the veil.

Disease, famine and internal dissension had done Charles's work for him, but this was certainly not good enough for the Monk of St Gall when he came to write his *Life of Charlemagne* for Charlemagne's son Louis. The end had to be worked up to heroic, epic proportions and, in doing so, the Monk was to help lay the foundations of the Carolingian legend. But, also in doing so, he transcends his usual bathetic style, giving too a sudden insight into the almost mystical source both of Charlemagne's authority and his means of imposing his will.

AMORBOMALO·Ł·

Left: The ox-cart of the Merovingian kings which aroused Einhard's derision

Below: Reconstruction of a 7th/8th-century village near Gladbach, in the middle Rhine area, after excavation

Foot: Model of a Carolingian villa. Though protected by a stockade and surmounted by a watch-tower it is undefended compared with the massive fortifications of later centuries

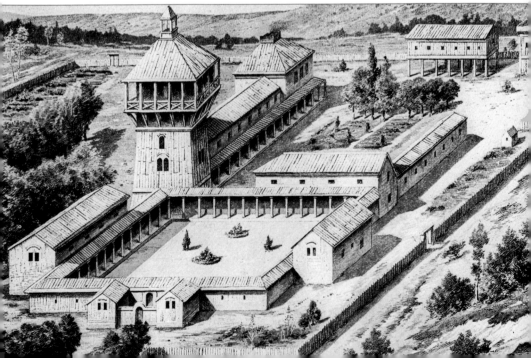

ET SYRIAM SOBAL · ET CONVERTIT
IOAB · ET PERCUSSIT EDOM IN VAL
LE SALINARUM · XII MILIA

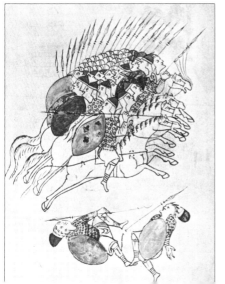

Above: Carolingian soldiers: from the St Gall Psalter. Clearly distinguishable are the stirrups, which helped to revolutionise warfare, and the longitudinal bar on the spear to prevent too deep penetration

Left: The fact that the invention of the stirrup was not widespread is shown in this manuscript, illustrating soldiers from the Book of Maccabees. Although it was produced at least a generation after the St Gall Psalter, the horsemen have no stirrups

BEATISSIMO PAPAE DAMASO
HIERONIMUS

Nouum opus me facere cogis ex ueteri · ut post exemplaria scrip
turarum toto orbe dispersa · quasi quidam arbiter sedeam ·
& quia inter se uariant quae sint illa quae cum greca consenti
ant ueritate decernam · Pius labor · sed periculosa praesump
tio · Iudicare de ceteris Ipsum ab omnibus iudicandum · senis muta
relinquam · & canescentem mundum ad initia retrahere paruu
lorum · Quis enim doctus pariter uel indoctus cum in manus uo
lumen adsumpserit · & a saliua quam semel Inbibit uiderit discre
pare quod lectitat Non statim erumpat In uocem me falsarium
meclamans esse sacrilegum · qui audeam aliquid In ueteribus
libris addere mutare corrigere · Aduersus quam Inuidiam du
plex causa me consolatur · Quod & tu quisummus sacerdos es
fieri iubes · & uerum non esse quod uariat etiam maledicorum
testimonio conprobatur · Si enim latinis exemplaribus fides est
adhibenda respondeant · quibus tot sunt exemplaria pene quod
codices · sin autem ueritas est quaerenda depluribus · Cur non
ad grecam originem reuertentes · ea quae uel á uitiosis Inter
pretibus male edita uel á presumptoribus Imperitis emendata
peruersius uel á librariis dormitantibus aut addita sunt aut
mutata corrigimus · Neque uero ego de ueteri disputo testimo ·
quod á Lxx senioribus In grecam linguam uersum tertio gradu
ad nos usque peruenit · Non quaero quid aquila · quid sremmachus
sapiant · Quare theodotion Inter nouos & ueteres medius Incedat ·
sit illa uera Inter praelatio · quam apostoli probauerunt · De nouo

The advance of literacy: (*right*) the semi-barbaric
script of the Merovingians; (*above*) the 'Carolingian
minuscule', readable even to an untrained modern eye

The international nature of Carolingian architecture: interior west wall of S. Maria in Valle, Cividale, Italy

Interior of S. Michael, Fulda, Germany

AD TROPAEVM AETER
NAE VICTORIAE SVSTI
NENDVM EINHARDVS
PECCATOR HVNC AR
CVM PONERE AC DEO
DEDICARE CVRAVIT

The high level of Carolingian art: (*left*) ivory triptych from book cover of Lorsch Gospels showing profound classical influence; this reliquary, Einhard's personal gift to his abbey at Maastricht, shows (*above and right*) the still overwhelming influence of classical Rome, an influence that also permeated Einhard's writings

commendauit au eum beata helena
epo qui illo tempore exet. qui & bap
tizauit eum in xpo.

cum mortem adhuc beata hel
na in hierofolyma. factum est
beatum eum in dormitione ad
pem in xpo;

Left: Baptism by total immersion. The convert shown here would have been a notable: mass baptisms were carried out in rivers

Below: The abbey gateway of Lorsch. Following classical design, it may have been erected to commemorate Charlemagne's visit to the monastery

According to the Monk, Otker (who had, in fact, been captured at Verona) was in Pavia acting as Desiderius's adviser.

When the near approach of the dreaded Charles was known, these two went up into a very high tower from which they could see everyone approaching from a very great distance. When therefore the baggage wagons appeared, which moved more swiftly than those used by Darius and Julius, Desidirius said to Otker, 'Is Charles in that vast army?' And Otker answered, 'Not yet'. Then when he saw the vast force of the nations gathered together from all parts of his empire he said with confidence to Otker, 'Surely Charles moves in pride among these forces?' But Otker answered, 'Not yet, not yet'. Then Desidirius fell into a great alarm and said 'What shall we do if a yet greater force comes with him?' And Otker said 'You will see what he is like when he comes. What will happen to us I cannot say.'

And behold, while they were thus talking, there came in sight Charles's personal attendants and Desidirius saw them and cried in his amazement 'There is Charles'. And Otker answered 'Not yet, not yet'. Then they saw the bishops and the abbots and the clerks of his chapel with their attendants. When he saw them [Desidirius] hated the light and longed for death and sobbed and stammered, 'Let us go down to hide ourselves in the earth from the face of an enemy so terrible.' And Otker answered, trembling – for once, in happier days he had thorough and constant knowledge of the mind of Charles – 'When you see an iron harvest bristling in the fields, and the Po and the Ticino pouring against the walls of the city like the waves of the sea, gleaming black with glint of iron, then know that Charles is at hand'. Hardly were these words finished when there came from the West a black cloud which turned the bright day to horrid gloom. Then could be seen the iron Charles, helmeted with an iron helmet, his hands clad in iron gauntlets, his iron breast and broad shoulders protected with an iron breastplate; an iron spear was raised on high in his left hand; his right always rested on his unconquered iron falchion . . . All who went before him, all who marched by his side, all who followed after him imitated him as closely as possible. The fields and open places were filled with iron; the rays of the sun were thrown back by the iron; a people harder than iron paid universal honour to the hardness of iron. 'Oh the iron! Woe for the iron!' was the confused cry that rose from the citizens. The strong walls shook at the sight of iron: the resolution of young and old fell before the iron. Now when the truthful Otker saw in one swift glance all this which I, with my stammering tongue have been clumsily explaining with rambling words, he said to Desidirius 'There is the Charles that you so much desired to see' and when he had said this he fell to the ground half dead.

Einhard knew nothing of such high drama, but his restrained remark that 'The sum of this war was the conquest of Italy', though not literally true, grasped the essence of the matter. It is difficult to account for the sudden and ignoble collapse of the kingdom of the Lombards, a collapse as mysterious in its way as the collapse of the Incas or the Mayas. This resourceful, intelligent and courageous race had not only carved out a kingdom and held it against the power of the emperors, but had built up a culture as rich as anything the Merovingians had achieved. They had, perhaps, opted for monarchy – the one sure means of national survival of these dark centuries – just too late. Aistulf and his successor Desiderius had possessed neither the personal magnetism of a Clovis to impose their will upon their people, nor had they the mystique which had allowed the *rois fainéants* to act at least as a constant centre for the growing kingdom of the Franks. It was probably inevitable that they would succumb to a man who had both personal power and monarchical mystique.

Charles marched into Pavia and took up the Iron Crown of the Lombards, a simple circle in which, it was said, was embedded material from the Holy Nails. Pavia not only gave him a powerful base in Italy but also opened up direct communication with Constantinople, for royal emissaries could go by ship from the very heart of Europe along the river-road of the Po and out into the Adriatic. The Iron Crown now added *rex langobardum* to *rex francorum*. The Frankish kingdom had passed the great barrier of the Alps and was now, in all but name, an empire.

6 The King in His Kingdom

At the fall of Pavia in June 774 Charles was about thirty-three or thirty-four years old. He had been actively engaged in politics and warfare for over fifteen years. In the six years that he had been upon the throne he had had the good fortune to be able to turn the bisected kingdom into one unit, and the good skill to bring Aquitaine, finally, into the Frankish ambit; moreover, he eliminated, finally, the Lombard problem and, in so doing, dramatically extended his kingdom. He had also established that quasi-mystic relationship between Italy and what would be Germany, a relationship which would bring more harm than good to both parties over the centuries but which was, inescapably, one of the factors in the shaping of Europe. Rome loomed large in his imagination, large enough for him to be prepared to spend blood and gold in its defence, but he never evinced the slightest desire to become Romanized, a lure which beckoned more than one of his successors to their misfortune. He remained a Frank of the Franks, so much so that he would not even take up residence in one of the beautiful Roman cities of southern Francia. He seems to have regarded Provence precisely as the Romans had regarded it, as an extension – a 'province' – of Italy – and while he made very sure that it was held within his kingdom, he made his home by preference in that colder north whence his people had come. Like his predecessors, he still had no fixed capital. Aachen was still little more than a spa, a pleasant place to spend a week or so bathing in the hot sulphur springs, or hunting in the immense woods. He had other palaces at Compiègne, Duren, Frankfurt, Attigny Liège, Thionville and Ingelheim being among those most frequently referred to by contemporary chroniclers.

Shortly after his triumphant return from Italy, and probably about the year 777, Charles began a major reconstruction of the Ingelheim palace. Until then, he and his predecessors both among the Merovings and the Arnulfings had been content to use one or other of the Gallo-Roman villas which had so richly studied Roman Gaul, adapting them to their own use but still, in effect, lodging in them as a hermit crab lodges in the empty shell of another species. But as though that giant step he had taken across the Alps into Italy had taken him also into the future, Charlemagne now found a new, indubitably 'Carolingian' architectural form in which to express himself. In the words of the French architectural historian Jean Hubert, it was 'a well-ordered architecture, designed on a scale that aspired to give man the taste for grandeur. At no other stage in the formation of Europe was architecture so directly and forcibly the expression of a political ideal.' The new architecture did not turn its back upon the classical past. On the contrary, the masons and sculptors could, when needed, display a skill in copying Roman motifs which all but defeats the attempts of modern archaeologists to place them in their correct chronological sequence. But these early creators of the 'Carolingian renaissance', like their successors in the later, better-known Renaissance, in taking classic forms would also place their own subtle imprint upon it.

The building of the Ingelheim palace extended over some years and, in due course, Charles's son Louis, when ruler in his turn, rebuilt and adapted it to his own requirements but maintained its overall form. None of the Carolingian palaces has survived intact, and contemporary descriptions of them are sparse. But they followed closely the layout of monasteries which have not only survived in part, but were well described by their occupants. In addition, archaeological research since World War II has enabled sparse documentation to be filled out. An outstanding feature of the Ingelheim palace was its remarkable series of murals, following the Carolingian delight in highly coloured, richly decorated interiors. The frescoes of the Great Hall were fully described by Louis's biographer and though they have disappeared with the rest of the building, murals in such places as the crypts in St Germaine Auxerre, the gateway of the abbey at Lorsch and, above all, the little church of St Benedetto in Malles in north Italy, give a clear indication of the bright colours and lively style adopted. Not until the Renaissance of the fifteenth century was the human figure treated with such skill and subtlety, placed in settings which followed the classical Roman style of illusionism. The decoration of the hall on the upper floor of the Lorsch Abbey gateway, which was probably used to entertain the emperor on his visit, is purely Roman. Chequer-work occupies the lower part of the wall while, apparently resting upon these coloured squares, are paintings of elegant columns which, in their turn, support a delicately moulded architrave. Even in their faded state the paintings give the spectator the liveliest impression of being in a loggia open to the sky instead of an enclosed room.

The Ingelheim frescoes showed the legendary and epic history of the Franks from antiquity down to the conquests of Charlemagne himself, their size and importance testimony to the importance which Ingelheim had for Charles himself until it was eclipsed by the great palace at Aachen which he built towards the end of the century. In general, the palace would have followed the ground plan of a Roman villa with a large atrium or forecourt, probably furnished with fountains, and a complex of separate buildings grouped around the chapel (always an important and separate building in a Carolingian palace) and the great throne room. Standards of comfort were high and, again, would not be equalled much less surpassed for another eight centuries. It was well heated in winter, probably with a combination of fireplaces and piped water. But perhaps the most outstanding characteristic of Ingelheim and of all Charlemagne's other palaces was its total lack of military defence, clearest possible evidence of the stability of Frankish society. In a century's time men would be frantically encasing themselves in stone, building ever higher and more solidly, sacrificing comfort and hygiene in order to defend themselves against their fellows. Charlemagne's palaces were as open as the Roman villas, and for the same reason: the nearest enemy was hundreds of miles away beyond the frontiers of the state.

Contemporary commentators referred to the king and his court in two quite distinct ways. When they wished to refer to the court as a whole – that is, to the whole machinery of government, together with members of both sexes near the king – they used the term *palatium* (palace) even though that 'palace' was an idea more than a place. But when they wished to refer to the group of men around the king, his advisers and aides and close friends, they returned to Tacitus and used the word *comitatus*. The nearest translation possible, perhaps, would be that of 'company' and it is worthwhile going back to Tacitus's admirable, clear description of the *comitatus* written in his *Germania* in the second century for, though it had modified itself over the centuries, it was still of enormous potency. Out of it, indeed, would grow that legend of Charlemagne and his Paladins, the noble band of comrades who would ride with him even into the Valley of the Shadow of Death, that would haunt European imagination for centuries.

When the young nobles have received their arms and are enrolled in the ranks of warriors, they take their places by the side of the hardy veterans, nor do they blush to be seen among the 'comrades' [*comites*]. Each receives his rank in the comradeship according to the judgement of him they follow, and great is the rivalry among the comrades which shall attain the highest place beside his chief, and of the chiefs as to which shall have the most numerous and the most eager comrades. This is their dignity, this their strength; to be ever surrounded by a cluster of picked youths is in peace a distinction and in war a defence. When the day of battle comes, it is disgraceful for the chief to be excelled in bravery by the comrades, disgraceful for them not to equal the chief's valour. Yea, and base for the rest of his life is he accounted by himself and others who has escaped alive from the battle, leaving his chief behind. Him to guard, him to defend in his glory to merge every brave deed of his own, this is the one great point of honour with the comrade. The chiefs fight for victory, the comrades for their chief. If the community in which they were born grows sluggish with too long peace and restfulness, most of the young nobles seek of their own accord those nations which may then be waging war elsewhere, both because this race hates rest, and because renown is more easily won on well-balanced battlefields. Each comrade claims from his chief that great warhorse of his, that gory and conquering spear. For the rest, the seat at the banquet, the bountiful though coarse repast, are taken as sufficient pay.

Charlemagne himself was to make significant modifications to this programme: in particular he, far from supplying 'that great warhorse, that gory and conquering spear' expected his 'comrades' to bring horse and war gear to battle in return for the lands that he had granted them. But in Tacitus's lucid account can be seen not only the seeds of legend both of the Paladins and later the Knights of the Round Table, but also one of the dynamics which was to keep Charles at war year after year, decade after decade. He, personally, took little delight in actual battle and is recorded as personally leading the charge on only two occasions. But apart from the geo-political necessity that kept him steadily pushing out the frontiers of the state was that recognition of the nature of his subjects who 'if the community in which they were born grows sluggish with too long peace . . . seek of their own accord those nations which may then be waging war elsewhere'. And finally, more important even than the clues to the later legend and one of the causes of the endless war, is the clue that Tacitus gives as to the inevitable development of feudalism, *the* shaping factor of the European Middle Ages.

The survival of the spirit of the primitive *comitatus* in a sophisticated modern court was at once cause and result of the king's own sturdy conservatism. On the one hand, Charles was capable of shaping and promoting ideas far in advance of his time. But on the other hand, he determinedly clung to the traditions and customs of his Frankish forebears. This was clearest of all in his attitude to dress. Where his distant forerunner, Clovis, had hastened to adopt – quite illegally – the gorgeous costume of a Roman consul, Charlemagne was most reluctant to wear the robes of a Patrician of Rome to which he was fully entitled. Only twice did he ever appear in this distinctive dress and that was in Rome itself, at the direct personal request of the pope.

Einhard goes out of his way to emphasize that the king

wore the national – that is to say, the Frankish dress. His shirts and drawers were of linen, then came a tunic with a silken fringe and hose. His legs were cross-gartered and his feet enclosed in shoes. In winter-time he protected his shoulders and chest with a jerkin made of the skins of otters and ermine. He was clad in a blue cloak, and always wore a sword, with the hilt and belt of either gold or silver. Occasionally, too, he used a jewelled sword but this was only on the great festivals or when he received ambassadors from foreign nations. He disliked foreign garments, however beautiful, and would never consent to wear them except at Rome on the request of Pope Hadrian and again upon the entreaty of his successor, Pope Leo, when he wore a long tunic and cloak and put on shoes made after the Roman fashion. On festal days, he walked in procession in a garment of gold cloth, with jewelled boots and a golden girdle to his cloak, and distinguished further by a diadem of gold and precious stones. But on other days his dress differed little from that of the common people.

He expected, but did not command, his courtiers to adopt the same sobriety and the Monk of St Gall tells a delightful story of how the king provided them with an object lesson. The court, according to the Monk, had just returned from a holiday visit to Pavia where the courtiers like all holiday-makers had loaded themselves with foreign exotica 'strutting in robes made of pheasant skins and silks or of the necks, backs and tails of peacocks in their first plumage. Some were decorated with purple and lemon-coloured ribbons and some in ermine robes.' Charles, wearing a comfortable old sheepskin, proposed a hunt on a wet day and deliberately led the dandies through the thickest part of the forest. Later, when the wretched courtiers assembled in their torn, filthy, shrunken, finery he lectured them on their foolishness, pointing out that his old sheepskin, which had cost a single piece of silver, was far more useful than their beribboned splendour 'which you bought for pounds – nay, for many talents'.

The administrative head of the court was the Count of the Palace. Under the firm hand of a man like Charles, there was little likelihood now that the count would have temptation or opportunity to emulate the late Mayors of the Palace and usurp power. But he was still a very important man, not only running the palace but also with considerable legal powers, in particular during the king's absence. The staff of the court divided into two main bodies, lay and clerical, and the names of some of their offices would enter all European languages, though somewhat changed in meaning. Thus the clerics were known as *capellani* because in their care was the most sacred relic of the Franks, the *cappa* or cloak of St Martin which had been acquired by one of the Arnulfing mayors. (St Martin, the soldier-saint, cut his cloak in two to share with a beggar.) In due course, the *capellani* would emerge as 'chaplains', even as their *cappella* would emerge as 'chapel', giving two new words to European languages. The duty of the chaplains was both religious and administrative because it was to them, being among the few people able to read and write, that there fell the duty of composing – under the king's close supervision – the king's correspondence and the equivalent of state papers. In the early days of Charles's reign, he was particularly fortunate in that his arch-chaplain, through whose hands passed most of the state's affairs, was Abbot Fulrad his old tutor and his father's counsellor. Fulrad occupied this vital position for at least sixteen years, from Charles's accession, until his death in 784.

Charles never followed the lead of his Byzantine and Muslim opposite numbers by the creation of a salaried staff, his officials obtaining their quid pro quo in the form of privileges and, above all, of gifts of land – a fact which was to have a profound effect upon both the future economy and constitution of the state. The lay officials of his palace were very important men in their own right although, by a quirk of etymology, the names of the offices they filled have either become wholly archaic (such as the 'seneschal') or downgraded into that of domestic servants – such as 'butler' and 'steward'; or they have become that of minor officials – such as 'constable'. The seneschal probably acted as deputy to the Count of the Palace, and as an official was certainly important enough to find a leading role in the *Song of Roland* where the Seneschal Eggihard fell at Roland's side at Roncesvalles. The butler's duties included the purely domestic affairs of the court, but he also took part in affairs of state, one butler actually going as a legate to Charles's rebellious young cousin, Tassilo of Bavaria. The *comes stabuli* – the 'count of the stables' whose name eventually emerged as 'constable' – had both important military and domestic roles to play in the organization of transport, perhaps the most important domestic role of all, so that the 'constable' survived as a high state official into late medieval France. The Carolingian court, like all medieval courts, was ever on the move from one estate to another, the endless movements around the state having two motives, the administrative and the domestic. Administratively, it enabled the king to keep in close touch with affairs all over the kingdom. Domestically, it was far easier to bring mouths to food, rather than food to mouths. The peripatetic nature of the court allowed it to move from one estate to another, consuming the products of one before moving on to the next.

Francia still had an excellent road system, inherited from the Romans. Early in his reign, Charles promoted a major programme not only of restoration and repair, but also of building anew. Now the least impressive of his achievements was the building of a bridge over the Rhine itself at Mainz, a task which took ten years and whose accidental destruction by fire a few weeks before his death was seen as an omen. Elsewhere, bridge-building was a private enterprise with the bridge-builder allowed to charge tolls. In addition, the king reinforced the custom whereby people living beside a road were responsible for a section of it. The road system of Carolingian Europe was probably better than the road system of early eighteenth-century England.

Along those roads and over those bridges at frequent intervals there travelled the court composed of scores or, at times, of hundreds of people. It was the duty of the constable not only to ensure that transport was available but that the baggage, which in actual, practical fact constituted the physical palace, was adequately protected. About the only historically accurate part of the *Song of Roland* is the fact that it was in defence of the baggage that the epic heroes met their end. Arrived at the next 'palace' or the next 'villa' or estate, the baggage would transform a mostly empty building into the heart of the state.

Charles ruled his country through the medium of edicts known as capitularies: 'They compose not a system, but a series of occasional and minute edicts for the correction of abuses, the reformation of manners, the economy of his farms, the care of his poultry and even the sale of his eggs.' The slighting picture presented of the king as a parsimonious farmer was accurate enough in fact, if unkind in interpretation. Gibbon undoubtedly had in mind Charles's edict known as *Capitulaire de Villis* in which the king did indeed lay down, personally, the most minor details of how his villas should be conducted and which, as by-product, provides posterity with a rare and priceless view not only of the Carolingian domestic economy but of agricultural life and product in the Europe of the dark centuries.

All land belonged to the king. The terms *villae regales* and *villae publices* were interchangeable but for sheer practical convenience certain areas of the vast landscape were recognized as being 'royal'. Significantly, their original Latin name of *fiscus* means 'basket' and this, in fact, was exactly their function – the means by which the produce of the land was gathered together for royal use. The *fisci* or villas had accumulated into the rulers' hands over centuries and in a variety of ways. Some of those which now supplied Charlemagne's needs had originally belonged to the Merovingian kings and came into the hands of Charlemagne's family along with the rest of the goods of the 'sacred kings'. Others had been acquired by conquest or confiscation. The most powerful man who held land did so only at the king's will and he could be deprived of that land by a wide change of legal devices: thus a certain Godber lost his estates near Angers on being convicted of incest though, in this case, the estates went to the Abbey of Prumes and not the king.

Charlemagne's villas were mostly concentrated in what had always been the Frankish heartland, in what is now the Ardennes and between the Moselle, the Meuse and the Rhine. But others were scattered far away, partly through the accident of acquisition but also because each villa represented a royal foothold in any given area, very useful indeed for such humdrum but vital purposes as providing shelter and protection for the royal servants on their endless journeys around the vast realm, the main means whereby it was given some choate form. An *index major* had the overall control of each villa, with a number of mayors beneath him. Inevitably, the more distant the villa was from the centre of affairs and the more rarely visited by the king, the more powerful became its controller. In certain areas, indeed, Charles simply appointed a local magnate who ran the villa virtually as his own estate in return for a cash rent, one of the few examples of cash transaction in the Carolingian rural economy. Such a system made perfect good sense and worked well under such a king as Charlemagne, but proved one of the divisive factors in the reigns of his weaker successors.

Each superintendent had to provide a report and inventory of the villa at around Christmas time, money dues being paid the following Palm Sunday. One such report, for a small villa called 'Asnapius', has survived in detail. The main building of the estate was built of stone, the seventeen houses that surrounded it were of wood. There were eleven apartments for women – probably workrooms for female serfs rather than the harem which the concept implies, for throughout Charlemagne's reign men and women mixed freely – too freely in the eyes of moralists – in his palaces and estates. This particular estate was only sparsely provided with linen, probably because it was relatively small and any visiting party would bring its own. But Charlemagne, with that extraordinary eye of his for the minutest detail, later specified that all the royal estates should be fully equipped with all necessary domestic furniture, including blankets and pillows – incidentally providing some insight into the royal wealth that expensive linen could be kept perhaps months in readiness.

The inventory specified the iron carpenters' tools that the estate possessed – one chisel, one axe, one knife – but simply recorded that there was a 'sufficiency' of wooden utensils: metal objects were still scarce enough and expensive enough to warrant being detailed separately. This does, however, point to the probability that the inventory was made relatively early in Charlemagne's reign. Later, when great new iron-mines were opened up, the metal became relatively cheap and far more widely used and, used in ploughs and axes particularly, had an immense effect on that agricultural revolution which was as vital, if unsung, a part of the Carolingian renaissance as the more obvious and glamorous advances in art and literature.

The main crops at Asnapius were grains and legumes. Wheat, here as elsewhere, was a luxury, the carefully protected crops being raised in special walled compounds. Most of the grain consisted of oats and barley, much of the latter being used for beer. In the year of the inventory, there were 178 head of cattle, ranging from calves to old beef stock. Pigs, as was to be expected, out-numbered all other forms of animals with 260 hogs and 100 gilts: this hardy, self-sufficient animal, most of whose food was obtained from the forests and every part of whose body could be consumed, underpinned European rural economy for centuries. There was a considerable number of geese, chicken and the like and, characteristically for the time, a flock of peacocks all of which would find their way, ceremonially dressed, on to the banquet table. Peacocks were not particularly palatable and on a cost-for-value return their flesh was economically inferior to most other forms of poultry. But they made a splendid show. No mention is made of that other showy, but highly nourishing, dish of the Middle Ages, the swan.

Another omission in the inventory is that of blacksmith – again, an indication of its relatively early compilation for with the more wide-spread use of iron the smith began to become a major feature of all rural communities, and would remain as such till the coming of the motor car. Certainly, in the *Capitulaire de Villis*, compiled about 770, Charles insisted that all of his estates should have resident smiths.

In most of his capitularies, the voice of the king can be heard, if dimly muffled by the legalisms, and in none more so than that pertaining to the running of his estates. Its very incoherence, leaping from subject to subject, strengthens that impression. One receives a clear picture of the king, wearing his favourite casual dress, riding round his estates accompanied by a crowd of attentive and occasionally crest-fallen stewards rapping out questions in that high-pitched voice of his, half turning his head to dictate an opinion, a comment, an order to one of the clerics accompanying the party. And in due course those opinions, comments, orders would find their way on to parchment, frequently only slightly modified into formal language.

The entire household, of all degree from high official to serf, was known as the *familia*. Though this does not have the same concept of a powerful bond as its English translation 'family', it does convey the idea of a unit. And the king was a good master. Tenants of the estates not only received a remission of taxes during times of genuine hardship, but also a free distribution of essential seeds. And he also permitted the disposal of surplus crops from the estate in the local markets, though making it very clear to some of his more high-handed mayors that the estate was run for the royal benefit not as a private fief of their own.

Despite his dislike of dunkenness, Charles took a keen interest in viticulture, establishing vineyards first in his own country and later, as emperor, in such outlying places as Hungary – where their remote descendants would be producing wine into the twentieth century. His main reason seems to have been to reduce the dependence on foreign wines: the science of economics was not yet born, but he was perfectly aware that what was spent on foreign goods was taken out of the country and he imposed taxes on imports, imported wine in particular bearing a burden. For some extraordinary reason he forbade the ancient method of treading grapes by peasants in bare feet, the most efficient method ever adopted for turning grapes into wine. The prohibition probably arose from that preoccupation of his with cleanliness, which amounted to an obsession: it was probably one of the factors which led the little spa town of Aachen, with its abundant hot springs, to become the capital of the Carolingian empire.

Even a cursory reading of the *Capitulaire de Villis* leaves the reader impressed with the detail and range of the king's interests. Nothing was too trivial or too complex: cowsheds and pigsties must be repaired before their dilapidations made a new building necessary; certain textiles and dyes should be made available for 'women's work'; if fish were sold from the vivariums in times of surplus they must rapidly be stocked with fry; wagons must be roofed with leather and they must also be watertight so that the contents would not be harmed while fording deep streams (though here it is Charles the general rather than Charles the farmer who is talking, for these wagons were vital for military service). But perhaps of all the minutiae of the capitulary, historically the most valuable is the list of vegetables which were to be grown on the estates. There are seventy-one varieties, and the king's list presents a priceless check of indigenous European vegetables before the expansion of later centuries brought in plants from all corners of the world.

It was during Charles's reign that the Franks began to turn away from the traditional pattern of agriculture in favour of the three-field rotation system, an innovation which has been described by a modern economist as 'the greatest agricultural novelty in the Middle Ages'. In discussing the effect of this agricultural revolution, the American historian Lynn White notes how almost entirely it has been disregarded by scholars. 'Nowhere are the urban roots of "civilisation" more evident than in the neglect which historians have lavished upon the rustic and his works and days . . . While our libraries groan with data on the ownership of land, there is an astonishing dearth of information about the various, and often changing, methods of cultivation which made the land worth owning.' And of all these changes, the three-field system was the most potent, as shown by the extraordinary speed with which it was adopted: the first indication of it comes in the year 763, some five years before Charles came to the throne, the next in 783, the third in 800. The first two references come from monastic sources, monks always alert to the recording of novelties, but thereafter the references are casual and frequent, implying the widespread adoption of the new system at a speed quite remarkable among a notoriously conservative peasantry.

It is only with the comparatively recent development of the science of palaeobotany that we receive a clue to the origin of the process.

Pollen analysis has shown that the early inhabitants of the Baltic countries favoured spring planting for their main crops, in contrast to the Mediterranean countries' favouring of autumn. The Carolingian empire, stretching between Baltic and Mediterranean, acted as a bridge along which ideas could move and fuse. Some time in the 770s Charles evidently became aware of the fusion between Baltic and Mediterranean agriculture, saw its potential value, and set about promoting it. The three-field system not only increased the yield of crops (hitherto one half of the land was left fallow whereas it was now necessary to leave only one-third) but it also increased the fertility of the land by alternating nitrogen-rich legumes with cereals. So revolutionary a development would inevitably have spread across Europe whether or not the King of the Franks had a hand in its propagation. But the remarkable speed with which it spread was almost certainly related to his deliberate policy of education.

A bird's-eye view of western Europe would have shown, in this eighth century after Christ, solid masses of green not unlike the great Amazon rain forests viewed from an aircraft today. The forest covered great areas from Baltic to Atlantic, creating their own myths: where the Mediterranean peoples spoke of the noon-day devil, that spirit born of intense heat and stillness in open country, the northerners would speak of goblins half seen in the underwater light of the forests. In due course their ceremonial architecture, too, would be infused by the sense of upward rushing of the giant trees, the pillars of a Gothic church being the outside forest petrified and tamed.

But such architecture was centuries in the future. Stone-built cities survived: Roman cities like Cologne adapting themselves to new conditions; tribal capitals like Paris or Soissons rooting themselves and flourishing. But here, in the north, the towns, though connected still by the roads of Rome, were like island universes calling to each other before the night and silence descended upon them. Far more frequent were the villages. To the south a thousand miles or so away were great cities, urban complexes rivalling those of the twentieth century with infra-structures of sewage and law and markets. Here, in the north, the bulk of Charles's subjects lived in communities of a few hundred at the most. Their homes were made of wood drawn from that all-encompassing forest, single-storey huts with straw and clay stuffed into the chinks of the planks to make them solid. They were scattered around in no particular order, their centre point being the church and the hall of the local lord, bigger than the peasant's hut and with more elaborate decoration but of the same material – different in degree, not in kind.

At the very bottom of society, its foundations, the peasant whether virtual slave tied to the land or freeman was not in that abject state of dependency he would know a century or so hence, treated as a chattel. The capitularies that regulated his life as well as that of his superiors gave him freedom of movement, unlike his wretched descendants who would be legally tied to one spot of earth for their life-span. In actual fact, that freedom meant little: no man would willingly give up the area of arable land so painfully clawed from the forest and worked into some form of loam with primitive tools. But the concept of 'the frank' percolated down into this lowest stratum of society. The lord no more 'owned' his land than did the peasant, for all were leaseholders of the king. But within that all-encompassing arm, the peasant was free to build and own his own wooden hut, a number of strips of land scattered around which would provide him and his family with sustenance and, in good years, a little surplus which could be exchanged for cash or kind. Just as the mayor above him owed certain dues to the king, so did the peasant though his was a payment in the only means available to him – labour. In general, a peasant would expect to give half his week's labour to the estate. He was specifically protected from being obliged to work on Sundays, by the all-seeing, all-encompassing capitularies.

Charles's agricultural reforms began on the estates most directly under the royal eye. Life and work for the bulk of the population superficially appears unchanged over the centuries. But there was, in fact, a ferment at work, demonstrated by the appearance in some of the larger and richer rural communities of a curious new implement: it had wheels and a complicated arrangement of blades set at a carefully determined angle. The locals knew it as a *charrue* or *carruca*: we would recognize it today as a plough.

A mechanized means of tilling the soil employing the far greater power of a quadruped had been known for centuries. The earlier form of plough – the 'scratch-plough' – consisted essentially of three long, strong spars of timber joined together at the base (and, if metal were available, shod at the base) and held apart by cross-pieces. An animal – ox if available, if not a donkey or even a cow – when harnessed to the front of this contraption would pull the pointed end through the ground while the ploughman carefully held it at the correct angle. It altered the very face of primitive agriculture and, indeed, was still in use in Francia for it required no outlay to make and, in dire necessity, could be pulled by a human being. It was quite useful in light soils but because it only scratched the surface, every few years the ploughed field would have to be laboriously dug with a spade. It was also quite useless in the heavy soils of the north, particularly in the root-choked glades of the forests being cleared so painfully slowly.

Like the three-field system, the heavy wheeled plough came into Francia as a result of contact with alien peoples and, historically, its course is traced neither by archaeology, nor by palaeobotany but by etymology, to its origins among the Slavic peoples of eastern Europe. The Lombards took it with them into northern Italy and in due course the Franks took it from their Lombard relatives. Certainly by the year 730 the farmers of the Rhineland were familiar with the *carruca* and Charles, as a boy, would probably have seen no other form of plough on the royal estates.

Unlike the scratch-plough (or *araire*), the *carruca* bit deep into the soil which was then turned over in a wave – exactly as the prow of a ship turns over the water – by the mould board. The blade cut through all but the toughest roots, while the mould board, in throwing the new-cut earth aside, ensured that the soil was aerated and the valuable humus buried to form fertilizer for next year's crop. There was no longer any need to dig the field·over by hand, the area of arable land increased dramatically, and the soil itself was enriched producing heavier crops per acre. But it was, for its time, a high-technology tool. It could not be knocked together by a handyman, but was the work of skilled craftsmen using expensive materials. It could not possibly be pulled by a human being but required heavy, expensive oxen and it operated best not on a smallholding, but on larger plots of land. In this, it contributed substantially towards that gradual coalescence of small strips which would change the face of European society with the small, independent peasant dropping further and further out of sight.

But throughout Charles's reign as king and as emperor, the small 'free' man was still the last unit of society. He owned his home, he had grazing rights in common with his neighbours, his lean, black pigs snuffled for acorns in the forest as of right. He was only just balanced on the edge of existence: for every two bushels of grain he sowed, he would get back only three so that a bad year would see a village near starvation. Grains provided his basic food – 'bread' was quite literally a synonym for 'food'. The watermill, which turned the grain into flour, was so vital a piece of rural equipment that over the centuries it would remain as part of the monarch's personal appanage. Some indication of the role that bread played in diet is provided by the term for almost all other foods – vegetables, meat and the rare fruits were regarded simply as *companaticum*, 'that which accompanied bread'. The basic meal probably consisted of a kind of purée of thick soup of vegetables with an occasional flavouring of meat, washed down by a sour wine or thin beer. Barley beer was for the relatively well-to-do: the poorest drank concoctions made from rosemary or bog myrtle.

Under the strong hand of the king, the land was safe from external enemies but there were internal enemies enough, both human and animal. The forests gave shelter to some of the fiercest predators known, wolves, bears and even the occasional lion. The capitularies emphasized what needed little emphasizing: crops must be protected. The fields were therefore frequently deeply ditched in the form of a moat or solidly fenced just as the villages were fenced. Bandits thrived. Their punishment, when caught, was swift and draconian but in that vast forested landscape an entire band could melt away a few yards from a settlement. The shortage of species alone hampered their activities: the loot they were after was usually mobile, on four legs.

The seasons imposed their unaltered rhythms. Autumn was a time of intense activity preparing for the long, cold, dark and hungry days that lay ahead. Cattle which were not ear-marked for breeding were slaughtered and salted: in the *Capitulaire de Villis* the king enjoined every estate, where possible, to produce its own salt; without it, hunger loomed over the community. Fish from the vivarium would be soaked in brine; pork and beef salted down. Sour wine, converted in verjuice, pickled those fruits which could not be dried; small sour apples were turned into cider; great masses of firewood would be stacked against the savage winter.

With the onset of the first blizzards of December the pulse of life slowed. For some, the very poor, it would cease altogether if the winter proved very severe and prolonged, for their margin of survival, measured by what they had in store, would prove just too slender. But for most, it was a species of hibernation. Darkness, occurring by 5 p.m. in these northern climes, would bring what little activity there was to an end, the family crawling into the communal bed at one end of the hut to remain there for twelve hours and more until the red winter sun signalled another short day at around 8 or 9 a.m. For the men, during the day, there might be perhaps the excitement of a hunt: the capitularies preserved large areas and certain species of game for the king but the laws were neither enacted, nor executed, with the savagery of later years and the monotonous diet of dried and salted foods could be supplemented occasionally with fresh meat. A limited amount of stock care for the handful of animals set aside to breed in spring; the repair of tools and weapons constituted the day's work for the men. Women had a fuller day. It was they who provided the entire clothing for the household and it was now that spinning and weaving became a main preoccupation.

With spring, the tempo increased again, the life of the household responding to the warmth and hours of daylight precisely as the life of the natural world responded. In Charlemagne's calendar, March was Spring-month, the time when the whole world came to life and went about its business, when the early crops were sown, the new generation of animals made their appearance – lambs and calves, piglets, foals. These latter in particular were of enormous importance, for some time during the early years of the king's reign the Franks evolved finally into a race of horsemen. And the same kind of horse bred for strength and stamina on the battlefield was ideal for working the farm. Equipped with the newly evolved horse-collar, which meant that the animal thrust with its shoulders instead of pulling with its neck (and so suffering slow strangulation), the horse worked at least 50 per cent more efficiently than the oxen and, despite its relative appearance of slenderness, could work for a good two hours a day longer. The ox would survive side by side as a beast of burden with the horse, if for no better reason than that an old ox made better eating than an old horse. But the relative value of the two is shown by the fact that a measure of ploughland came to be recognized as that which could be worked by two oxen or one horse in a given period. In terms of agricultural output, yet another boost had been given to food production.

The feudalism that shaped Europe for a millennium was only, as yet, dimly apparent. The king, admittedly, recognized the basic pyramidal shape of society when, in one of his capitularies, he enjoined: 'Let no man renounce his lord after he has received so much as the value of one *solidus*, with these exceptions if the lord desire to kill him, or beat him with a stick or to defile his wife or daughter, or to take from him his inheritance.' The nature of Frankish society had begun to change, slowly but irrevocably, when the first great Merovingian king, Clovis, gave vast tracts of land to his followers in return for their service – in effect, buying their loyalty. No longer were the generous young men of Tacitus's *comitatus* content with a great sword and a seat at the banquet. Loyalty now had a very real financial value in the form of land gifts. And land was useless without a peasantry which could be induced, bullied or bargained to work it. A system began to emerge of delegation, of a free man offering his services on the land in exchange for certain privileges extended by he who held that land of the king. This free relation would become fossilized centuries later into that extraordinary relationship illustrated by the *chanson de geste* of Raoul of Cambrai. According to the *chanson* Bernier, vassal of Raoul, hears that his mother has been murdered, with attendant atrocities, by his lord. Raoul humiliates him, mocks the very tie that binds them, but Bernier can do nothing but stand with limp hands for the act of homage that he has made to Raoul has created an artificial force stronger than the natural force that links him to his mother. He has only one remedy – to abandon Raoul – and this he does but even this is heinous. The true vassal would have continued not merely to serve Raoul, but serve him with active love, the memory of his murdered mother an irrelevancy. Such a relationship would have been monstrous to Charles, who had specifically provided a man with an escape clause if his lord prove unmerciful – the kind of far-seeing, humane vision which characterized most of his enactments.

Ironically, the office of count which Charles established in order to ensure that justice was available for the lowest of his subjects, probably contributed towards the feudal process. The division of Francia into counties was as old as the nation, for the Franks had introduced it into Gaul after their conquest. The counties varied very considerably in size, and their shape changed according to need; their numbers, too, varied and during Charles's reign there were probably about three hundred including the counts he established in Italy in place of the arrogant Lombard dukes. They were the king's deputy and, subject to that overriding but distant presence, they were all but absolute in their counties. The count's was the law court which could condemn a man to death. His was the tax office – and the fact that he was allowed by law to retain one-third of all taxes, and one-third of all fines, was an obvious temptation to corruption and oppression. The king did his best to check this tendency by ensuring that the count in his capacity of judge exercised power in effect as a member of a bench, one among an assembly of freemen – yet again, the spirit of the *comitatus* was still strong enough to check the tendency towards tyranny. Each year the count had to present himself in person at the royal court, wherever it might be, to render the king a personal account of his conduct of affairs as well as to hand over to the royal treasurer the revenues he had obtained on the crown's behalf. The paucity of the records of counties in surviving archives throws light on a major problem of administering the kingdom – the lack of literate administrators. Charles was obliged to attempt to run a modern state with rule-of-thumb methods evolved by nomadic tribesmen and, even with an honest and competent count, he would have had only a very general idea of the finances and general administration of that particular county.

As was inevitable, not all counts were by any means honourable. By a quirk of history, we have a vivid picture of the administration of provincial justice, and the corruption of local counts, not from any of the king's archives but from a poem written by a bishop. This was Theodulf, Bishop of Orleans, who gravitated to the court and there became part of that brilliant if brief-lived 'Rome of the North' which provided the dynamic for the cultural renaissance.

Theodulf begins by remarking: 'I have often perceived that when I inveigh against the bribery of judges, the secret thought of my hearers is that I, if I had the opportunity, would do even as they.' In order to refute this he tells the story of a journey he made down the Rhone on the king's behalf. At every place he was offered bribes: one man offered him a beautiful silver vase if he would cancel a deed of enfranchisement which had freed a number of slaves belonging to his parents. Another, in a dispute over the ownership of cattle, offered him a superb Saracen robe. Theodulf remarks percipiently that he would not have been so approached unless his predecessors too had been approached and successfully bribed. He then goes on to describe the ideal judge at work, giving incidentally a valuable impression of life in a small Frankish town as seen by a visiting lawyer:

When you are on your way to the court, perhaps some poor man will address to you words of entreaty, some man who may afterwards say that he could not have speech of you while you walked surrounded by your people. You go forward, you are received within those proud doors while the common people are shut out. But let some faithful and compassionate person walk near you to whom you can say 'Bring into our presence that man who uttered his complaint in such a loud voice.'

If you ask my advice when you should go to the Forum [court] I should say 'go early' and do not grudge spending the whole day on the judgement seat. I have seen judges who were slow to attend the duties of their office, though prompt enough in taking their rewards. Some arrive at eleven, and depart at three. Others, if nine o'clock will see them on the bench, will rise therefrom at noon. Gluttony is always to be avoided, but especially at the time when the duty awaits you of handling the reins of justice. He who devotes himself to feasting and slumber, comes with dulled senses to the trial of causes and sits in his court flabby, inactive, mindless. Beware of too abundant banquets and especially of the goblets of Bacchus.

The janitor of the court must control the gaping crowd and not suffer the lawless mob to rush into the hall and fill the building with their noisy complaints. But he too must be a man of clean hands, and must be expressly admonished not to take any douceurs from the people. Alas, this is a vice which every janitor loves. The janitor loves a bribe, and among his masters, the judges, you will scarce find one in a thousand who hates it.

Theodulf was so well informed because he belonged to an élite group, the *missi dominici*. The 'Messengers of the Lord' were the means by which the king kept himself informed of what was happening in the kingdom, promulgated his edicts and checked abuses on the spot. The *missi* were invariably men of high social standing – not infrequently, they were personal friends of the king's – and were sent out annually in pairs to tour the kingdom, usually in areas with which they were familiar. Where possible, one was a layman, the other a cleric and they were, in effect, plenipotentiaries, the king's representatives with powers to conduct their own law cases, overturn the rulings of the count if necessary (and, indeed, arraign him before the highest court in the land, that of the king's, for grave transgressions of duty). They were an attempt to resolve that oldest of all civic problems: Who shall judge the judges? Who shall oversee the overseers? And, to a remarkable extent, the system worked in that the *missi* really do seem to have lived up to the high moral concept of their office, really do seem to have attempted to translate into humdrum, everyday activities the visions dreamed up by their king. The limitation of the system was that there were just not sufficient men of the right calibre to discharge the office. Setting out in spring, they had to cover immense areas in relatively little time, so that their visitation to any given place was brief. Like lay magistrates in modern society, they had their own personal preoccupations: a bishop acting as a *missus* might well be obliged to cut short his tour to attend some crisis in his own diocese, leaving his companion with a suddenly doubled workload. But looking back over the pattern of Charles's reign it becomes evident that, with all its limitations, the system of *missi dominici* was the single most important factor in linking together the widely differing regions of the kingdom, making of 'Francia' an idea not simply a more or less chance collection of peoples and localities.

Another powerful binding element was that spirit of the *comitatus* which found its expression nationally in the two great assemblies of the people. These found their origin in the primitive past of the Franks when every able-bodied man passed in review of the chief once a year during spring, the so-called March Field. This was the assembly which, long ago, had approved King Pippin's invasion of Italy and so commenced the relationship between Franks and Romans and which, even now, modified the autocracy of the king. It still had a strong military significance: as cavalry increased among the Franks so the assembly was moved to May, ensuring a sufficiency of fodder. But it was now also the nation in parliament and was divided into two assemblies. The March Field was the general assembly when representatives of the entire Frankish nation gathered together to discuss the propositions put before them by the king. They could not, themselves, initiate subjects for discussion but they could, and did, subject royal proposals to a very cool and detailed analysis. In a few years' time the suffix Magnus would be added to their king's Christian name and a little after that he would be Imperator. But even now he was regarded essentially, in the Frankish manner, as the first among equals. The second assembly took place in October and was far more select, the nobles alone working out, with the king, the issues which were to be placed before the March Field the following year.

It was out of these assemblies that there emerged the capitularies which provided the legal structure for the nation's life, and provide posterity with a priceless insight both into the working of the king's mind (for they reflect his preoccupations) and the activities of the kingdom. They took their name from the articles (capitula) into which they were divided and though each capitulary was concerned with a specific subject, whether it be the mobilization of the army or the conduct of priests, they tend to cover wide-ranging subjects as though the king were saying 'Oh, yes, that reminds me . . .' Nevertheless, each article is short and to the point, each subject ticked off firmly.

The first known capitulary of the reign, issued in 779 after his triumphant return from Italy, shows the king grappling with the problems of violence in his kingdom. The Franks were removed by only a generation or so from the time when violence was an accepted way of life, the means by which a man proved himself among his peers. Directed against external enemies of the state it was still an invaluable asset to the community: directed inwards it could destroy that homogeneity being built up so slowly. Murder, robbery, and rape were crimes which no man, civilized or barbarian, could defend: far more difficult was it to outlaw the concept of the blood feud, the ancient custom whereby a man was honour-bound to take on the vendetta when his nearest male relative had fallen to it. It could not be banned outright, and the king did not attempt it, but he could and did enjoin that when *wergeld* (monetary compensation) was offered, the relatives of the victim could not refuse it.

Thereafter the capitularies emerge in astonishing numbers and variety, blueprints for the society the king was creating. It is a peculiar irony that not one of them survives in the original, considering the enormous importance their author placed on documentation and the care to which he went to preserve correspondence. But later copies were assembled either within his lifetime, or shortly after his death, accurate enough to allow posterity to detect the subjects that were uppermost in the king's mind at a particular time. No detail seems too small: the actual types of apples that are to be grown on his estates are specified; no detail seems too remote, whether it is the minimum age at which a girl should take the veil or the paying of tolls on bridges.

The capitulary for the mobilization of the army in 802 provides a valuable clue as to the physical means of promulgation. Four copies of each capitulary were made: one for the *missi*, those all-powerful emissaries charged with the execution of these laws, one for the local count, one for the army administrators and the fourth, for the chancellery, as permanent record. As much as the remains of Carolingian art and architecture, the capitularies are monuments both to the king and to the man. It is entirely appropriate that one of the very rare authentic portraits of Charlemagne should be associated with a capitulary. And it is appropriate, too, that it should show him in an admonitory mood, for the watchword of all capitularies is 'Reform'. Do better: try harder: love one another: these are the constant themes of his laws.

PART III · *Imperium*

The place where the head of the world resides may indeed be called Rome.

Modoin, Bishop of
Autun AD 804

7 The General

At the battle of Poitiers, fought some ten years before Charlemagne's birth, the Frankish army fought entirely on foot as they had always done, in the words of the chronicler 'standing rigid as a wall and like a belt of ice frozen solidly together.'

At the battle of the Dyle, fought in 891 some eighty years after Charlemagne's death, the chronicler of that time noted that 'the Franks are unused to fighting on foot'. In other words, some time during Charlemagne's reign the Franks changed from their role of infantry to cavalry and that, in turn, triggered off profound changes not only in the manner of warfare but in the very structure of society. Among much else, it signalled the eclipse of the poor but free man, for only a rich man could afford to be a horseman.

'The historian of Frankish institutions too often recalls to the wearied mind Eliza on ice: hypothesis clutched to bosom, he leaps from charter to ambiguous capitulary, the critics baying at his heels.' So, feelingly, records the American historian Lynn White in his epochal work on medieval technology. Documentary evidence for eighth-century military history is sparser even than for social history. The clerical scribes who held up the mirror to their society were interested, in descending order, in theology (mostly miraculous), politics and law. They would occasionally record some aspect of social life of significance to their largely monastic world. They could, and did, describe warfare at length, but only in its effects – usually to pillory an enemy of their church or their community. Equipment and tactics were of little interest to them. Until Charlemagne's capitularies give us at least a bird's-eye view of warfare, posterity has to build up a picture from archaeology, and by the linking together of apparently unrelated factors, in an attempt to account for the revolutionary change in military technology. Three apparently unrelated factors are that a small piece of metal linked to a U-shaped piece of leather appeared in Francia; that Charles Martel went to hell after his death; and that the Carolingian lance had a cross-bar a few inches below its murderous point.

Charles Martel, Charlemagne's grandfather, went to hell because he confiscated Church lands on a grand scale, giving them to his followers. Or so says a prelate, who was given the facts in a dream. But though the great Mayor's ultimate destination might be debatable, the fact of those confiscations was very real. Later, his son Carloman was to apologize to Pope Zacharias about it – but also explained he was obliged to retain those rich Church lands in order to defend Christendom from its foes, and Pope Zacharias, with something like a sigh, agreed that it was necessary. For by then the new shape of warfare had become evident, and it was an expensive shape to maintain. Martel had risked external damnation because that was the only means whereby he could finance the new weapon of cavalry.

The probable reason why Martel departed from the centuries-old fighting tactics of his forebears was the advent of that U-shaped piece of leather with its metal jointure: the stirrup. It is an astonishing fact of history that, though cavalry had been used for centuries in both the civilized and the barbarian worlds, and though some variation of the stirrup had in fact appeared in widely distant places at widely distant periods, it did not become universally adopted until taken up by the Franks in the early eighth century. Without the stirrup, the horseman can function only as an archer or, to a limited extent, as swordsman and spearman. With the stirrup, horse and man are transformed into one immense projectile with the weight of the charging beast transmitted down the heavy lance which the horseman could now wield, bracing himself against the stirrup for the impact. Had he attempted such a manoeuvre without a stirrup, he would simply be swept off the back of his mount at the moment of impact. So violent was that impact, that the lance would penetrate right through its victim, rendering the lancer defenceless at a critical moment and, to obviate this, the little cross-bar appeared a few inches below the iron point so preventing too deep penetration. It became customary, too, to tie gay ribbons to the cross-bar as an aid to sighting and this gave a festive air to a column of horsemen on the march with lances raised and pennons fluttering in the wind. In addition, the horseman could, by standing on the stirrup, raise himself in the saddle to strike with his sword down on his left-hand, or blind, side.

It is impossible to say why a non-cavalry people like the Franks should have adopted this crucial device at this crucial period. But it was to have an effect upon medieval warfare comparable, in proportion, to the effect that the invention of aircraft was to have on twentieth-century warfare. Its social effect was as great, beginning the sundering of the classes, with 'aristocrat' and 'horseman' being virtually interchangeable terms; 'footman' and 'peasant' too were related. In the annual mustering of the host, only a man with four hides of land was expected to present himself, fully equipped, as a cavalryman. Charlemagne, in order to increase his cavalry potential and, perhaps too with that eye of his to the importance of social balance, decreed that wherever possible among poorer men, one should be chosen as horseman and his neighbours should band together to equip him. But the system, depending on a complicated series of calculations, never really worked and the poor man simply turned up at the muster on foot as his ancestors had always done.

From the first year of his reign until the last Charlemagne was at war either personally or through his sons in later years. The mustering of the host therefore became a standard military exercise, its time and place varying according to the objective of the campaign. Usually, it took place in spring and very rarely indeed would a campaign extend into winter – although, when necessary, Charlemagne would even cross the Alps in winter, a feat which added to his awesome reputation. But the dramatic effect of his campaigns was the result of endless, minute, humdrum planning where even the number of thongs in a hide-cover for a cart would be specified, the kind of meticulous detail which would not be seen again until the era of modern wars. Most of the military capitularies date from the later years of the king's reign, the result of experience and a clearer appreciation of need. But through them can be seen the gradual steps which turned a mass of courageous but individualistic men into a disciplined instrument for controlling an empire.

The development of the Frankish army operated on the snowball principle: the expansion of the kingdom was the result of an efficient fighting force – but the larger the kingdom became, the more streamlined it was necessary to make the fighting force. The old annual musters with thousands of men milling casually around, probably accompanied by their wives and children in a holiday atmosphere, was of no use to the king. He cut down the size of the force by eliminating ill-armed, untrained peasants, substituting contributions in cash or kind from them. As the frontiers of the kingdom expanded ever deeper to north, south and east, so cavalry simply as a means of transport, quite apart from its tactical role, became ever more important. And, like all great commanders, the king adopted the best weapons of his erstwhile enemies. Thus, the spearhead of his cavalry formations were those supreme horsemen, the Lombards. Significantly, a very high proportion of the subjects of his military capitularies issued in the early years of his reign deal with the newly conquered Lombards. They, too, as with the Franks, were now subject to the *hereban* – the call to the host – and were liable to the death penalty for desertion. And the recognition of their dominant military skill lay in the fact that the king's *ban*, or order to the Lombards, applied only to cavalry.

After that recognition of the value of cavalry, Charlemagne placed in importance the possession of armour. In his very first military capitulary he strictly forbade export of the *byrnie* or mailed shirt, a prohibition repeated again and again in successive capitularies. A merchant caught smuggling mail out of the country had his entire property confiscated and, similarly, any man subject to the *ban* who owned a mail shirt and failed to bring it to the muster, not only forfeited the *byrnie* itself but also the land which he held.

The muster continued to be a national event, but now organized on much more disciplined levels. A man who failed to answer the *ban*, or to be enrolled in one of its contributing groups, was fined 50 per cent of what he owned, and as this 50 per cent was decided by the local court it could well amount to a death sentence not only on the man but upon his entire household, depending upon which 50 per cent was taken. In theory, the confiscation of 'half a man's substance' related to specie – three pounds of gold for any man valued at six pounds, or thirty *solidi* for a man valued at three pounds. In practice, owing to the scarceness of precious metal, fines were levied in kind – an irritation or discomfort if the fine levied took the form of household goods, but a threat of actual starvation if it took the form of seed crops or animals. Later in the reign, there came an edict which accelerated the now inevitable movement towards feudalism. All Franks who held land were automatically subject to the *ban* but hitherto this had been a fairly free and easy arrangement. The king now delegated responsibility: every Frank who held four hides of land must march under the local count and, in their turn, the counts were responsible for seeing that all who should be under their banner were, in fact, present. It was this same capitulary which sought to even out the discrepancy between rich and poor in the matter of furnishing cavalry. The measurement of ability was four hides of land: any man who possessed only three hides was expected to come to an arrangement with a neighbour who had only one hide and pro rata. The two men were then supposed to agree as to who was to go as horseman: if the richer of the two answered the *ban*, the poorer man paid a quarter of his equipment. If the two men decided that, on balance, it would be better if the poorer man went, his neighbour would pay three-quarters. It worked reasonably well during Charlemagne's reign but, under his weaker successors, the fact that it was the local count who made the decision as to who paid what encouraged yet again the trend towards local despotism and separatism.

Charles turned his attention then to the discipline of the host itself. Starting from the date of the muster, any man who arrived late was deprived of meat and wine for the same number of days as he was late. The king's hatred of the drunkard found its way even into a muster consisting of thousands of men: any man found drunk and incapable in camp was forbidden all alcohol until the end of the campaign – a particularly grievous punishment condemning the delinquent to a regime of water, much of it brackish, unpleasant and at times down-right dangerous. Each man was to bring with him provisions for three months, consisting usually of flour, bacon and wine. He was to be fully armed, carrying lance, shield and club. Charlemagne's ability to draw on experience is shown by his later edicts that all foot soldiers should be armed with bow and arrows. This was a weapon quite unknown to the Franks until the kingdom's remorseless expansion to the east brought the host into contact with Hungarian bowmen. The Franks never became good bowmen, however, despite the king's insistence that every man should have a bow, two bowstrings and twelve arrows. The rations and other heavy equipment were carried in carts following the host and the specifications even for these were minutely detailed. Each cart carried twelve bushels of corn, an equivalent quantity of dried or cured meat, or twelve small barrels of wine. Each cart was to be supplied with a leather covering, to protect the contents from the weather; this covering was pierced with holes around the edges so that, when stuffed with hay and laced together with leather thongs, it could be used as a raft or pontoon in emergency.

In addition to the weapons of war, every man brought tools – pickaxes, hatchets and the like – and as these would have been taken from the already sparse equipment of his farm, a campaign would bring hardship upon his home where his wife was striving to run his farm in his absence. The three-month length of service, too, would inflict further hardship although the king tried to mitigate this by adjusting length of service according to the distance a man had to travel to join the host. In general, service was reckoned to commence from arrival at the border, but for any man coming from, say, the Rhineland for an expedition into Aquitaine or, later, into Spain, service was reckoned as commencing with his arrival at the Loire; while any man bound for a campaign into Saxony counted his service as beginning from the Rhine – giving, in each case, a leeway of about a week in the man's favour. Consciously or otherwise, Charles was following the Roman example of carrying his fort with him for among the equipment carried were iron-shod stakes and spades. With these, and with the massive carts, a temporary encampment could be turned swiftly into a fortified place.

The date and place for the muster would be transmitted to the host via the local counts, each of whom was responsible for the standard of equipment brought by his tenants. The summons which Fulrad, Abbot of Altaich, received is typical of the rest in its precision and its firmness of language.

> You shall come to Stasfurt on the Boda by May 20 with your men prepared to go on warlike service to any part of our realm that we may point out: that is, you shall come with arms and gear and all warlike equipment of clothing and victuals. Every horseman shall have shield, lance, sword, dagger, a bow and a quiver. On your carts you shall have ready spades, axes, picks, and iron-pointed stakes and all other things needed for the host. The rations shall be for three months, and clothing must be able to hold out for six. On your way out you shall do no damage to our subjects and touch nothing but water, wood, and grass. Your men shall march along with the carts and horses and not leave them till you reach the muster place, so that they may not scatter to do mischief. See that there be no neglect as you prize our good grace.

The prohibition against plunder is a clear indication of how Charlemagne saw the host: at home, it was essentially a policing instrument and even in wars against external enemies it was controlled in a civilized manner. The realization that their goods would not be stolen, their wives and daughters raped, their houses destroyed, must have made up the minds of many a citizenry deciding whether or not to surrender. But the prohibition against plunder was hard on a soldier for whom a campaign meant little more than privation for his wife at home and hard knocks for himself. It says much for the king's charisma (and, perhaps, for that ferocity of the Franks which centuries of civilization had still not eliminated) that his soldiers fought as they did, their financial return being limited to what they could find on the bodies of the slain and the permitted plunder of fortified places which had foolishly resisted.

In addition to the heavy carts, the baggage train included herds of cattle and flocks of sheep which were replenished en route sometimes through straightforward requisitioning, but more often as part of their owners' dues to the king. Except in emergency, each campaign would have been planned the previous year, forward scouts having covered the route up to (and frequently into) enemy country to make arrangements for provisions. The actual cutting edge of the army, the wedge of fighting men who would turn the king's wide-ranging policies into military fact, consisted of about half the host but even the auxiliaries – the herdsmen, cooks, carpenters and the rest – were accustomed to the use of arms. The Frankish host on the march would less resemble a modern army than a nomadic tribe with the king riding with his nobles somewhere in the centre. Usually his wife would accompany him and, in their childhood, his sons learned at their father's side the meaning of war – but learned it not as some great game, but as a grim and unavoidable extension of politics.

The Assembly of January 775 turned again and again to the seemingly unending problem of the Saxons. The punitive raid of 768 when the Irminsul had been destroyed had not had the hope-for long-term effect upon these resourceful and dangerous neighbours. Every summer saw Saxon incursions across the border, sudden armed raids that were little more than pinpricks in the vast body of the Frankish state but nevertheless were a standing insult to its ruler. Every murdered farmer, every burnt village, made a mockery of his claim to universal authority. There were retaliations: a Frankish force would swoop across the border and inflict upon the unfortunate Saxon farmers the same treatment as had been inflicted upon the Franks. But the main body of the Saxon host remained ever just beyond reach, melting into their forests and swamps in that familiar, exasperating manner.

All this was according to a long-established pattern. But a new dynamic was becoming evident behind that pattern: the Saxons were belatedly, painfully, feeling their way towards the same concept of nationhood as the Franks had done long before, the dozens of small units gradually coalescing into a handful. In particular, they had found a focal point, the Saxon equivalent of the long-dead Clovis, a nobleman called Widukind. And how one would like to know more about this man who deliberately allied himself with serfs and peasants instead of his fellow nobles, who gave Charlemagne the hardest of all his tasks and goaded him into committing the greatest crime of his life. Even so short and cautious a biography as Einhard wrote of Charlemagne would have served to flesh out this extraordinary figure from the heroic past. But the Saxons had no literary tradition and the Franks were certainly not going to honour so determined an enemy, and we can only guess at the man's character and motives according to Charlemagne's reaction to him. The king's address to the January Assembly gives a clear enough clue. The time had come, he said, 'to wage war upon the perfidious and oath-breaking Saxon people until they were conquered and converted to the Christian religion or wholly destroyed'. The king knew well the Saxon aversion to Christianity, how they would glibly accept baptism but shrug it off as soon as the pressure was removed; his announcement therefore was little less than an announcement of a policy of genocide. And so, in part, it would prove.

The host met in early summer at Duren, half-way between Aachen and Cologne and, after the muster, turned north-east towards the Rhine. And it was here that one of the seemingly pedantic provisions of the military capitulary – that whereby the covers of the carts could be turned into pontoons – came into its own. The Rhine, that broad, powerful river sweeping irresistibly through its spectacular landscape, marked the boundary between civilization and barbarism. Even the Romans had been content to halt at its western shore: Charlemagne intended to carry civilization over to the eastern shore – even if it were civilization presented in a mailed fist. The great bridge he built across the river at Mainz was at once a symbol of the unity he was imposing on Europe, but also a very practical means of crossing Europe's greatest river. But the building of that bridge lay some time in the future: his early Saxon campaigns usually began with a battle with the Rhine itself, the river which in 1944 checked the greatest mechanized army in history. And to cross it, he had at his disposal rafts, leather bags stuffed with hay and flimsy boats. No description exists of one of these crossings which must rank high in military history.

The Saxons retreated before the ponderous onslaught of the Frankish host, leaving their two main fortresses, the Sigeburg and the Eresburg, in the king's hands. He strengthened their defences and left garrisons within them for now he was determined on the permanent occupation of the country. He had evolved his own technique for the process. Hostages were taken in every area that surrendered to him and a fortified post built. Like the Romans, he followed a standard pattern for all these posts: established where possible on a hill near a river they were surrounded by impressive entrenchments and palisades. And, like the Roman camps which in the course of time became cities, some of the burgs he created in the north-east developed into flourishing towns, among them Magdeburg, Paderborn and Bremen. But that was in the future. The Saxons saw the King of the Franks now not as a civilizing force but as one of destruction and terror. For two months he unleashed the host in a deliberate campaign of terror quite at odds with his normal military strategy. It seemed to work: certainly, when a plaintive message came from Pope Hadrian that there was a Lombard rising in Italy, he felt free to make the journey to the south having established a Frankish governor in the captured Saxon lands. In one of his lightning campaigns he crossed the Alps in winter, fell upon the rebellious Lombard dukes like a thunderbolt, quashed the rebellion and swiftly returned to the north. So secure did he feel in Saxony that he actually called the annual Assembly of 777 in Paderborn, in the very heart of what had been enemy country. Saxons were included in the *ban*, and they obeyed. There were mass baptisms to which they submitted with their usual resignation; the mysterious Widukind retreated to the court of his kinsman, the King of Denmark, and the 'Saxon troubles' seemed to be at an end. The king must have felt very pleased with himself, very sure of his ultimate destiny when there appeared at Paderborn a deputation of exotically dressed, dark-skinned men – slender, almost fragile compared with the ponderous Franks but with a wiry strength and agility that made them formidable enemies. Saracens, led by no less a personage than Suleiman, governor of Barcelona, come to make a proposal.

To the outside world, it seemed as though Islam was one great monolith directed to one overwhelming end. Internally, it was split with divisions as mutually ferocious as any of those which split the Christian world. In the Christian year of 750 the Ommayyad dynasty, ruling in Baghdad, was overthrown by the Abbassids in a sequence of events reminiscent of the Carolingian overthrow of the Merovingians, an energetic new dynasty thrusting aside a worn-out one. But where the Carolingian coup had been legalistic and bloodless, the Abbassid had been murderous. Only one member of the old dynasty, Abderrahman, had survived and it was he who, fleeing to Spain, established a caliphate in opposition to the Caliphate of Baghdad. Suleiman, the Abbassid governor of Barcelona, declared that he would rather make a pact with the infidel than be subject to an Ommayyad and, hearing of the great

Assembly taking place at Paderborn, unwittingly followed in the footsteps of the pope in appealing to a King of the Franks to settle internal matters. His promises to Charlemagne were expansive, to say the least: not only would he help Charles to reduce the great fortress of Saragossa but he would turn over to the king all the cities under his control. In return, Charles would help him to throw out Abderrahman, calling on all Spanish Christians to join in what would be a crusade. Charles accepted.

In that manner began the Spanish campaign which was to end in disaster but, by one of the ironies of history, produce as by-product the first great epic to appear in Europe since Virgil's *Aeneid*. It is difficult to adduce Suleiman's motive in this tangled affair. He must have realized that he would need a very long spoon, indeed, to sup with the Frankish devil who, once established in Spain, would be very difficult to dislodge. Charles's motives are fairly obvious. Still a young man of thirty-five or so, he was in the expansionist phase of empire-building and the temptation to take up where his great uncle, Charles Martel, had left off a generation earlier and carry Frankish arms into the Saracen heartland was great. There was also the purely practical fact that the whole south-west of his kingdom was a troubled area, for ever on the brink of rebellion. It made good sense to push the borders of the Frankish kingdom beyond the Pyrenees, so cutting off any help that might come thence to the endlessly restless Gascons who submitted only reluctantly to northern rule. The king was aware of the size of the task, even with the somewhat suspect aid of Suleiman, and his preparations were on a commensurate scale.

The army that was assembled early in the following year was probably the largest and most heterogeneous since the days of Rome: Burgundians and Lombards, Goths, Provencals, 'Romans' from Italy, Austrasian and Neustrian Franks – even Bavarians sent by Charles's cousin Tassilo, still sulking in Ratisbon – came together to take part in the first Christian counter-attack upon Islam, the opening stages of a war which would continue for 700 years.

What happened when the army crossed the Pyrenees is best told in the words of Einhard. It is a very tight-lipped account, clearly carefully edited, but it is the last objective view we have of the action before it disappeared finally in a rainbow mist of legend and romance:

> He [the king] attacked Spain with the largest military expedition he could collect. He crossed the Pyrenees, received the surrender of all the towns and

fortresses that he attacked, and returned with his army safe and sound, except for a reverse which he experienced through the treason of the Gascons through the passes of the Pyrenees. For while his army was marching in a long line, suiting their formation to the character of the ground and the defiles, the Gascons placed an ambuscade on the top of the mountain (where the density and extent of the woods in the neighbourhood rendered it highly suitable for such a purpose) and then rushing down into the valley beneath threw into disorder the last part of the baggage train and also the rearguard which acted as a protection to those ahead. In the battle which followed, the Gascons slew their opponents to the last man. Then they seized upon the baggage and, under cover of night, they scattered with the utmost rapidity in different directions. The Gascons were assisted in this feat by the lightness of their armour and the character of the ground where the affair took place. In this battle Eggihard, the surveyor of the royal table, Anselm, the Count of the Palace and Roland, Prefect of the Breton frontier, were killed, along with very many others. Nor could this assault be punished at once, for when the deed had been done, the enemy so completely disappeared that they left behind them not so much as a rumour of their whereabouts.

The first part of the campaign did not go quite as smoothly as Einhard suggests. The Christian Spanish, far from welcoming their co-religionists from across the Pyrenees, joined forces with the Saracens to resist them. The promised support from Suleiman and his Abbassids disappeared into a morass of internecine feuds. A handful of Spanish towns, Barcelona and Gerona among them, did surrender to him but the fortress of Saragossa firmly kept its gates closed, its citizens declining to accept the rule of an infidel, and Saragossa was the key to northern Spain. There was, it appears, a number of pitched battles whose results were inconclusive – sufficiently so to decide the king that the time was not yet come for Spain to be included in the Frankish empire. In that undramatic, indeed, somewhat humiliating manner, the great crusade came to an end. Returning back, the army paused to sack Pamplona. In the absence of any other great deeds this stood out so that when, six centuries later, the king had been transformed not only into a hero but also a saint and the Spanish expedition had been similarly glorified, the sack of Pamplona was deemed to be worthy to be immortalized in gold upon his tomb. The army then retreated back through the Pyrenees, through the pass of Roncesvalles.

It is clear enough what happened at Roncesvalles even from Einhard's wary account. Far from being an heroic action on the part of a noble rearguard, it was the result of a quite remarkable incompetence amounting to a dereliction of duty. The vanguard, consisting of some

40,000 men under the direct command of the king, passed safely through the narrow valley. The rearguard, with its tempting baggage, was under the command of high-ranking soldiers, including that Roland who was to pass into legend as Charlemagne's nephew, and it is impossible to say why these veteran soldiers failed to take the elementary precaution of sending out scouts to guard the flanks. At the point where the pass narrows (marked today by the Chapel of Sancti Spiritus, supposedly founded by Charlemagne as Roland's tomb) the wild Gascon mountaineers overwhelmed the rearguard. Einhard was correct in assuming that 'the Gascons were assisted by the lightness of their armour and the character of the ground'. They would probably have had no armour at all while the northerners, gasping in the heat of a Spanish August day, were burdened with mail painfully hot to the touch. The Gascons, too, knew every inch of the ground – so steeply sloping and littered with boulders as to cancel out wholly the use of cavalry. An avalanche of boulders would have wiped out a substantial part of the rearguard even before the mountaineers came to close quarters: thereafter it was simply a question of wearing down the ponderously accoutred northerners and slaughtering them as they collapsed. The mountaineers then plundered the baggage and escaped before Charlemagne even knew that the rearguard had been attacked.

Such was what really happened at Roncesvalles on 15 August 778. And, just as puzzling as the incompetence of Roland and his comrades, is the fact that legend turned them into heroes, and the humiliating defeat into an act of noble self-sacrifice, immortalized in that *Song of Roland* which the minstrel Taillefer would chant to uplift the spirit of the Normans before the battle of Hastings. In it, the half-naked mountain shepherds became Saracens:

> the paynim warhost,
> Never was huger beholden by men that on earth abide
> Ranked shields a hundred thousand of men-at-arms have I seen
> Seen laced on their heads their helmets, their mail all glittering sheer
> Strong dark-brown staves of lances, like a forest of pines, they bear

In it, the incompetence of Roland is transformed into the treachery of Ganelon, a purely imaginary figure invented to explain that humiliating defeat. Some blame is, indeed, attached to Roland, but it arises only from his noble refusal to call for help by sounding the great horn Oliphant:

Sound Oliphant, Roland my brother, so Charles shall hear it and back
Will he turn, and will strike with his barons on our side in the battle wrack
So please God, Roland answered, never my kindred through me
Shall be brought to reproach, nor our country be stained with infamy.

But, at last, as they fall before the overwhelming force of the
paynims, Roland is persuaded to sound the horn and here the unknown
poet created an enduring image that would haunt the consciousness of
Europe for centuries, the blast of the great war-horn calling to the king:

But now with pain Count Roland, with striving of strong strain
With pangs of endeavour, soundeth Horn Oliphant again
From between his lips is streaming the blood bright-crimson now:
That voice of the great horn crying is beyond all measure great
And again King Charles hath heard it afar at the mountain gate.

Despite the second attempt of the traitor Ganelon to persuade the
king to ignore the cry of the horn, Charles returns and finds his Paladins
all dead. There is nothing now but vengeance, and God obligingly halts
the sun in its course so that the work of slaughter can go on and at the
end the king buries the men who were both his comrades and his
subjects and returns grieving to Francia.

The king's sorrows and humiliation were not at an end in this
disastrous year for scarcely had he crossed the Pyrenees back into his
own land again when there came news that the Saxons, despite the mass
baptism of the previous year, despite the oaths of loyalty and gifts of
land, had risen in the most savage of all their acts of defiance. Einhard
sums up the Saxon deviousness fairly and succinctly. He believed that
the long-drawn-out war would have soon come to an end.

had it not been for the perfidy of the Saxons. It is hard to say how often they
admitted themselves beaten and surrendered as suppliants to King Charles:
how often they promised to obey his orders, gave without delay the required
hostages, and received the ambassadors that were sent to them. Sometimes
they were so cowed and broken that they promised to abandon the worship
of devils and willingly to submit themselves to the Christian religion. But
though sometimes ready to bow to his commands they were always eager to
break their promise so that it is impossible to say which course seemed to
come more natural to them for from the beginning of the war there was
scarcely a year in which they did not promise and fail to perform.

The Saxons might have replied, with justice, that it was scarcely
'perfidious' to reject an oath that had been forced upon them by

superior strength and there was no doubting their almost desperate courage in attempting, again and again, to throw off the yoke that had been accepted by so many other peoples, not least the Lombards. Charles was beside himself with rage, but there was nothing now he could do about it. The great muster of troops for the ill-fated Spanish expedition and the unusually long period of the campaign season had drained the land of reserves. He sent a punitive force to the Rhine and the Saxons, as usual, retreated out of range, but obviously one more major expedition would be necessary before the 'perfidious Saxon' could be brought finally under the control of the Frank.

There was one cheering piece of news in that dismal year: his wife Hildegarde had given birth to boy twins. The queen could not yet have been more than twenty-two years old but she had already given her husband three sons and three daughters. She combined courage and stoicism with almost saintly gentleness, invariably accompanying her husband upon his campaigns, willingly exchanging the comfort of the court for the rigours of open-air life – one of the factors which undoubtedly bound her to Charles. On this occasion, however, she had been so near her time that he had refused to take her into the hazards of the Spanish campaign, leaving her behind in Aquitaine. One of the baby boys did not long survive but the other, Louis, was destined to be his father's sole survivor and became, in due course, the second emperor of the Carolingian empire. The king now had three legitimate heirs: his namesake Charles, born in 772 and now a sprightly little boy of six years old, and Carloman, born the previous year.

The birth of a third son turned the king's mind towards that problem of inheritance which always plagued the Franks. He himself was barely middle-aged and had, in fact, a good thirty years of active life before him but already, it would seem, he was realizing the need to arrange the succession. There was the problem, too, of the increasing size of the kingdom with all the attendant difficulties of running it with the rudimentary communication network at his disposal. In the event, he solved both problems by creating what were three sub-kingdoms for his three sons, beginning now with Aquitaine for the new-born Louis. Many years later, Louis's biographer summed up the king's reasons:

> Since the most wise and percipient King Charles knew that a kingdom is like a body and is agitated now by this and now by that trouble if it is not cared for by good advice and strength as a doctor keeps a body in health . . . he established throughout Aquitaine counts, abbots and many men who are popularly called *vassi*, drawn from the Frankish people – men of courage

and foresight – to whom he gave the care of the kingdom, so far as he judged it of benefit, the guardian of the frontiers and the management of the royal estate.

What Charlemagne had done on the borders of his kingdom, in fact, was what Edward I was to do on the borders of his kingdom when he created the first Prince of Wales – that is, he created the machinery for controlling a vital but dangerously volatile border country while simultaneously laying some salve on wounded local susceptibilities by giving them his own son as titular monarch. The two other kingdoms within the greater kingdom were that formed from the heartland of the old Frankish *Reich* and Italy itself so that, for the first time for centuries, the potent name King of Italy was again in use, even though applying initially to a baby boy. It was not simply a ceremonial role. The new kingdoms were locked firmly into the body of the state: there would be no nonsense about independence during the lifetime of their creator. But the court of each was a true court, a mirror image of the central court, run by competent men who had their master's complete trust and confidence and who gradually moulded his sons into the forms he required. And he gave the boy-kings the potent new ceremony of coronation in Rome itself two years later when, in answer to Pope Hadrian's ever more urgent pleas, he descended into Italy bringing with him his entire family as well as a formidable military presence.

'Great tribulations had fallen on Italy after the Frankish conquest: by the sword, by famine, by wild beasts many persons perished so that some villages and towns were left altogether bare of inhabitants.' So recorded a chronicler in the little northern city of Bergamo. The chronicler's implication that Italy's tribulation was a result of the Frankish conquest was certainly not intended, for, from the moment of crossing the Alps, Charles was under continual pressure from litigants and suppliants seeking his aid as the one sole, constant centre of power and authority in an increasingly distracted peninsula. Beyond the Alps, Charles regarded himself, and styled himself, 'King of the Lombards', establishing himself in the great Lombard palace of Pavia, the capital of northern Italy until the rise of Milan three centuries later. This remained his headquarters in Italy but, following his usual restless practice, he travelled from city to city. And in every city the people flocked to the court to receive justice dispensed by the towering blond northman. At Parma he gave a charter for the merchants of Comachio:

at Mantua he held a solemn general assembly to hand down yet more capitularies, this time designed for his Lombardic people. Following his well-tried practice he made few alterations to their laws. After the brief rebellion of 776 he had diminished the power of the old Lombard dukes and in their place established Frankish counts in every major city as his direct representatives. And he made a move towards breaking down the old hostility between Romans and Lombards by repeating Aistulf's law forbidding any form of contact, commercial or social, with the hated 'Romans'. Aistulf had carried this to extremes, even decreeing that unpatriotic traders should, as well as being fined, have their hair cut in the Roman manner: 'Since you are ashamed of the flowing locks of your fathers and will trade with these well-trimmed dainty citizens of Rome we will shear away all the hair that Nature has given you and send you, bald-pated, a derision to all men, to cry your ignominy through the city.' That prime example of chauvinism, too, was removed from the statutes.

So, briskly applying the royal authority, the king moved south with his family, entering Rome again on Easter Day, 15 April. Seven years had passed since he and Pope Hadrian had taken the measure of each other and liked what they saw. There was still an underlying, mutual respect tough enough to survive their differences. Nevertheless, on this occasion there was a distinct chill in their attitudes to each other for each had become aware of the long-term motives of the other. Again and again, Hadrian had sent complaints winging over the Alps: complaints not only against the rump of the Lombard kingdom existing in the south; but also against a fellow bishop, Leo, Archbishop of Ravenna. 'Soon after you returned to Frankland this man, with tyrannical and most insolent intent, turned rebel to St Peter and ourselves.' Charles must have sighed to himself as he flipped through the only too familiar catalogue of papal complaints. If it wasn't Leo Archbishop of Ravenna who was defying St Peter's representative it was the Duke of Clusium stirring up trouble in Tuscany; and if Tuscany was filially devoted to St Peter's representative, then the citizens of Spoleto were showing insubordination. Each letter of complaint was a veiled reproach to the man styled 'Patrician' for not abandoning his trivial pursuits in the north to come to the support of St Peter's representative in the south. Nor were the reproaches always veiled. There was a celebrated occasion three years earlier when Hadrian's representative, the chamberlain Anastasius, was evidently foolish enough to mistake Charles's amiability and courtesy for weakness and began upbraiding him 'in most insolent tones' for breach of faith. It was probable that Anastasius, a Roman born and with a Roman's light-hearted attitude to the concept of loyalty, did not fully appreciate the nature of the insult he had levied at a Frankish king. He very rapidly learned. In one of his rare but most terrifying explosions of rage, Charles had the man dragged out of his presence and hurled into prison, refusing to let him return to Rome. Hadrian held his hands up in horror. 'Never since the beginning of the world had it been known that an envoy of St Peter, great or small, had been detained by any nation,' and begged for Anastasius's return, a plea which Charles ignored for some months.

Much delicate negotiation was needed to re-establish the old cordial relationship. There was, first, the unsavoury business of Hadrian having seemed to have countenanced slavery, allowing Roman citizens to sell fellow Christians to 'the unspeakable Saracens'. Hadrian indignantly repudiated the charge and, in so doing, gives some substance to that picture of privation to which the chronicler of Bergamo had referred. 'Never have we fallen into such wickedness, nor has any such deed been done with our permission.' It was true, he said, that Greek ships had been prowling along the Lombard coast in quest of slaves: 'The Lombards themselves, as we have been told, constrained by hunger have sold many families into slavery. And others of the Lombards have of their own accord gone on board the slave-ships of the Greeks, because they had no other hope of livelihood.' There was nothing the Romans could do about it, because they had no ships. One more problem had been passed over, to be placed on the burly shoulders of the Frank.

Charles then turned to his personal affairs: he wanted his two little sons Carloman and Louis crowned as kings of Italy and Aquitaine respectively. And he wanted Carloman to be re-baptized as Pippin.

The re-baptism of Carloman as Pippin was no casual whim. Rather was it an act of sympathetic magic, a recognition of the enormous power of a name. To modern ears, Pippin has a slightly comic, if charming, connotation: in the ear of a Frank it sounded as the name of the great founders of the Arnulfing dynasty. Since the founding of that dynasty, the name of its leading male had alternated between Charles and Pippin. There was again a Charles, the eldest son of Charlemagne, a boy of about five left at home, on this occasion at Worms. But the current bearer of the name 'Pippin' was that hunchbacked, illegitimate boy, now about fourteen years old whose likelihood of succeeding to his great father became ever more distant as one legitimate son after another made his appearance. The king now made it plain that this unfortunate son of his was now removed from the succession when his very name was given to another.

Charles had had an additional reason for bringing his wife and family with him, apart from his usual reason of family affection. Among his children was a pretty, fair-haired little girl of eight years of age, Hrotrud, and for her was intended a destiny which would measure the distance her race, her family and, above all, her father had travelled, for she was intended to be the wife of the boyish emperor of Constantinople, Constantine. He was firmly under his mother Irene's tutelage and it was she who had conducted negotiations which would turn a Frankish maiden into an empress. Waiting in Rome now were two high dignitaries of the Byzantine court, the Treasurer Constantine and the Grand Chamberlain himself, the haughty Mamulus. But not so haughty that he could not abase himself in that wholeheartedly subservient manner which startled the Franks. It was an occasion not only of historic significance but also of some social difficulty, an occasion that must have tried Byzantine skill at protocol. In theory, they were the emissaries of the Lord of the World, the Roman Emperor, but they could scarcely have been unaware of the fact that Pope Hadrian had quietly dropped the imperial formulae from his documents. No longer were these dated by the year of the emperor, or issued in his name and Mamulus, coming to his feet after abasing himself before the Frankish king, must have cast a speculative if respectful eye upon the man who, calling himself simply King of the Lombards, was so very evidently Lord of Italy. A vacuum existed in western Europe: would this man, Mamulus must have wondered, in time come to fill it?

Meanwhile the decencies were observed, the marriage treaty drawn up and signed with the king's elaborate monogram, and in due course the Byzantines returned to report the affair to their distant mistress. But they returned without the little girl whom they, twisting their tongue around that outlandish name of hers, christened in their mellifluous language 'Erythro'. Charlemagne was happy to betroth his beloved little daughter, but had not the slightest intention of parting with her until it was necessary. The Greek party, however, did leave behind one of their number, the eunuch Elisha, to instruct the little girl in 'the language and literature of the Greeks and the customs observed in the monarchy of the Romans'. Her father might have smiled at the lofty pretensions of that phrase 'monarchy of the Romans' but, with that passion of his for knowledge, welcomed Elisha into his court, adding one more potent ingredient to the cultural brew he was creating.

Afterwards, the royal party leisurely began its northward journey home, calling in at Monte Soracte to make a pious offering at the cell of Charles's uncle, that unhappy Carloman who had sought to prevent the Frankish invasion so many years ago but, despite that, whose memory was still revered in the royal family. At Florence and Pavia and Brescia there were yet more disputed legal actions to be heard, the press being so great that the king was obliged to restrict the right of appearance at the court. At Milan, his newborn daughter was christened and given the name of his much-loved sister, Gisila. Little King Pippin, just four years old, was left as viceroy of Italy in Pavia. He would grow up there, frequently crossing the Alps to visit the Frankish heartland, but growing up as his father intended as a native of the land he was destined to govern – a true hybrid, not a Frank, not a Lombard, not yet an Italian but pertaining to all three. He would prove to be a formidable ally of his father's – liable to explode into rage when thwarted, but strong and competent – like his brother Charles but, singularly and sadly, unlike their brother Louis, the one destined by fate to survive them all.

In that manner the Italian journey came to an end, a satisfying end; indeed, a flattering one with its seeming acceptance of the King of the Franks as the universal law-giver; a journey during which that king had dealt on equal terms with the Byzantine emperor, given orders that were swiftly and respectfully obeyed by the citizens of Rome and the Vicar of Christ on earth. But what Italy gave, Saxony took away, for it was after his return beyond the Alps that the universal law-giver, the polished equal of the Byzantine emperor and the Patrician of Rome committed the great and bizarre crime that thrust him back into the barbaric past, stamping him as one, after all, with Attila the Hun and Clovis the Merovingian, a barbarian who would drown the world in blood.

It was not, entirely, Charlemagne's fault. After the great assembly at Paderborn, when Saxons had come in their hundreds and then in their thousands to be dipped in pure water and so be born again as Christians, he could have reasonably concluded that the endless Saxon conflict had, in fact, reached its end. Saxon auxiliaries were now actually enrolled in the Frankish host as infantry, employed not only outside their own country but within it as police. For Charlemagne could now regard that once dangerous piece of country stretching from

Rhine to Elbe as a part of the Frankish *Reich*, a turbulent part perhaps but no more so than Aquitaine, perhaps, or Bavaria, whose insubordinate duke had still to be brought to book. He therefore felt perfectly justified in holding the May Field of 782 deep in the heart of this newly won land. So large was the assembly, and so lacking in urgency, that it was well into July before the ox-drawn carts creaked to a halt not far from the modern city of Hanover and the tents began to go up at the head of the river Lippe and the ancient machinery of the 'gathering of the host' commenced to turn over.

It was no longer simply the annual meeting of the tribe but a truly international affair, testimony at once to the problems of governing a great state and the fact that, as that state expanded, it was attracting attention – alarmed, interested, or hostile attention – from those touched by its new frontiers. Among the ambassadors were those from Sigifrid, King of the Danes, whose southern border now touched the northern border of the Frankish state – always assuming, of course, that Saxony was now indeed part of the Frankish state. Danes and Franks were, as yet, on parallel, not collision, courses. Later, Sigifrid would think it worthwhile to go to the immense expense of actually building a massive set of fortifications across that southern frontier of his, separating him from that remorselessly advancing state. And in the last years of his life Charlemagne was touched with a prescience about these handsome, vigorous, murderous new neighbours: 'I foresee what evil things they will do to my descendants and their subjects.' At the moment, however, all was in reasonable amity. The Danes, actually come to measure the stature of the new neighbour, entered a routine protest at the treatment he was meting out to their fellow pagans – for the Danes were even more determinedly anti-Christian than had been the Saxons. And Charles, for his part, complained energetically at the fact that the Danish king had given shelter to the trouble-maker Widukind.

The majority of those waiting audience in the royal pavilion were northerners – big men with fair or reddish hair and fair skins. There was a sprinkling of Italians and southern Gauls – slighter built, with olive skins and black hair, but still recognizably fellow Europeans. One group of strangers therefore stood out – much smaller in stature than either northern or southern European, with a tendency towards bandiness, swarthy complexions and a curious hairstyle (pigtails woven with bright colours) that attracted the astonished attention of the Frankish poets: Avars – distant relatives of the Huns but partially settled down now in a vast robbers' camp in what today is Hungary. Frank and Avar must have again exchanged measuring and speculative glances, aware that the expanding Frankish *Reich* must inevitably lead to a trial of strength. But again for the moment all was amity, with the Avars assuring the King of the Franks that they came 'on account of peace', whatever that might mean and Charles, ever fascinated by strange people and ideas, received them hospitably.

The assembly came to an end, the thousands of men began to disperse. Charles himself had crossed the Rhine on his way home when word came that a formidable band of Slavs had crossed the Elbe and were terrorizing the Saxons living near the river. The Saxons were perfectly capable of handling the intruders but the king was morally obliged to take action. More than his honour was at stake for not only did the whole ethos of the *comitatus* demand that he extend protection to those who had given allegiance – his very credibility as the governing centre of the state would be called into question if his new subjects were supposed to fight off aggressors on their own. There was no need for him personally to turn about and make the long, uncomfortable journey back into Saxony, but there was every reason to ensure that this, the first testing of his role as protecting King of the Saxons, should be efficiently handled. He therefore confided the task to three high-ranking officers of his court, men personally known to him who would defend the honour of the king – the Chamberlain Adalgis, the Constable Geilo and Worad, the Count of the Palace in person. By including this last man, Charles gave some indication as to how important he regarded what was, in essence, a police action.

The three men crossed the Rhine with their contingent of cavalry to find, as in one of those slightly nightmarish German folktales, that everything had changed since they had left the assembly. No more were the Slavic raiders heard from – it is by no means impossible that they had been bribed or otherwise attracted to act as a decoy. For what the three Frankish soldiers found was that the supposedly pacified land of Saxony was aflame with hatred, that the auxiliaries whom they had planned to use against the invaders had reverted to being the deadly enemy of the Frank and that Widukind, the elusive, indestructible Widukind, was back in the country, stirring up his fellow Saxons, calling on the peasants to oppose their own nobles if necessary – their own nobles who had made that humiliating agreement with the hated Frank and who deserved to go down into destruction with him. In distant Francia Charlemagne, too, heard of the return of Widukind and, correctly divining the scale of trouble, he sent off his cousin

Theoderic with reinforcements to join Adalgis, Geilo and Worad. They met near the Weser where Theoderic took command and gave certain orders.

The Frankish reaction had, up to this point, been both correct and effective and had the action that followed gone according to the plan which Theoderic outlined it would have ended in yet another Saxon defeat and, possibly, the elimination of Widukind's influence. The Saxons, infantrymen all, had established themselves on the upper slopes of the Süntel mountain. Theoderic, following that battle-plan which had served his cousin and master so well in countless engagements, planned to divide his force and catch the Saxons in a pincer movement. Adalgis, Geilo and Worad nodded agreement at the conference and, as soon as Theoderic had departed to commence the complex manoeuvring of his own wing, they moved to the attack. Their motive was, apparently, simple jealousy; resentment of the fact that a kinsman of the king should reap the military glory that they deemed belonged to them. It was the same kind of indiscipline that had resulted in the disaster at Roncesvalles, and it had the same kind of result here. Charlemagne knew how to use cavalry; quite evidently, they did not. They did not know, or they affected not to care, that massed and disciplined infantry would always check a cavalry charge, no matter how brave. The Saxons, too, had the decided advantage in having seized high ground. Nevertheless, the three leaders of the Frankish cavalry charged as though they were chasing fugitives; instead they were hurling themselves upon a bristling hedge of lances. The Franks died almost to a man. Of the three, only Worad survived and the spirit of the *comitatus* served to condemn all the followers of the other two.

The king came raging back across the Rhine.

The stupidity and selfishness of his three trusted counsellors must have been, for him, as difficult to accept as their defeat. After nearly thirty years' campaigning, thirty years of experimenting and training, thirty years of driving home the fact that war was simply a political instrument and not a means of glory, it must have been supremely disconcerting to discover how quickly even a sophisticated man could revert to the old ways. In addition to this bitter discovery was the discovery that the Saxons, far from being tamed, had also reverted to the old ways, but more skilfully than the Franks had done. Charlemagne had brought massive reinforcements which, with those already under the command of Theoderic, were more than sufficient to destroy the core of Saxon resistance. But there was no core of Saxon resistance.

Following their own, well-tried battle-technique, the Saxon soldiers melted away into the population; there was no anvil upon which the Frankish hammer could descend.

Posterity would dearly like to have some idea as to Charlemagne's state of mind at this point. One can only guess, from the causes that brought him here, to the appalling effect at Verden, that he must have been beside himself with rage and frustration. He summoned the Saxon nobles – those men who had taken no part in the rebellion – and demanded to know the name of the ringleader. The answer came as a chorus: Widukind. The nobles certainly had no affection for one of their number who had made such a spectacular class betrayal but neither was there any reason to keep his name a secret. Because Widukind was nowhere to be found. He, too, had skilfully reverted to the Saxon device of melting into the background and was now safe beyond the Danish border. Charlemagne may have toyed with the idea of launching an attack upon the King of Denmark, but dismissed it; even the capture of Widukind was not worth stirring up that particular hornets' nest. But the idea that the Saxons – those endlessly 'perfidious Saxons' – should escape unpunished was intolerable. And bad politics. News of that disastrous battle on the Süntel had sped throughout Europe. Even in distant England the compiler of the Anglo-Saxon Chronicle had raised his myopic eyes from what was happening in England and, departing from custom, actually recorded what had happened on the Continent. 'The Old Saxons and the Franks fought,' the writer noted in his monastery and perhaps briefly felt a twinge of racial pride that his distant kinsmen were still giving trouble, before going on with his terse record of what was happening around him.

No, Süntel could not go unpunished and so the king moved on to his crime. He ordered the Saxon nobles to identify, individually, every man who had fought under Widukind. The nobles did so, 4500 men were brought to the king, and he cut off all their heads at a place called Verden.

The twentieth century has put a certain gloss on violence. The century which has seen the incineration of hundreds of thousands of innocent and helpless people at Hiroshima and Dresden, which has seen the slaughter of millions of the defenceless in Kampuchea and Treblinka and Auschwitz, will view the violent death of 4500 savage young men with a certain detachment. But Charlemagne's contemporaries, and his commentators for many centuries after, were deeply shocked. Posterity began to put its own gloss on the action. As the

Carolingian empire receded down the perspective of time and its great founder became larger than life, first as an epic hero and then as a duly canonized saint, so it became ever more difficult to equate this titanic, shining figure with such an action. In time, it even became fashionable to say that no massacre ever happened, that the whole thing was a myth brought into being by a simple, single act of illiterate orthography and that the scribes who recorded what happened to the 4500 had written, or intended to write, *delocare* (to relocate or remove) and not *decollare* (to behead). Charlemagne, in fact, followed a highly organized policy of transporting troublesome subjects from one part of the state to another. Sometimes it might be a handful of carefully chosen young men – hostages in fact; sometimes there were wholesale forcible evacuations. In the long run such transportation proved beneficial to the state, in enforcing a mixing of population, and not infrequently beneficial to the individual, particularly if he were a bright young lad, taken out of some forest village and brought up under the eye of the king.

But the reaction of contemporaries makes it plain that the unknown scribe had been traduced by posterity, that he had indeed correctly written *decollare* and not *delocare*. Einhard kept silent about the matter, but the Englishman Alcuin, the greatest intellectual influence on the king, returned again and again to the theme that violence produced only violence, that the Saxons who were, after all, Alcuin's own distant kinsmen, would never yield to force. It is at about this time that the otherwise smooth flow of the king's career meets checks, not abroad but at home in the very heart of his family. It is at about this time that the first of the conspiracies against him began to be hatched, the epitaph and gravestone of those 4500 dead. The sheer mass of dead flesh itself appalled. Even among the pugnacious Franks, brought up to warfare as an ordinary, acceptable part of everyday life, the dead of the most prolonged and bitter of battles rarely rose above the hundreds – a few years later, the last violent attempt of the Byzantine army to reconquer Italy produced only 3000 dead Greeks. At Verden lay 4500 headless corpses, 4500 severed heads, the grass made noisome, if enriched, by the blood pumped out of 4500 trunks.

Yet, even now, the King of the Franks had not finished with these Saxons. Outwardly unperturbed ('the king went into winter camp at Thionville after having thus taken vengeance and there celebrated Christmas as usual'), ignoring the advice of his counsellors, Charles began drawing up the most savage of all his capitularies, savage not only in itself but because, employing Christianity as it did as a weapon of control, it foreshadowed the axes and ropes and fires of the Inquisition.

Included in the army of tradesmen which followed the host on campaign was a large number of skilled masons. Their work, for the most part, was concerned with the erection of fortifications, Charles continuing to follow his Roman model by establishing permanent camps in conquered areas. But the masons had an additional task, too, to which they turned after having ensured the military safety of the garrison and that task was the building of a church or chapel nearby.

Looking back on the ferocious wars of religion which have wracked Europe again and again, it is difficult for the late twentieth century to appreciate the medieval belief in the civilizing powers of Christianity. Yet that belief continued almost down into living memory, the nineteenth-century European missionaries in Africa and the Pacific islands obeying the same impulses as the eighth-century Carolingian missionaries in Saxony. In both cases the ultimate motivation was a genuine desire to save souls, a genuine belief that the gospel of Christianity would bring peace and light into savage, darkened places. But behind the missionaries were administrators – again, men with perfectly sincere Christian beliefs but who cannily saw Christianity, whose rigid moral code was upheld by threat of hideous, never-ending punishment, as a very useful tool with which to mould a savage and wayward people into a form acceptable to the conqueror.

Until the massacre of Verden, Charles had been content to follow the accepted pattern of conversion. The would-be Christians, either individually or in the mass, would repeat a formula after a priest, a formula which not simply renounced the devil and all his works but specifically and clearly rejected the devil's personal assistants, those supernatural entities whom they had earlier believed to be gods, Woden, Saxnot, Thunar and the rest. The candidate or candidates would then affirm belief in the Trinity and would then be baptized by total immersion, high-ranking candidates given the indulgence of a personal tub, mass baptisms for the mob being effected through any convenient river or stream of pure water. Thereafter, the new Christian would follow the path to salvation as best he could, obeying the dictates of his conscience under the guidance of his priest. In his terrible *Capitulatio de partibus Saxoniae*, Charlemagne turned the voluntary into the compulsory with one, simple, clear-cut punishment for all offences, moral, civil or religious: death.

Death was the penalty for eating meat in Lent or killing a priest. Death was the penalty for any Saxon who tried to escape baptism by hiding. Death was the penalty for any who believed in witchcraft or practised it (and it was specified that execution should be by the horror of burning – probably the earliest such action against witchcraft in Europe). Death was the penalty for any Christian who conspired with pagans, or who entered a church with intent to rob it or who offered sacrifice to demons (i.e., the old tribal gods). So the hideous catalogue went on, its terrorizing intent all the more evident in that, within the Frankish law code itself, death was a most rare penalty, treason alone being certain to attract it.

The *Capitulatio* was not all negative, the king seeking to strengthen the power of the clergy itself by decreeing that the local priest could give absolution, and hence bring about the remission of the death penalty if the 'criminal' genuinely made confession and penance. The local church, too, was turned into a sanctuary increasing its attraction to otherwise reluctant new Christians. And, finally, the *Capitulatio* included provision for a tax which not only placed an incomprehensible burden on farmers who were still pagans at heart, but would enrage Christian farmers throughout Europe for the next thousand years and more: 'We enact that according to the command of God, all men, whether nobles, freeborn men or serfs shall give the tenth part of their substance and labour to the churches and priests, so that as God shall have given to every Christian he shall restore a part to God.' The high-sounding decree lost some of its majesty when put into practice, when a hungry peasant saw one pig in ten, one bushel of wheat in ten, one chicken in ten – and that the best one in each case – taken away to be consumed by the local clergy. Over the next millennium the pattern of Christianity would change as profoundly as the pattern of Europe itself, but the law of tithes would march on, unchanged in a changing world, the most constant single source of friction between clergy and laity. Alcuin, the king's great counsellor and intimate friend, spoke for all reformers down the centuries when he shook his head over this enactment and said truly: 'If the light yoke of Christ were to be preached to the stubborn Saxons as insistently as the duty to render tithes, perhaps they would not reject the sacrament of baptism.' But in this matter, at least, the civilized Anglo-Saxon was ignored by his Frankish king.

8 The Sowing of
the Seed

The mixed group of north-western Europeans, known to history as Anglo-Saxons, who settled in England from the fifth century onwards, developed a remarkably precocious civilization. So precocious were they, indeed, that even before Alcuin's day moralists among the clergy were sharpening up their invective, giving incidentally a picture of Anglo-Saxon society markedly different from that of a simple, essentially rural society which has been transmitted to posterity. The writer, a monk, was as usual inveighing women's dress (always a good index to a society's wealth):

> A woman of rank wears an undervest of fine linen of a violet colour and over it a scarlet tunic with full skirt and sleeves and hood, both striped or faced with silk. Her hair is curled with irons, ornaments of gold in the form of crescents encircle her neck: bracelets are on her arms and rings with precious stones on her fingers, the nails of which are pared to a point to resemble the talons of a falcon. Her shoes are of red leather and stibium is used to paint her face.

The men were scarcely less gorgeously dressed, and addicted to drunkenness, the characteristic Saxon vice.

But behind all was the threat of a paganism which was so very slowly in retreat and which, unless the vigilant servants of God stood guard, would overwhelm their frail charges.

> You tattoo your bodies like the pagans who obey the notions of the Devil: you wear your clothes in the same way as the heathen whom your fathers conquered by the help of God. Truly wonderful is it that you should imitate the very men whose manner of life you have ever detested. Following a shameful custom you mutilate your horses, slitting their nostrils, fastening

their ears together. We hear, too, that in your disputes you cast lots in pagan fashion . . . many of you eat horseflesh, a thing which no Christian among the Orientals do.

So the diatribe runs on, over-coloured perhaps, but probably giving a not inaccurate picture of a vigorous people barely a generation or so removed from those ferocious heathens on the other side of the North Sea. In this seemingly pagan landscape, the godly city of York stood out like a Christian beacon. Founded upon the ancient Roman capital of Eboracum, it became a centre of learning that, in due course, influenced its Continental neighbours, as though it were reflecting back something of the Latin virtues which had led to its founding. There was here a kind of Apostolic succession of learning. Egbert, Archbishop of York, had been the favourite pupil of the now almost legendary Venerable Bede, the humble monk of Jarrow whose great *History of the English Church* laid the foundations of the history of what, in time, would be the English nation. And it was in York, at the Cathedral School, that Alcuin spent his childhood.

He was born, of noble Northumbrian parents, some time about the year 735. An anecdote about his boyhood gives some indication of his surroundings. He was sharing a cell in the school with an old monk who habitually slept on heavily after the call to rise to vigils. On one occasion Alcuin himself was awakened when the cell was filled with an unearthly light and he saw a number of evil spirits surrounding the old monk's bed, beating him and taunting him: 'Thou sleepest soundly brother. When all the brethren are keeping their vigil in church why art thou alone snoring here?' Alcuin desperately prayed for deliverance, vowing that he would never again neglect the vigils but the spirits, having done with tormenting the monk, turned their attention to the boy. 'Who is this other sleeping in the cell? We will not chastise him with stripes because he is still raw [presumably, still a novice] but we will punish him on the hard soles of his feet and make him remember the vow he has just made.' They pulled the bedclothes off him, but he made the sign of the Cross and they disappeared. Unless the boy really did have some kind of hallucination, or most vivid nightmare, it is decidedly ironic that such a story should be told of a man for whom reason was the highest of the faculties, who despised superstition and spent his life combating it. But it illustrates how his formative years were not so much shaped as imbued by the Church. Yet side by side with indwelling Christianity was a deep and passionate love for the old pagan literature and learning. He himself was never a great or even an original scholar. A later commentator said of him, with a touch of unkindness: 'The best that can be said is that he gave to western Europe imperfectly understood fragments of the wisdom of the ancients.' But above all else, he was a teacher, with a teacher's instinctive understanding of the needs and limitations of the pupil. In his own vivid metaphor, he likened his task of teacher to that of a man striking a flint to release the spark that is within it – an attitude to education light years from the dreary cramming by rote that had passed, and would again for centuries pass, for education.

He was also a very practical man. When the great cathedral was burned down in April 741, he was one of those placed in charge of rebuilding its successor, and left, in poetic form, one of the very rare contemporary descriptions of a Saxon cathedral. And he combined both sides of his character, the practical man of action and the contemplative, when he immersed himself more and more in the building up of the cathedral library. It already had a considerable reputation but under Alcuin's enthusiastic direction its fame became international and continental scholars made special journeys to study and to copy. Learning was very much a matter of finding, of tracking down those priceless volumes which held within them the distilled culture of Greece and Rome. Alcuin threw himself into the task with delight. He had what the good hunter must always have, a 'nose' for his quarry, the ability to follow a casual lead which would take him – days or even weeks later – to some remote monastery to find one more manuscript. In his quest, he criss-crossed Europe and, in so doing, got to know the scholars and clergy of the Frankish court, certainly coming into contact with Charlemagne. One of his poems, in which he lovingly mentions the learned friends he had made, is virtually a check-list of Frankish scholarship: Albrich, Bishop of Utrecht, Riculf, Bishop of Cologne, Lul, Archbishop of Mainz, Abbot Samuel of Epternach, Peter of Pisa, Paulinus of Aquileia, all of whom were members of the royal court.

In seeking to illustrate the almost magical view of learning held by his contemporaries and, in particular, Charlemagne's role in promoting it, the Monk of St Gall relates an anecdote which reads like a folktale.

Now it happened, when he [the king] had begun to reign alone in the western parts of the world and the pursuit of learning had almost been forgotten throughout all his realm, two Scots came from Ireland to the coast of Gaul with certain traders from Britain. These Scotchmen were unrivalled for their skill in sacred and secular learning: and day by day, when the crowd gathered round them for trade, they exhibited no wares for sale but cried out and said, 'Ho, everyone that desires wisdom, let him draw near and take it from our hands; for it is wisdom that we have for sale' . . . So long did they make their proclamation that in the end those who wondered at these men, or perhaps thought them insane, brought the matter to the ears of King Charles who always loved and sought after wisdom. Wherefore he ordered them to come with all speed into his presence and asked them whether it were true, as fame reported of them, that they brought wisdom with them (and) asked what price they asked for it. They answered, 'We ask no price, O King; but we ask only for a fit place for teaching and quick minds to teach; and besides food to eat and raiment to put on, for without these we cannot accomplish our pilgrimage.' This answer filled the king with a great joy.

The Monk of St Gall was, as usual, relying as much upon his vivid imagination as on historic fact but, in his naïve way he did – again, as usual – encapsulate a truth: the king did indeed regard 'wisdom' as a vital commodity and went to great lengths to attract those to his court who could provide it. He had obviously already marked down Alcuin as a potential prize but it was not until 781, during his Italian campaign, that he took definite steps to entice the Englishman to Francia. Alcuin himself was on a visit to Italy, having been commissioned by the new archbishop of York to go to Italy to receive the episcopal pallium from the hands of the pope, as was customary. Journeying back north, Alcuin called in at Parma and met the king and it was during this visit that Charles urged the Englishman to join his court as Master of the Palace School. Alcuin hesitated for a long time. He was forty-six years old – not an age at which to make light decisions about the future. He was deeply, personally, attached to York and his friends and colleagues there. Years later he was to write from his voluntary exile: 'Keep me in mind, dearest of fathers and brothers, for I shall be yours in death as in life. And it may be that God in his concession will grant that you, who nurtured my childhood, will also bury my old age.'

But there were also very strong reasons for accepting the invitation. The Golden Age was passing in England, the country entering upon the convulsions attendant upon the birth of a new society. A few years after Alcuin left, the ferocious Viking sack of the holy island of Lindisfarne proclaimed that the Saxon kings could no longer defend their own. 'Fierce foreboding omens came over the land of Northumbria and terrified the people. There were great whirlwinds, lightning storms and fiery dragons were seen flying in the sky. These signs were followed by great famine and shortly after the ravaging of heathen men destroyed

God's church on Lindisfarne through brutal robbery and slaughter'; so said the Anglo-Saxon chronicler.

The Frankish state, by contrast, appeared firm and stable under a single powerful ruler, a fact that must have been of very considerable attraction to so unwarlike a character as Alcuin of York. But, to be fair, there was an even greater attraction, the fact that this great state was not only wealthy enough but, under its ruler, most eager to act as a patron of scholarship. There was the attraction of moulding young minds which, in their maturity, would be deciding the destiny of Europe – the perennial attraction that the idea of the 'philosopher-king' holds for the great educationalists. And Alcuin, though a teacher from first to last, as with all teachers had the need and the desire to replenish his intellectual forces among his peers. He would, too, have been almost inhumanly modest if he had not been excited by the idea of guiding the guider, of acting as mentor to the most powerful man in the western world. The Monk of St Gall was not far out when he wrote, 'Charles received Albinus kindly and kept him at his side to the end of his life, except when he marched with his armies to his vast wars: nay Charles would even call himself Albinus's disciple: and Albinus he would call his master.' Einhard, who in due course became one of Alcuin's pupils in the Palace School, tersely agreed with the loquacious monk. 'For his lessons in grammar he [Charles] listened to the instruction of Deacon Peter of Pisa, an old man: but for all other subjects Albinus, called Alcuin, was his teacher – a man from Britain, of the Saxon race and the most learned man of his time.'

The Palace School was not an invention of Charlemagne's. The early Merovings, their bloodthirsty habits notwithstanding, were genuine patrons of culture and had established such a school in their palace. This had virtually flickered into extinction with all else during the rule of the *rois fainéants*, but Charles's father, Pippin, had caused it to be revived to a certain extent. His reasons were purely pragmatic: he needed people who could read and write and was farseeing enough to realize that a seed had to be sown before a crop could be reaped. Charles took this simple, practical approach and extended and deepened it. It is tempting to regard the Carolingian Palace School as a species of formal academy, a nascent university centuries ahead of its time. But like so much that this king founded, it existed in outline rather than depth, in intention, rather than execution. A worthy successor might have filled in that outline and brought about the execution but there was no such successor and what could have altered the whole pattern of European civilization joined the other great might-have-beens of history. But the outline is clear-cut, and that outline was very largely the work of Alcuin.

It is extraordinarily difficult for posterity to assess the stature of a teacher for, unlike an artist or scholar or writer, he leaves no tangible evidence of his skill. If one were to judge Alcuin by his formal written work alone, it would be to dismiss him as the most arid of pedants. Some modern scholars have seen in his treatise *On Rhetoric* a kind of *vade mecum* in the practice of kingship intended for Charlemagne – in effect a foreshadowing, if a virtuous foreshadowing, of Machiavelli's *Prince*. Such an intention can be quarried out of it, but only a dedicated medievalist could get much pleasure or profit from the process. The theological treatises he wrote, usually at the king's request, during the course of the endless religious controversies of the day were highly relevant and probably explosively exciting when they hit their mark as they invariably did. His attack on the heresy of Adoptionism (the theory that Christ was not God's natural son but had been adopted by him) was a major factor in eliminating that particular bizarre version of Christianity. But, as with all his formal writings, the reader tends to admire the skill with which the argument is presented rather than be warmed by it.

As it happens, a fragment of dialogue has survived which not only gives insight into his teaching methods, but also a most rare insight into the operation of the medieval mind – or, at least, the medieval mind that had gone through the Anglo-Saxon school. The speakers are Alcuin himself, and one of the young princes, Pippin (it is not clear if this is the illegitimate little hunchback or the half-brother who later took his name). Pippin is asking the questions, Alcuin giving the answers.

P: What is a letter?
A: The guardian of history.
P: What is a word?
A: The mind's betrayer.
P: What creates the word?
A The tongue.
P: What is the tongue?
A: Something which whips the air.
P: What is the air?
A: The protection of life.
P: What is life?
A: The joy of the blessed, the sorrow of sinners, the expectation of death.
P: What is death?

A: An unavoidable occurrence, an uncertain journey, the tears of the living, the confirmation of the testament, the thief of man.

P: What is man?

A: The slave of death, a passing wayfarer, the guest of a place.

P: To what is man [*homo*] like?

A: A fruit [*pomo*].

P: How is man situated?

A: Like a lamp in the wind.

P: Where is he situated?

A: Within six walls.

P: Which?

A: Above, below, before, behind, right and left.

P: In how many ways does he vary?

A: In hunger and satiety, repose and labour, in wakeful hours and sleep.

P: What is sleep?

A: The image of death

What is immediately evident from this dialogue is the lack of classification, the leaping from idea to idea (one is irresistibly reminded of the psychiatrist's test of association of ideas). Later, Alcuin became aware of this to some degree when, in establishing cathedral and monastic schools, he experimented with specialization. But, in general, the dialogue shows that medieval view of the universe as being made up of an infinite number of separate items, rather than that concept of a basic unity which had underlined classic thinking. Evident, too, is that love of riddles – a very Anglo-Saxon trait. Later in the dialogue Alcuin changes places with Pippin and does the questioning: 'I lately saw a man standing, a dead man walking, even one who never was. What was it?' Answer: 'A reflection in water.' (The king himself became particularly fond of these exercises, he and Alcuin seeking to cap each other with messengers scurrying between them bearing what seems to the modern reader to be somewhat puerile examples of the genre but which apparently gave them considerable pleasure.) The juggling with names which bore an accidental similarity with each other (as in *homo* [man] and *pomo* [fruit] and hence the idea that man falls like an overripe fruit) was later to be developed into the elaborate fantasies of the bestiaries. Thus the hedgehog was typecast as the devil because, at the time of the grape harvest, the animal shakes the vine and impales the fallen grapes upon its spine just as the devil impales the souls of men at death. The fornicator is urged to consider the fate of the antelope. This shy and reasonably chaste beast does not seem to be the most obvious symbol for this kind of sin, but it uses its needle-sharp horns to scythe down trees and the hunter captures it when it entangles itself in a bush. In this it is like man to whom God has given two horns, the Old and New Testament, with which to scythe down the trees of sin. Women, however, form a snare in which he can entangle himself and the Infernal Hunter then captures him. By the time the bestiary was fully developed, in the early Middle Ages, reality had so completely parted from it that the panther could be typecast as Christ; the panther's breath is so sweet that it attracts all animals in the forest and in this is like Christ whose sweetness attracts all men. The religious interpretation buttressed the imaginary characteristics until the existence of the sweet breath of the panther is proved by the fact that it resembles Christ. The evidence of the few men who might have had the leisure to smell the breath of an actual panther would have done little to weaken such a chain of logic.

Alcuin's poetry and letters, in contrast to his formal writing, is clear, infused with humour and filled with human touches. His little poem addressed to idle boys, far more than his overtly didactic material, shows just why he was revered as a teacher, for he was able to make learning fresh and exciting.

> You lads, whose age is fitted for reading, learn. The years go by like running water. Don't waste the learning days in idleness. The flowing wave, the hastening hour return not. Let early youth thrive in the pursuit of virtues that the mature man may shine with the full lustre of praise. Let each read a book and use the happy years. Learn, my boy, that ready speech may plead thy causes that thou mayest defend, protect and succor thy people. Learn, I pray, my boy graceful movement and habits, that thy name may be praised throughout the globe.

One major preoccupation of Alcuin's, and one which posterity is fortunate in that he was able to impress his master with its importance, would seem to posterity the ultimate in pedantry. He was obsessed with spelling and orthography and, to underline its importance, made the light-hearted remark that the letter *h* carelessly prefixed to the word *ara* turned it from 'altar' to 'pigsty' (*hara*). Latin was not simply the universal, but the only language of communication among scholars: if it became corrupted all else must, of necessity, become corrupted and again and again he hammers home that *b*, *v*, and *f* must not be mistaken, that a carelessly written *b* will turn *beneficus* (benefactor) into *veneficus* (poisoner). That such transformations were not fanciful is shown in the work of the French chronicler, Gossuin, who created an entire tribe of people who drank nothing but sea-water because he had mistaken *ex mari viventes* (living by the sea) for *ex mari biventes* (drinking sea-water).

It is difficult for posterity fully to appreciate the extent and significance of Alcuin's work in this unglamorous field. It is not simply that we have immediate and easy access to a range of printed works that would have seemed, to Alcuin, all but infinite, but those clearly printed works are constructed with a flexible, universal system of punctuation and spelling – the whole vital underpinning of written language which is noticed only when it is absent, as when a comma is missing or misplaced. Alcuin had to deduce the need for such a system, work it out and then struggle to see it universally applied 'in daily fights with rusticity', in his own phrase. An awareness of the importance of orthography led, logically, to the recognition of a need for a good clear script and in that manner would have been born the famous 'Carolingian minuscule'. The actual designer seems to have been a scribe, Adalbert by name, but its Anglo-Saxon characteristics, together with Alcuin's known crusade for the clarity of interpretation, argues his close involvement in its development. It is not often that one can obtain so clear a picture of a culture in the process of development as one can by comparing the spiky, ugly, confused Merovingian script with the Carolingian. Seven centuries later the Carolingian minuscule would be rediscovered by the Italian humanist scholar, Poggio Bracciolini, and, launched under his name, in due course became the model chosen by the first Italian printers for their founts, and, hence, the progenitor of all modern print.

From a preoccupation with the structure of language, progression into the dangerous field of scriptural exegesis was inevitable. And dangerous because, in the theocentric world of the eighth century, all human experience was deemed to be connected with Revelation and that, in turn, meant that the information transmitted about that unique Revelation through the Gospels and through the writings of the Church Fathers must be 'correct' – uncorrupted. And here the scholar had the wholehearted and formidable backing of the monarch. Charles once settled a dispute among Frankish scholars regarding the relative pre-eminence of Frankish and Latin sources by asking, rhetorically, which was the purer, the brook or the spring. Again and again requests were sent to Rome asking for this or that authentic text of the sacred writings: when received the precious original was carefully housed in the king's own collection, all copies made from it being duly certified as made from the authentic source. If Rome could not supply such a text, or that which was supplied fell under suspicion, then Alcuin went back further and further in quest of that pure spring not simply with the king's encouragement, but at his insistence. Inescapably, the trail led back to the source of all sources, the Bible itself, and in due course Alcuin, working with a group of scholars, produced an acceptable Vulgate. It disappeared along with so much else in the wrack of empire following Charles's death but it left behind a memory that the Word of God, though divinely inspired, depended for its transmission on the work of fallible man.

It is almost exclusively through the illustrations in the sacred writings that posterity gains a rare, authentic and pricelessly direct vision into the Carolingian life-style. Like the Carolingian minuscule, it is necessary only to compare these elegant, sophisticated paintings with that which came both before and after to appreciate the degree of Carolingian culture. The art springs up from a void, flourishes brilliantly, achieving its apogee some years after Charlemagne's death and then gutters out. The first of the illuminated Carolingian manuscripts was produced, by an otherwise unknown scribe called Gundohinus, to mark the epochal visit of Pope Stephen to King Pippin, that visit which began the long train of events that would lead to an imperial crown. The figures in the manuscript are still crude, but vigorous with a curious underlying grace. Significantly, they follow Lombard models: the figure of Christ wears his hair plastered down on each side of his head in the distinctive style described by the Lombard historian Paul the Deacon and the Lombards, in their turn, are evidently deeply influenced by the still vigorous Byzantine culture flourishing on the eastern seaboard of Italy. The work of the scribe Gundohinus is an almost textbook example of the way in which cultural influences move from people to people: from Constantinople to Ravenna, from Ravenna to Pavia thence across the Alps to the rising new kingdom of the Franks.

The next oldest manuscript also marks an important event in Frankish history: Charlemagne's journey to Rome in 781. But though only thirty years separate the two works, their difference is almost that of two civilizations. The book is a Gospel, and the artist was a personal friend of Charlemagne's, a Frank by the name of Godescalc who dedicated his work to the king in the warmest terms. The Byzantine tradition is still strongly evident in his work but the fugitive element of grace in Gundohinus's figures has developed into flowing elegance, the sturdy, rather squat bodies becoming elongated while the expressions on the faces of the evangelists are lively, expressive, each with its own identity so that one wonders if here, perhaps, are portraits of some of the courtiers. A few years later there is a second jump and this will prove the final, the moment when a completely distinct 'Carolingian art' comes into being. It takes place about the year 795 – probably about the time that Charles moved into his newly completed palace at Aachen. Gone now are the rather fierce Lombard expressions of Gundohinus; gone the plump faces, with their last hint of Byzantium, which appeared in Godescalc's work. The inspiration from here onwards would be classical Rome, reflecting the fact that in the year 800 Charles, King of the Franks, became Charles, Roman Emperor. But in addition, too, there is an inventiveness, an almost virtuoso display of imagination which, while still remaining safely within religious orthodoxy, edges into the realms of fantasy. Outstanding is the Gospel Book made for Charlemagne's personal use, which passed to his son Louis and was given by him to the Abbey of St Médard at Soissons in 827. The artist has thrown down images pell-mell to build his pictures, some drawn from reality – as, for instance, an antique column which still exists in St Peter's in Rome – but combining them in fanciful scenes as in the remarkable composition, the Fountain of Life. This is technically easily faulted as the living creatures created by the fountain are not placed in perspective, but look like wallpaper ornaments. But the whole does convey a feeling of mysterious fecundity, an image drawn from some parallel universe. In illustrating the Adoration of the Lamb the artist has simply gone back to classical Rome and created a stage setting, complete with proscenium and curtain. In addition to the recognizable figures from natural history is the now confident delineation of the human face and form, gradually becoming recognizable portraits, as in the portraits of Charlemagne's grandsons Lothair and Charles the Bald. One can only regret that the convention of introducing identified figures into the Gospels had not commenced at an earlier date to include at least one portrait of Charlemagne himself.

The illuminations make quite clear what is implicit in the literary work of scholars: the Carolingian renaissance, unlike its more famous successor, sprang from one source – the royal court. It is not simply that the style falls within a pattern which, in turn, can be traced to a single source, but it is possible to follow individual artists as their style develops. Much of the work was done under Alcuin's eyes at Tours, and was so firmly rooted that the distinctive style would continue long after his own death and that of his master's. At Tours, for instance, it is possible to follow the development of one particular artist from his first, hesitant beginnings, his confident maturity to his sudden disappearance, probably death as an old man, in 869. Even more dramatic is the evidence presented by the so-called Metz Sacramentum for the portrait of Charles the Bald. Begun with great detail, it is left unfinished with Charles's deposition in 842: one can almost see the artist shrugging his shoulders and walking away.

One area of learning which must have astonished the king's more conventional scholars, and examples of which posterity would dearly like to possess, is the collection he made of vernacular stories and poems of the day. Nothing, perhaps, more vividly illustrates the originality of the man's mind, its depth and scope, than that he should anticipate folklorists by nearly a thousand years and seek to preserve the despised jingles and tales of swineherds and footsoldiers and peasant women rocking their babies. Their evaluation by the more conventionally minded is shown by the fact that no one bothered to preserve them after his death, to the very great loss of European literature.

Some time in the 780s a letter, drawn up by Alcuin and the king in concert, went out to all the prelates in the State. It drew the attention of all bishops and abbots to the deplorable standard of learning, as expressed by writing, of the clergy as a whole. Some of the letters received at court from the provincial clergy were all but illiterate, 'the unlettered tongue failing through ignorance to interpret aright the pious devotions of the heart'. It followed logically, the letter went on,

> that if their skill in writing is so small, so also their power of rightly comprehending the Holy Scriptures may be far less than is benefiting. We exhort you therefore not only not to neglect the study of letters but to apply yourself thereto with that humble perseverance which is well pleasing to God . . . Let the men chosen for this task be such as are both themselves able and willing to learn and eager withal to impart their learning to others. And let the zeal with which the work is done equal the earnestness with which we now ordain it. Fail not, as you would enjoy our favour.

And with that hint of steel within the velvet, Charlemagne and his counsellor Alcuin launched what has been called a 'charter of universal education'. Over-enthusiastic commentators have taken it even further, one French historian declaring that, at the moment of the letter's publication, the Frankish state was instantaneously turned into 'one vast Athens'. But though they exaggerated, for, as with so many of the royal projects, it was an outline and an intention rather than a con-

Left: The 'Karlsgrab': last surviving trace of the ambitious canal planned, and partially executed, as a means of transporting troops to the East

Below: The Iron Crown of Lombardy whose acquisition marked the first, major expansion of the Carolingian empire. According to legend it contained nails from the True Cross

Presumed portraits of Charlemagne: (*top left*) the king with one of his sons and a scribe obsequiously (but industriously) recording what seems to be their altercation; (*left*) the admonishing giant: the woman has been tentatively identified as one of the king's wives; (*above*) the balance of power: St Peter confers spiritual authority on the pope, temporal authority on the king (mosaic placed by Pope Leo III in the Lateran)

The horse is from a much later period but the figure of the rider is the only surviving piece of Carolingian sculpture in the round. It is certainly that of a Carolingian monarch and may possibly be that of Charlemagne's grandson, Charles the Bald, but is usually identified as being that of Charlemagne himself; (right) early 16th-century representation of Charlemagne in imperial guise, made for the Emperor Maximilian's tomb in Innsbruck

kayser karl der
groß

The palace of Aachen: (*left*) model of the palace and chapel. The proportions remain much the same today, with the Rathaus now occupying the site of the great hall, shown at the bottom; (*below*) general view of the chapel showing how later buildings have been added to, but not altered, the original mystical octagon at the heart of the complex; (*right*) west (main) entrance to the chapel, seen from the atrium and showing bronze doors

Left: Close-up of the bronze doors at the main entrance to the chapel at Aachen, contemporary with the original building, showing lions' heads

Below: Detail of the contemporary bronze railings of the gallery in the chapel

Above: The seat of majesty: Charlemagne's simple throne in the gallery of the chapel. After his canonisation, pilgrims would creep through the short passage under the throne

Right: Detail of the candelabra presented to the chapel by the emperor Frederick I (Barbarossa) on the occasion of Charlemagne's canonisation

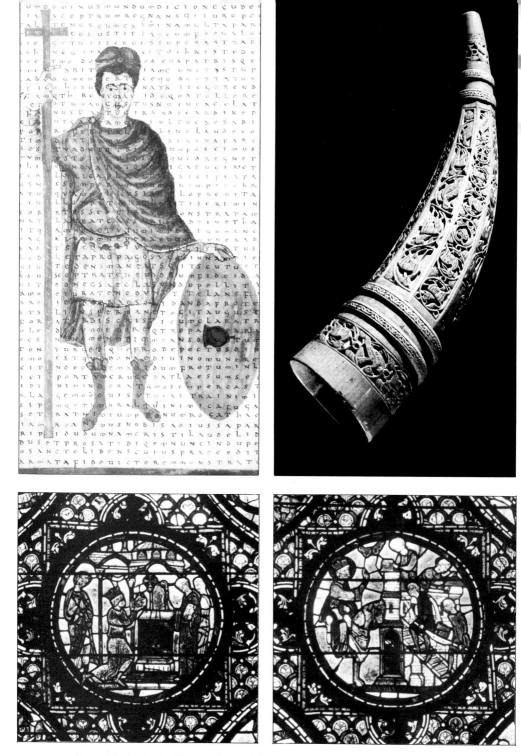

Above left: Louis the Pious, sole surviving son and eventual heir of Charlemagne

The growth of the Legend: Charlemagne presenting relics to Aachen chapel and giving orders to soldiers who are building a church (both details are from windows in Chartres cathedral); the supposed 'Horn of Roland' (Auch) from Toulouse (*above right*)

tinuing execution, nevertheless it did lay the foundation for a system which, had it survived and been developed after Charles's death, would have incalculably altered the history of Europe.

That first circular letter was backed up by a series of tough capitularies, steadily expanding the concept until it did indeed resemble a system of universal education. The first capitularies limited their intention to the clergy. *Missi* were to visit the provincial clergy to check that they were not only able to recite the offices, but understood the meaning of ecclesiastical formularies, an obligation which throws a bizarre light on the casual manner in which some of the more ignorant clergy used Latin in such vital ceremonies as baptism. Later capitularies extended the range of matters of which 'every ecclesiastic' should have some knowledge and finally insisted that every man should send his son to school where he would have to remain until he had received a fitting education. The extent to which the capitularies were adopted depended to a considerable degree on the enthusiasm of the local bishop but most appear to have acted energetically on the king's commands. Thus Charlemagne's personal friend Theodulf, the poetic bishop of Orleans, ordained that in every village, and on every estate, priests should organize schools which every Christian father could send his son without fee. Leidrad, Bishop of Lyons, reported that he had successfully established schools in his diocese. The very least that was expected of the children was the ability to read and write while, as far as the clergy was concerned, it was made very clear that ecclesiastical promotion depended upon scholastic ability, Alcuin with the consent of the king harnessing self-interest to the cause of learning. It is interesting to compare this attitude towards learning in the so-called Dark Ages with that prevailing among Italian clergy in the sixteenth century when the majority of parish clergy remained quite ignorant of the supposedly prevailing 'Renaissance' spirit.

The type of education differed according to whether the school was attached to a cathedral or a monastery. Education in the cathedral schools was essentially practical, training young choristers, readers and copyists. The practical skills of copyists and readers were certainly not neglected in the monasteries, but the emphasis was on higher learning, theology in particular. Alcuin set great store by that system of specialization which he had introduced into the cathedral schools, warmly recommending its adoption in a letter to his old colleagues in York. In time, specialization spread to the schools themselves. The cathedral school of Metz and the abbey school of St Wandrille became famous throughout Europe for their music. Orleans under Bishop Theodulf produced exquisitely written and illuminated manuscripts; in Bavaria, Bishop Arno founded the Salzburg library, launched the invaluable Salzburg chronicle, and repaid the state's debt to Alcuin by collecting and preserving his letters. Some of the monastic and cathedral libraries rivalled that of the king's: Reichenau possessed over 400 volumes, St Riquier some 250. Arno, that dedicated bibliophile, arranged for the copying of 150 volumes, classical as well as religious.

In all of this the king took a warm and personal interest. The Monk of St Gall gives a lively picture of the king presiding over a kind of informal examination when the boys recited to him letters and verse of their own composition. According to the Monk, there was a decided difference between the attitude to learning of lower-class children and the sons of the nobility: 'Now the boys of middle or low birth presented him with writings garnished with the sweet savours of wisdom beyond all that he could have hoped, while those of the children of noble parents were silly and tasteless.' The king complimented the lower-class boys, promising them promotion and favours, then turned to give the idle lads of the nobility the rough edge of his tongue. 'You nobles, you sons of my chiefs, you superfine dandies, you have trusted to your birth and your possessions and have set at naught my orders to your own advancement: you have neglected the pursuit of learning and you have given yourself over to luxury and sport, to idleness and profitless past-times.' He then cursed them with some vigour, ending by warning them that they had no hope of advancement 'unless you make up for your former sloth by vigorous study'.

Despite his love of England and of York, Alcuin was never to return permanently to his native land. He did, however, make visits on behalf of the king, the oddest of all being his mission to Offa, King of Mercia. There had been marriage proposals between the two courts in which Charles's eldest son, also called Charles, was to marry Offa's daughter. All was going well until Offa, delighted at this opportunity of tying himself in with the great Frankish monarch, proposed a double ceremony: why should not his son Egfrith marry Charles's daughter Bertha? Enraged, Charles promptly broke off all negotiations. It was a deeply mysterious episode, the reason for which was an enigma even to Alcuin but presumably the result of that ambiguous relationship between Charles and his daughters at which Einhard hinted. Later the King realized the danger of antagonizing such a man as Offa, and Alcuin, as a fellow Englishman, was sent to smooth things over. He does not seem to have succeeded on this occasion and certainly the marriage proposals were never revived, although later a commercial treaty was drawn up between the two kings – the first such treaty ever signed by a king of England. The condition of England at that time was not such as would attract a man like Alcuin and he had no difficulty in deciding that his duty continued to be beside the Frankish king.

The demands placed upon Alcuin were heavy. He was forty-six years old when he entered Charles's service, an age all but patriarchal in a period when few men expected to live beyond their fifties. He refused to join the king on his endless campaigns, a refusal which Charles accepted amiably, but his journeys around the kingdom setting up that great educational project and the stress of life at the court were wearing to one of his sedentary and retiring habits. In 796, after he had served Charles at the centre of affairs for some eleven years, the abbacy of St Martin at Tours became vacant. It says much for the high esteem in which the king held his mentor that he had no hesitation in giving him this plum. It was said that the abbey was so rich that its abbot could cross from the North Sea to the Adriatic and never have to spend the night in any lodging but one of the abbey's own houses. Its abbot would rule over some 20,000 serfs alone, quite apart from the monks, and in his care was the most famous shrine of the Frankish state, that of St Martin.

Thither Alcuin went in the evening of his days, in his own poignant words: 'I have laid aside the pastoral care and now sit quietly at St Martin, waiting for the knocking at the gate.' But he was by no means idle. The abbey had declined from its great days and he threw himself now into the task of giving 'the rusticity of Tours' the polish of learning. His removal from the royal court is fortunate for posterity, for communication between himself and Charles, as well as with his old friends and colleagues at court, had to be conducted by letter. Through those letters, far more than through his formal work, we have some indication of his personality: a gentle, rather pedantic sense of humour; a total dedication to the cause of learning; deep loyalty to friends. His habits were abstemious, amounting almost to the austere; he shared with Charles a hatred of drunkenness, regarding wine essentially as a medicine (although on his trips back to England he made sure he was adequately supplied in a land addicted to ale). Through those letters, too, we see clearly the complex relationship between the scholar, well aware of his value, and the all-powerful king, well aware of his responsibilities and status – a delicately balanced relationship in which each knew exactly the role he must play if the intimacy was to survive.

Only once was the harmony between them broken. The abbey had given sanctuary to a prisoner who had escaped from Theodulf, Bishop of Orleans. The bishop promptly sent in armed men who violated the sanctuary and, when Alcuin complained, Theodulf forcefully pointed out that the prisoner had been a common criminal. Charles came down on the unfortunate Alcuin like a thunderbolt. The monks who had resisted the bishop's demands were to be arraigned before a special tribunal, Alcuin himself was severely censured, the king adding cruelly and somewhat unfairly that he regretted to note that the abbey's 'evil reputation' had not yet been reformed by the new abbot. The correspondence is, tantalizingly, incomplete, so how the matter ended and just why the king adopted this harsh attitude to the most loyal of his counsellors is not known. But Alcuin must have been deeply hurt.

It may well have been that the king resented being obliged to arbitrate between two equally valued friends and counsellors. For if Alcuin of York was his mentor in intellectual matters, his guide through the minefield of theology, Theodulf was, one suspects, the companion of his lighter hours. Born in the old Gothic province of Septimania – probably in the town of Narbonne – about 760, Theodulf was some eight years younger than his patron, friend and king. His birthplace shaped his intellectual development, for of all those of Frankish or English origin at the court, his was the more Latin mind. Lightly, he called himself 'the Goth' but his copious poetry indicates a very considerable background of classical learning. That poetry is almost intolerably flowery, entangled in far too many verbal conceits for modern taste. It is difficult to take seriously a poet who could devote endless hours of labour to producing a set of verses of 'prayer for king Charles' which when read perpendicularly, horizontally or as a rhomboid, yield eight more similar pieces of trickery.

Nevertheless, through Theodulf, one obtains an immediate and vivid insight into the daily life of the court and the characters of the people in it. The long poem entitled simply *Ad Carolum regem* was written about the year 796 when the court had finally come to rest at Aachen and the sons and daughters of the king were in their teens or early twenties. The day begins with prayer in the chapel after which the king proceeds in audience at the palace. There is a remarkable degree of informality, the great doors of the palace standing wide open with the ordinary people coming and going. After the audience, the children come flocking round, vying with each other to do some little service for their father. The eldest son, Charles, takes off the heavy *pallium* which has clothed his father in majesty during the audience while Louis takes his sword. Then come the daughters: Bertha brings roses, Hrotrud lilies, Rothaid apples, Hiltrud bread, Theoderada wine. They are all beautifully dressed, smothered in jewels – golden clasps, bracelets, necklaces – wearing strong colours of red or green. One of them charms her father with her dancing, another delights him with jokes. They are joined by the king's sister, the Abbess Gisila, whom the girls welcome respectfully, and the king greets affectionately. They exchange kisses and Gisila brings up some problem of scriptural interpretation which the king resolves.

Surrounded by his chattering, laughing, beautiful daughters and stalwart sons, followed by his personal friends, the king makes his way to the dining table where he personally cuts vast portions, piling the plates of his family and guests. Theodulf now introduces one by one the other prominent figures of the court. Most of them have nicknames, a practice introduced by Alcuin as a means of eliminating social differences and ensuring that, while in company, they are part of a family. The king himself is David, Alcuin is Flaccus, Arno of Salzburg Aquila, Gisila Lucia; even little Hrotrud has her pseudonym which suits her gentle personality: Columba – Dove. Theodulf brings on Alcuin first, even as the king places this wisest of his wise men in the seat of honour. 'Flaccus is the glory of our bards, mighty to shout forth his sons, but also a powerful sophist, able to prove pious doctrines out of Holy Scripture and, in genial jest, propounds problems and riddles'. These 'Flaccidica' are sometimes easy to answer, but frequently defeat the cleverest; however, all enjoy them and seek to cap them.

Next comes the Chancellor, Ercambald. He sits near the king for it is his duty to record any order that Charles might make and for this purpose he has two tablets in his hand and, according to Theodulf, repeats the order in an inaudible voice as he writes it down. Somebody called Lentulus brings in apples in a basket – a faithful servant, but rather slow in speech and manner. Then suddenly, through Theodulf's eyes, we get a tantalizingly brief glimpse of a very important little man indeed – Einhard, who some day will encapsulate the king in his biography. Theodulf makes up his own nickname for him, Nardulus, a pun based on his name Einhard, meaning 'pony': he rushes hither and thither like a busy little ant. His body is small but inhabited by a mighty spirit. Then, abruptly, the tone of the poem changes, becomes charged with contempt and malice, giving some faint indication of the enmities at work in so enclosed a society. The person involved is given no name but is simply identified as a Scotsman: 'Such kisses will I give thee as the wolf gives the donkey. Sooner shall the dog cherish hares or the fierce wolf lambs than I, the Goth, will have any friendship with the Scotsman. Take away one little letter, the third in the alphabet, a letter which he himself cannot pronounce and you have the true description of his character, a sot (*sottum*) instead of a Scot (*Scottum*).'

After the banquet there is music and dancing and Theodulf mocks a certain Wibod for his lack of sophistication. Wibod seems to be a conservative Frank of the old school, puzzled by the wit and elegance around him: 'He shakes his thick head of hair three or four times at the minstrel and hurls out dreadful threats at him.' The king summons him and, Caliban-like but loyal, Wibod lumbers to his master 'with shambling gait and trembling knee, a very Jove with his awful voice but a Vulcan with his lame foot'. At the end, Theodulf signs off with an apology to his readers, hoping that they will not be offended by anything he has written. Considering that the poem was intended for circulation among those it described, the apology is necessary.

Einhard's 'official' nickname, the one bestowed upon him by Alcuin and used even by the king himself in intimate conversation, was Bezaleel, borrowed from one of the makers of the Hebrew tabernacle as related in Exodus. The bizarre name was appropriate, in fact, for this remarkable man was an outstanding craftsman and architect and, in due course, would be primarily responsible for the building of the great palace at Aachen. He was regarded by all, even the waspish Theodulf, with genuine affection. A nimble little man ('mannikin', 'midget', 'dwarf' are the terms commonly used of him), forever dashing about on some business, he was among the youngest in the informal academy. Born in 770, he would have been some eighteen years younger than the king and was destined to outlive him by twenty-six years. His father was a wealthy landowner in a village on the lower Main, in the eastern half of the state, and it was doubtless this proximity to the Saxon border country that gave him his insight into the causes of Frankish-Saxon hostility. He was educated at the great monastery of Fulda and his subsequent career gave testimony to the breadth and depth of education in a Frankish monastery of the late eighth century. He was one of the best Latinists of his time. But he had, in addition, very considerable technical and artistic skills, combining the skills of engineer, craftsman, scribe and architect with his academic work. He was about twenty years old when the abbot of Fulda recommended him to Charles and the king, ever alert to talent, brought the young man to court. There he stayed, at the centre of affairs, for the next forty years, for after Charles's death he remained in high favour with his successor, Louis the Pious. It was only with the tragic and inevitable outbreak of hostility between Louis and the sons who would bring about the destruction of the great design, that Einhard, heavy at heart, retired to the monastery that he had built and endowed. It was for this place, which he named Seligenstadt (City of the Saints), that he engaged in that dubious trafficking in relics from Rome.

Posterity owes an incalculable debt to him, even though the brevity of his *Vita Caroli* (*Life of Charles*) is tantalizing and his strange silences puzzling. There is no doubt whatsoever that he consciously prepared himself for the task during the king's lifetime, even though the actual writing was posthumous. The small, vivid, personal details that give the portrait three dimensions – even down to details of his clothes – are evidently not only the result of personal knowledge but of a continual act of recording in a manner that James Boswell would have recognized. There is a possibility that it was Einhard who was responsible for the editing of the chronicle which now bears his name, the so-called *Annales Einhardi*. Covering the years from 741 to 829, they reflect in fact the great period of the Frankish state from the death of Charles Martel to Einhard's own departure from the court. They give a terse but clear account of the chief events in the state, not glossing over such disasters as the defeats by the Saxons in 775 and by the Basques at Roncesvalles, and their latter part – that corresponding to the period of Einhard's own activity at court – bears the impress of contemporary judgements and observations. And these are precisely of the kind that at once bring his portrait of the king to life and give it credibility.

In an excess of modesty, Einhard says of his biography: 'There is nothing for you to wonder at or admire except his deeds – unless indeed it be that I, a barbarian and little versed in the Roman tongue, have imagined that I could write Latin inoffensively and usefully.' The major criticism of his *Vita Caroli*, indeed, is that it follows too closely its Roman model, for Einhard took Suetonius's *Life of Augustus* as an example so faithfully as to lift entire sentences from one to the other. But, like the contrast between the Carolingian minuscule and the clumsy Gothic which came before and after, the contrast between the cool, balanced clarity of Einhard's work, and the attempts at biography throughout most of Europe during the period until the Italian Renaissance, gives some indication of the quality of the light shed in the darkness by the Carolingian renaissance. Einhard's own epitaph equated his acquisition of those dubious relics with his service to

Charlemagne as his major claim to posthumous fame. Walafrid Strabo, the abbot and near-contemporary of Einhard who prepared the *Vita Caroli* in its modern form, lucidly summed up the man and his contribution to the Carolingian state:

> This little man – for he was mean of stature – gained so much glory at the Court by reason of his knowledge and high character that among all the ministers of his royal majesty there was scarcely anyone at that time with whom that most wise and powerful King discussed his private affairs more willingly. And indeed he deserved such favour for, not only in the time of Charles, but even more remarkably in the reign of the emperor Lewis [Charles's son and successor] when the commonwealth of the Franks was shaken with many and serious troubles, he so wonderfully and providentially balanced his conduct and, with the protection of God, kept such watch over himself that his reputation for cleverness which many had envied and many had mocked at, did not untimely desert him. This I have said that all men may read his words without doubting and may know that, while he has given great glory to his great leader, he has also provided the curious reader with the most unsullied truth.

In discussing the king's attitude to foreigners Einhard makes one of his rare criticisms: 'He had a great love for foreigners, and took such pains to entertain them that their numbers were justly reckoned to be a burden not only to the palace, but to the kingdom at large [causing] grave inconveniences.' It is an uncharacteristically narrow viewpoint for a writer who could find something to say on behalf even of the Saxons, and who assessed his own culture and talents from a Latin viewpoint, and therefore probably reflects some of the stresses at work in a seemingly harmonious court. But the king had reasons of state, as well as a personal liking for novelty, for including non-Franks among his advisers: the state he was creating was multi-racial. As it happens, the first known scholar to join his court was an elderly Italian, Peter of Pisa. Peter came back with him to the north after the first Frankish expedition, commissioned to teach grammar to the young nobles of the court and, according to both Einhard and Alcuin, the king himself frequently joined these classes. But a greater catch even than this esteemed grammarian was a member of the now subject Lombard race, Paul Warnefried, universally known as Paul the Deacon.

Paul came to live at the court of the destroyer of his nation's sovereignty under circumstances which do considerable honour both to himself and the conqueror. Paul's brother, Arichis, had been involved in the hopeless rebellion of 776 and had paid the price – not death but, according to the king's tough but humane policy, imprisonment. Paul had by then taken Holy Orders and was in the monastery of Monte Cassino when his brother's wife appealed to him to beg the king's mercy on her behalf. By now, knowledge of Charles's passion for learning, however couched, was widespread on both sides of the Alps and Paul adopted the technique which, above all others, was most sure to engage the king's attention – the couching of a plea for mercy in elegant Latin verse. Compared with the verse of Theodulf or even Alcuin, Paul's has a Biblical ring about it, a noble directness, eschewing flourishes and conceits.

> Hear, great king, my complaint and in mercy receive my petition
> Six long years have passed since my brother's doom overtook him
> Now is the seventh that he, a captive, in exile pines
> Lingers at home his wife to roam through the streets of her city
> Begging for morsels of food, knocking at door after door
> Only in shameful guise like this can she nourish her children
> Four little half-clothed babes, whom she in her wretchedness bore.

So the threnody continues, touching on the fate that awaits those in a conquered country:

> Reft of its scanty belongings is now the home of our fathers
> Us in our utmost need no neighbour will help or advise
> Gone is the pride of our birth. Thrust forth from the acres paternal
> Now we are equalled in rank with those the slaves of the soil
> Harsher doom we deserved, I own it. Yet merciful monarch
> Pity the prayer of the sad. End our distress and our toil
> Give but the captive back to his fatherland and his homestead.

Whether Paul crossed the Alps in person to deliver the plea or, more likely, being reluctant to leave the calm of the cloister entrusted it to a messenger, the king's response was immediate. Yes, the rebel Arichis could have his freedom – provided that his brother yielded himself up in his place. But not as prisoner or hostage but as most honoured guest at the court of the new King of the Lombards and of the Franks. Paul agreed, either from fraternal loyalty or out of curiosity to see this new court and to meet some of the scholars whose fame was already spreading through Europe. That first meeting between monarch and poet must have been one requiring very considerable social poise on both sides. Before entering Monte Cassino Paul had been high in favour at the court of Desiderius in Pavia and at no time did he disguise the fact that he was deeply attached to the last Lombard royal family, in particular to Desiderius's daughter Adalperga, sister to Charlemagne's first wife. But for the shifts of history, he might indeed have become the king's brother-in-law, for his devotion to Adalperga went beyond that of courtier, and his decision to enter a monastery was probably the result of the destruction of the court of Pavia by the Frankish monarch.

Paul stayed at the Frankish court for over four years, arriving there in 782 and returning to Italy in Charles's entourage in 786. At this period in European intellectual development, no real distinction can be drawn between one discipline and another, the word 'scholar' being used virtually interchangeably whether the man concerned was an engineer or a theologian or a grammarian. Einhard, as an outstanding example, moved easily from the field of Latin exercises to that of architecture to that of court recorder, while Alcuin expressed himself as readily in poetry as in prose, as an educationist or diplomat or canon lawyer. Nevertheless, specialization among them can be discerned even at this distance of time: in twentieth-century terms, Paul would be described as an historian with a strong interest in natural history of the kind pursued by eighteenth-century gentlemen of leisure. An outstanding example of this latter interest was when he measured his shadow on Christmas Day at the royal palace of Thionville and, comparing it with the length of his shadow in Italy also measured on a Christmas Day, calculated the declination of the sun according to its latitude, a combination of intuitive leap and meticulous observation that can be compared with Galileo's. But he was also a Greek scholar of considerable skill. The king, mistrusting perhaps the bias that would be given to his beloved daughter Hrotrud by the Byzantine scholar now engaged in instructing her in Greek, arranged for Paul to tutor the courtiers who would accompany the girl when – or if – she eventually made the journey to her imperial betrothed in Constantinople. A rather tiresome modesty about intellectual attainments seems to have been *de rigueur* at the court. Even as Einhard, that polished Latinist, modestly cast down his eyes declaring that he was only a barbarian with little skill in the great language of Rome, so now Paul felt obliged to say: 'I have heard and I exult in the news that your fair daughter, O king, is to cross the seas and grasp the sceptre so that through your child the power of your kingdom will spread over Asia. But if in that country the clerics who go from hence with your child shall speak no more Greek than they have learned from me, they will be as dumb as statues and will be derided by all.' Charlemagne took the ritual disclaimer to be just that, and Paul discharged the very useful function of, in effect, monitoring the education of the little girl expected to be, some day, empress of Rome.

Paul's 'captivity' was one which many a free but hungry scholar might have envied. He and the king were good companions, communicating on the same pragmatic, slightly ironical wavelength. He was commissioned, among much else, to write the history of Metz and so, for the first time, put the Arnulfing ancèstors of Charlemagne into historic perspective. He and Peter of Pisa indulged in elaborate banter which, though now meaningless to a modern student, evidently filled Charles with both amusement and admiration. The king himself would join in, sending by special messenger some complex joke or riddle demanding an answer. Paul leaves a brief sketch of one of these messengers arriving at his door at daybreak, a beautiful youth bearing one of the king's 'fire-tipped arrows' – perhaps the word 'cave' as an acrostic consisting of the three words 'caput, auris, venter' and the letter E – the kind of thing which might today be found in a child's comic but was then deemed worthy of recording.

All this was flattering enough, and life at the court of this most civilized king was doubtless exceedingly pleasant. But Paul continued to pine for the silence and calm of his monastery, writing again and again to his old abbot saying how much he missed his brethren and how only 'the silent might of our lord king' kept him so far away in a strange land. Eventually, Charlemagne relented and, on a royal visit to Italy, gave Paul permission to return to his little haven of peace. According to malicious gossip, Paul during his exile had thrice plotted against the king and, being brought to trial on the third occasion, said proudly: 'I was once faithful to King Desiderius, and that faith of mine remains for ever.' Charles was supposed to have given orders that his hands should be struck off, but then rescinded the order saying: 'When those hands are gone, where shall we find as elegant a writer?' Paul's enemies at court then urged the king instead to put out his eyes in the Byzantine manner, but the king responded: 'When we have blinded him, where shall we find another poet or historian as eminent as he is?' While the story might perhaps reflect some of the tensions and hatreds at work in the court, its inherent improbability is displayed by the fact that at about the time or shortly afterwards that Paul thankfully took up his residence in his old monastery, there was delivered there a poem in his honour from the hand of the king himself.

Poetry weaves its way throughout the complex relationship of the people of the court, the instinctive way in which they sought to express some fact or opinion about each other, of the condition of their times. But, to the outsider, it appears to be a poetry whose quality is in decidedly inverse proportion to its quantity. In his survey of Dark Age literature, M. L. W. Laistner records an all but universal opinion when he says: 'The first impression of the reader who peruses the four massive volumes of Carolingian poetry in the *Monumenta Germaniae Historica* is inevitably one of fatigued disappointment.' The reason was, he thought, 'the overmastering authority of the classical poets of Rome and the Christian poets of the later empire', an authority that all but smothered by its weight so that little that was individual or original could struggle through. But Laistner was writing just before there appeared in England in 1929 an anthology of translations simply entitled *Medieval Latin Lyrics* by an English scholar, Helen Waddell. In an astonishing cross-fertilization of poetic instinct and academic skill, she penetrated to the very heart of the poetry so that its essence was grasped by an alien people speaking a wholly alien language. In her preface she explained why certain poets were not present who should indeed have been present.

> I tried to translate them and I could not. To those born with this kind of restlessness, this curiosity to transmute the beauty of one language into another, although this baser alchemy is apt to turn the gold to copper and at worst to lead, a great phrase in the Latin, something familiar in the landscape, some touch of almost contemporary pain or desire may waken the recreative trouble; yet a greater phrase, a cry still more poignant, may leave the mind quieter for its passing. A man cannot say 'I will translate' any more than he can say 'I will compose poetry'. In this minor art also, the wind blows where it lists.

And scarcely minor, the reader may well decide on reading these exquisite verses, faithful to the original in spirit but boldly creating their own rhythm giving a rare – indeed, a unique – insight into minds dead these thousand years. Through her translation sounds clearly the sheer desolation of that lament for the dead which was forced out of Angilbert by the last, terrible battle at Fontenoy which brought the empire to an end. But in her translations, too, the staid Alcuin emerges as a lyric poet, celebrating the victory of spring over winter; mourning the loss of his beloved little nightingale; or, with a change of key, the sonorous majesty of the 'Sequence for St Michael' which Alcuin wrote for the Emperor Charles, or indeed his own epitaph, ending

> Alcuin was my name: learning I loved
> O thou that readest this, pray for my soul

Here, too, is the lament by his friend Fredugis, mourning his death, mourning his departure from that little house, 'O, dear and sweet my dwelling', the little house set in a flowering wood, girt about with streams and apple orchards and singing birds, where the friends would meet to talk or listen to the pure voice of singing boys. Walafrid Strabo is here, editor of Einhard's book, who sent his own book on gardening to the Abbot of St Gall. It is only a paltry gift, but Strabo sends it with all his heart, imagining his friend reading it perhaps

> in the small garden close
> In the green darkness of the apple trees
> Just where the peach tree casts its broken shade.

Here, too, is the poem that Charlemagne wrote for the Lombard Paul the Deacon, who had been his guest or his hostage but whom he had released as someone might release a linnet or a nightingale from its cage, watching with indulgent smile as he wings his way back to the shelter of the Benedictine monastery of Monte Cassino:

> Across the hills and in the valley's shade
> Alone the small script goes
> Seeking for Benedict's beloved roof
> Where waits its sure repose.
> They come and find, the tired travellers
> Green herbs and ample bread
> Quiet and brother's love and humbleness
> Christ's peace on every head

It is mostly through the poets, though with considerable help from Einhard, that an impressionistic picture emerges of the king at rest or at play with his family and his friends in the very heart of the great state he has built up. It is an impression, as is the picture of the state itself: here, the detail is clear but seemingly unrelated to the rest; there, it is only hinted at, merging into the background which is itself at times in perspective but at others little more than a wash of colours, sometimes rich, at others as pale as a watercolour. But one constant characteristic comes through: the affection, shot through with something like awe, with which he is regarded by those around him. It is as though they had, in their domestic setting, some enormous, handsome and amiable creature – a lion springs most readily to mind – a creature with whom they are proud and delighted to be associated, on whom they depend alike for status and livelihood but which they know can turn and obliterate them with a single almost absent-minded gesture.

The king was intensely gregarious. Even before he was dressed in the morning, people would be crowding in upon him, strangers as well as friends and relatives. If a law case was still unresolved, the Count of the Palace was free to bring the litigants to his private chamber where, perhaps half-clad, the king would listen and give judgement. This spontaneous audience at the beginning of the day would, centuries hence, develop into the preposterous *levée* of the French kings, where nobles of the highest rank would accept the most menial and disgusting of domestic offices in order to be near the sacred person of the monarch at this unbuttoned hour. But with Charles it was simply a bustling desire to get on with the day's work.

He was fluent and loquacious in speech – too much so, in Einhard's private opinion – reacting spontaneously, uninhibitedly to emotions, as ready to weep as to laugh. Despite his vast family, despite the fact that the survival of an infant beyond its fifth year was a matter of congratulation and delight, the death of any of his children devastated him. In Einhard's words 'he bore the deaths of his two sons and of his daughters with less patience than might have been expected from his usual stoutness of heart'. The death of the little baby Hildegarde was recorded by one of the loveliest of lyrics written by Paul the Deacon to console his host, with the poignant, unforgettable line, 'So small a maid to leave so great a sorrow'.

Despite, or perhaps because of, his gregariousness, the king disliked any kind of formal banquet. What he prized was the warm, casual give and take of conversation and song and debate between friends, the scholars striving to cap each other, the poets to weave some fragment of spontaneous, elegant comment. Here, at the dinner table, that ancient, powerful but crude spirit of association, the Frankish *comitatus*, flowers into a complex, potent tool of civilization. Here, in the place of honour as befits the oldest and wisest of the king's servitors, Alcuin propounds one of his tortuous Anglo-Saxon riddles or muses on some aspect of education. Here Theodulf, judge and poet, reminisces perhaps on one of his recent journeys as the royal *missus*, reflecting on the need to keep an eye on such and such a count who is suspected of extorting bribes. Ercambald the Chancellor with his tablets and his stylus sits somewhere near the king, ready to jot down any order Charles might wish to make or making a note to himself to follow up some detailed query. Paul Warnefried reflects perhaps on some natural phenomenon: why it is that certain species of birds move from one land to another at certain times of year; why one's shadow is lesser or greater at those times; or, with a certain discretion, he might touch on Lombard history, or raise some question of royal genealogy with the king to fill a gap in his history of the Arnulfings. Wibod, the stolid, unsophisticated Frank from the backwoods listens uncomprehendingly, with beetling brow, wondering why his tribal leader surrounds himself with these posturing foreigners; he is out of his depth, but nevertheless his place at the table is as secure as that of any of the stars, for at no point will the king forget his tribal origins. Opposite sits Hildegarde, the gentle, loving, but by no means submissive consort, presiding over her flower-garden of daughters. They have been brought up in the good, traditional virtues of Frankish womanhood, able to spin and weave and run a household. But something of the all-pervading intellectualism rubs off on them and they too take part in the conversation or listen, only partly understanding but aware of the great world that impinges on their little domestic universe. And somewhere at the table will be little Einhard, bright-eyed, alert, not saying very much but listening all the time.

One of the secrets of Charles's prodigious energy was his ability to switch off completely when he wished. Usually after the midday meal he would undress and go to bed for two or three hours. Conversely, he rarely slept the night through, but would awake three or four times, frequently even rising, perhaps simply to disperse that impatient energy, but sometimes too to despatch some business of state that had occurred to him. He exercised violently in the traditional royal sports of hunting and riding but, unusually for his time and his class, he was passionately fond of swimming. It was the existence of the hot baths of Aachen that led him to establish his centre of government there. 'He used to invite not only his sons to the bath but also his nobles and friends – and at times even a great number of his followers and bodyguards,' Einhard remarks with a hint of disapproval.

At the heart of the court lay the mystery of the king's relationship with his daughters.

His second legal wife, Hildegarde, the woman who had given birth to three legitimate sons and to three legitimate daughters, died at the age of about twenty-six in 783. Her death took place shortly after the massacre of Verden and, as Charles's mother, Bertha, died in that same year, there was no lack of whispers of divine retribution. His mother's death saddened him, for they had had a close and warm relationship, but she died full of years and honour whereas the gentle Hildegarde died just as she was flowering into mature womanhood. Her death, as with those of his children, devastated him but within a very short time he had married again. The third wife was Fastrada, a noble Frankish girl, beautiful, highly intelligent and, according to his closest friends, he had exchanged an angel for a she-devil. It was Einhard's opinion that the conspiracies and rebellions that threatened the stability of the throne in the 790s were due entirely to 'the cruelty of queen Fastrada'. On the face of it, it seems unlikely that a man of Charlemagne's stature, bearing the responsibilities that he bore, and with the strong sense of public duty that he possessed, would allow uxuriousness to threaten the state. Yet Einhard is a shrewd observer, finely attuned to the gossip of the court and there was, too, a precedent, at the very beginning of the reign, when the still untried king was perfectly prepared to embroil himself with the powerful Lombard monarchy in order to get the woman he wanted into his bed. It does seem, from what was to follow, that Queen Fastrada did indeed exert a strong and baleful influence over him.

She could not, however, affect his relationship with the daughters of his second marriage. And on this relationship we have the impeccable, though yet again mysteriously veiled, witness of Einhard. Discussing the fact that Charles's sons and daughters travelled with him wherever he went, Einhard described the line of march: 'His sons rode along with him and his daughters travelled in the rear. Some of his guards, chosen for this very purpose, watched the end of the line of march where his daughters travelled.' Then the writer goes on to make a very curious statement indeed:

> They [the daughters] were very beautiful indeed, and much beloved by their father, and therefore it is strange that he would give them in marriage to no one, either among his people or of a foreign state. But up to his death he kept them all at home, saying he could not forego their society. And hence the good fortune that followed him in all other respects was here broken by the touch of scandal and failure. He shut his eyes, however, to everything and acted as though no suspicion of anything amiss had reached him, or as if the rumour of it had been discredited.

Precisely as with his enigmatic statement about the king's childhood, Einhard has said just too much and just too little. To what 'scandal and failure' is he referring? To what did the clear-eyed, hard-headed ruler of half Europe 'shut his eyes'? A commonly accepted reason for the king's refusal to give his beautiful daughters in honourable marriage was that he was reluctant to set up any possible rival claimants to the throne in the form of ambitious sons-in-law. But all rulers must accept this problem and are prepared to do so because of the value of dynastic alliances. In any case, Charles eventually quite happily followed the tradition of dividing the realm into three, an act which in the long run was to prove far more disastrous than the claims of the most ambitious son-in-law. One is forced to ask why he was prepared to follow customary usage in one direction and not the other, and so come back again to Einhard's unhappy suspicion of 'scandal and failure'. Was Einhard really hinting at the possibility of incest? Because far from shutting his eyes to his daughters' activities, he was fully prepared to see them engaged in unofficial liaisons – in other words, they took lovers from among his friends and servants, by whom they had children. And in all those tangled relationships, none was odder than that between his eldest daughter, Bertha, and the gay, debonair, friendly, talented young man called Angilbert who also just happened to be the Abbot of St Riquier.* By one of those great ironies of history one of their two sons, Nithard, became an historian in his own right and it was he who recorded that doom-laden 'Oath of Strasburg' by which the grandsons of Charlemagne sundered his empire in two, turning Franks into 'Germans' and 'French'.

Angilbert and Bertha were childhood sweethearts, growing up side by side in the palace, travelling side by side in the king's restless perambulations around the country. The boy was from a noble Frankish family and, as was customary, was brought into the court as a child, proving so brilliant an addition to the king's personal *comitatus* that, instead of being returned to his family as was also customary, he remained with the court. He was educated personally by Alcuin, and proved to be so accomplished a poet that the nickname chosen for him was Homer. Alcuin was fond of the young man, but deeply mistrustful of his flippant manners and tastes, in particular his passion for the theatre. Writing to his friend Adalbert, asking him to keep an eye on his protégé, Alcuin dwelt on this failing, quoting St Augustine:

---

*No relation of the Angilbert who wrote the *Lament for Fontenoy* a generation later.

'Little does the man know who introduces actors and mimics and dancers into his house how great a crowd of unclean spirits follow them.' God forbid that the Devil should have power in a Christian home. I wrote to you about this before, desiring with all my heart the salvation of my dearest son, and wishing that you might accomplish that which was beyond my power.

Adalbert seems to have been able to bring about at least the partial reformation of the graceless young man, for a little later Alcuin is writing to him again:

I was much pleased to read what you have written about the improved morals of my Homer. For, although his character was always an honourable one, yet there is no one in the world who has not to 'forget the things which are behind and reach out to the things which are ahead' till he attains the 'crown of perfection'. Now 'one of the things that are behind' for him related to the actors from whose vanities I knew that no small peril impended over his soul, which grieved me. I was surprised that so intelligent a man did not himself perceive that he was doing blameworthy deeds and things which consisted not with his dignity.

Angilbert's reformation was either complete or, more likely, Charles did not hold quite so austere a view of the morals of theatre-going for he loaded the young man with favours. Although Angilbert could have been only a few years older than Pippin, the boy-king of Italy, Charles sent him to Pavia to act as his guide, counsellor and general mentor and, in addition, entrusted the young man with three important missions to Rome. In 790 he was made Abbot of St Riquier in Picardy and given the very important office of arch-chaplain. Charlemagne was deeply loyal to his friends, but he was also a veteran administrator and would never have appointed any person to such an office unless he was capable of filling it.

Through all this period, the young man maintained his relationship with Bertha. At first it was surreptitious. The story went round the court of how he had visited Bertha on a winter's night and, when preparing to leave her at dawn, was appalled to see that there had been a heavy fall of snow and his footprints would infallibly betray him and his princess. Bertha, though undoubtedly beautiful and alluring, was evidently both a strapping young woman and a quick thinker: she solved the problem by taking her lover on her back, leaving only one innocent set of footprints in the snow. But such precautions proved unnecessary. The court, despite the muttered protests of traditional moralists, took its lead from the king and simply recognized Bertha as the Abbot of St Riquier's common-law wife. In that manner, two more bastards were added to the Carolingian score, creating two more problems for future genealogists.

It is from Angilbert's fluent pen that there emerges a portrait of the court at play which, though artificial in its atmosphere, fixes it with the brilliant clarity of a manuscript illumination. The occasion is a boar-hunt at Aachen. The king, 'the Pharos of Europe', leads the way on a great charger which is smothered with heavy gold trappings, glinting dully in the autumn sunlight. He is followed by his sons, dressed plainly as is their father. But the six daughters who follow are in a blaze of jewellery and gorgeous costume, for their presence is decorative and they will be kept far from any danger, either to them or their clothes. Three of them are blood sisters, Hrotrud, Bertha and Gisila, the daughters of Hildegarde; the other three are half-sisters: Rothaid, daughter of a mistress (for socially their father draws not the slightest distinction between those born above or below the blankets) and Theoderada and Hiltrud, Fastrada's daughters. Even in the formality of the description Bertha emerges with a clarity of detail that bears evidence of the writer's particular interest. Her hair, like her father's, is fair almost to platinum; like her father's, her gestures are emphatic, expressive, the face lively, the eyes filled with humour and interest. She is also popular, being surrounded by her own little court of female friends: one suspects that, in modern parlance, she would be a chatter-box.

The boar is found and killed and the tents are then pitched in the middle of the forest. And in that vast green sea of primeval Germany, the little knot of humans form a warm, colourful island, the smell of woodsmoke and roasting meat arising, the sound of voices at play, backed with the plaintive music of wind and stringed instruments.

9   Consolidation

'*Hic annus fuit sine hoste*', the keeper of the royal annals recorded in 786, the fact that there was no general mustering of the host in that year being worthy of note. Year after year the men gathered in their thousands: year after year the economic life of the nation was disrupted for weeks or months at a time, peasants dragged from their farms, craftsmen from their shops. Nor was it simply a negative loss with a reduction in production, but food and equipment and money was diverted for the maintenance of the immense army, transporting it across half Europe and supporting it in the field. Even the Frankish taste for militarism, the ingrained loyalty to the tribal leader, weakened under the strain. In that same 'quiet' year of 786 there came a rebellion not on the peripheries of the state, but in its very heartland, in Austrasia and Thuringia; a rebellion, moreover, led by one of the men on whom the king relied for the administration of law and order, a count by the name of Hardrad. Judging by the speed with which Charles pounced before the rebellion could become dangerous, he must have established some sort of network of informers. The rebellion was rapidly suppressed, Einhard remarking on the king's clemency in that only three men were killed – resisting arrest – and the rest blinded or exiled, but it made evident the fact that the state was by no means as monolithic as it appeared from outside. Scarcely had that internal trouble been resolved when the Bretons in the south-west refused to pay tribute and an expedition had to be sent to winkle out the chiefs from their swamp-lands and haul them before the Assembly. They again swore homage, and paid the disputed tribute, but no one who knew these truculent, independent-minded people believed that was the end of the matter. Hard on the heels of these problems at home came the biggest threat of all, a three-way alliance between the Byzantine emperor, the Lombard duchy of Benevento in southern Italy and Charles's own cousin, Tassilo, all sworn to bring down the arrogant Frank.

Charles's intelligence service, backed up by that daunting ability of his to move fast, again stood him in good stead. Arichis, Duke of Benevento, was still negotiating with his widely separated allies, still in the process of preparation when the Frankish army stormed down out of the north. Arichis hastily sent his own son with rich gifts to the enraged monarch, and locked himself up in the impregnable fortress of Salerno. Charles was tempted to lay siege, but the looming threat of Tassilo in his rear, together with news of yet more trouble in Saxony, forbade any such luxury, particularly as Arichis was falling over himself to offer homage. Charles accepted, driving a breach in the triple alliance, a breach which was widened further when Byzantine envoys met him in Rome to try and urge forward the delayed marriage between his daughter Hrotrud and the boy-emperor. He temporized, turning his attention upon Tassilo.

Tassilo, Duke of Bavaria, considered he had grounds for grievance against his cousin and his suzerain. His family, the Agilolfings, had been dukes of Bavaria when Charlemagne's ancestors had been mere court officials. Tassilo still had that crime of *harisliz*, desertion of his lord, against his name, and the fact that even after twenty-five years Charlemagne had not brought him to book must have confirmed him in his contemptuous refusal to recognize him as overlord. There is little doubt, too, that his wife, Liutberga, daughter of the deposed and imprisoned Desiderius, was burning for revenge on the man who had destroyed the royal house of Pavia. For some reason, Tassilo had provided a detachment of Bavarians for the abortive Spanish expedition (and the disaster at Roncesvalles must have confirmed him in his low opinion of his cousin), but he ignored all the other duties and ceremonies of a vassal to his lord. He summoned councils in his own name, deliberately left out the name of the king on documents, inserting his own instead, and even loftily speaking in them of 'the year of my kingship'. The fact that now he had made common cause with Charles's enemies emphasized that the time had come to close this loophole in the kingdom. Charles had the wholehearted support of Pope Hadrian.

Warn Tassilo [Hadrian told the Bavarian envoys] that he prevent bloodshed and the ravage of his land by manifesting entire obedience to his lord king Charles and his sons. If otherwise, if with hardened heart, he refuse to obey my apostolic words then King Charles will be absolved from all peril of punishment and sin and whatever shall happen in that land, burning or homicide or any other evil that may light on Tassilo and his partisans, lord Charles and his Franks will remain thereafter innocent of blame.

With that papal dispensation to commit mayhem, Charles moved into action. First it was necessary to get the wholehearted support of the Assembly for this onslaught upon fellow Franks before, in October 787, Bavaria was invaded from three directions. From the south came his son, the eleven-year-old Pippin having his first taste of warfare as the titular head of an Italian army. From the north came a mixed force of Austrasian Franks, Thuringians and even a detachment of Saxons, avenging themselves on Franks at the behest of a Frank, while Charles himself entered Bavaria from the west by way of Ingolstadt. Faced with such a massive and co-ordinated attack, Tassilo collapsed. Humbly he waited upon the king, confessing that he had grievously wronged him and then, in a curious ceremony, resigned his country into the king's hands in the form of a 'wand, the top of which was carved into the likeness of a man'. Charles responded generously, returning the ducal staff of office to his cousin in token of restoring him to rule over Bavaria, and loading him with rich gifts, among them one of the famous Frankish chargers caparisoned in gold cloth. He could afford to be generous. In full assembly Tassilo had declared his subordinate status, making one of the earliest acts of formal homage in European history.

What happened next in Tassilo's palace at Ratisbon is obscure. The Franks laid the blame for what followed upon the passionate desire for vengeance of Tassilo's wife Liutberga. It is not unlikely. Her father lived, tonsured, in a Frankish monastery; her brother, Adelchis, was wandering the world homeless (he eventually arrived at the Byzantine court, stirring up trouble against the destroyer of the Lombards). Her mother and sisters – one of whom she believed was the rightful queen of the Franks – were immured in a nunnery. Tassilo seems to have been an unstable man, easy to persuade to a course of action without heeding its long-term result. News came to Aachen that he had committed the ultimate unforgivable sin for a European Christian: he had contacted the pagan Avars, those merciless enemies of Europe whose lands abutted his own. So serious was the charge that Charles called an assembly at Ingelheim and Tassilo was summoned before it.

In the light of the twentieth-century's wide experience of show trials there is an uneasy suspicion that the trial and condemnation of Tassilo was just one such, that Charlemagne had manoeuvred patiently, craftily, deceitfully over many months or even years to get himself in a position where he could eliminate, finally, a man who, after all, occupied a position in the nation second only to his own. The way in which the accusations were made by Tassilo's own subjects, men who owed their position in society to him and who now trooped forward to make the most damaging accusations, argues a very considerable degree of pre-planning. There was nothing particularly dishonourable in their action. They owed allegiance to the king through the duke, and they had doubtless become more than disenchanted with Tassilo's reckless toying with danger, his feckless changes of course apparently under pressure from his wife. There is, nevertheless, something distasteful about the fact that not a single Bavarian came forward to speak on his behalf. In addition to the charge of plotting with the Avars, he was accused of having threatened the lives of the king's vassals; of having ordered those obliged to take the oath of loyalty to the king to do so 'with a mental reservation'. He was even prepared to risk the life of his son, Theodo, whom Charles had taken as hostage, saying 'If I had ten sons I would lose them all rather than stand by my sworn compact with that king. It is better for me to die than live on such terms.' Tassilo made no attempt to defend himself and the Assembly, taking into account that ancient, still unexpiated crime of *harisliz* together with the treasonable contact with the Avars, condemned him to death. It was a just punishment in the context of Frankish law, *harisliz* alone carrying the death penalty. Charles, however, 'for the love of God and because he was his kinsman', commuted the sentence to confinement in a monas- tery. Tassilo accepted it with resignation, making only the plea that he should not be shamed by having his hair cut off and the tonsure made in public in the palace, and to this his victor agreed. Tassilo was to make one more, rather odd, appearance on the stage of history when he was summoned before the synod of Frankfurt six years later and obliged to admit his faults all over again, formally renouncing all his property in Bavaria – probably because of some technical defect in the Ingelsheim trial. But thereafter he disappears utterly, bringing to an end a dynasty which had ruled Bavaria for two centuries, for his two sons as well as his daughters and the wife who had probably brought this trouble upon all their heads, were also confined for life in monasteries and nunneries. Three centuries after Clovis the Merovingian had set out on his path of conquest, and a little over a generation after Charles the Hammer had welded the Frankish nation into a unit, the last Teutonic enclave had been brought finally and firmly under the control of the Frankish king.

Each expansion of the state brought it into conflict with new enemies, and those with whom it was now in contact upon its eastern border were the fiercest and most bloodthirsty of all: the Avars. In Einhard's view, the war with the Avars was second only to that of the Saxons and very much more bloody. 'How many battles were fought there and how much blood was shed is still shown by the deserted and uninhabited condition of Pannonia, and the district in which stood the palace of the Kagan is so desolate that there is not so much as a trace of human habitation. All the nobles of the Huns were killed in this war: all their glory passed away.'

The Avars moved into the region which the Romans knew as Pannonia, and which is today part of Hungary, some time at the turn of the fifth and sixth centuries – at about the time the Franks were establishing themselves further west. But where the Franks adopted and adapted Roman manners, turning themselves into a civilization, the Mongolian Avars remained, from first to last, plunderers and parasites. Small, dark, hardy people they were superb horsemen on their small, wiry, agile ponies. They would appear in a cloud thousands strong as if from nowhere, swoop down upon their victim, kill everything that moved and, their loot secured, race off back to their mysterious Ring, the unconquered and seemingly unconquerable heart of their nation.

The Monk of St Gall, usually addicted to something near fiction, provides, for once, a description of this Ring which convinces because of the odd manner in which he acquired it. It was told to him by an old man called Adalbert, a veteran of the Avar and Saxon wars. 'When I was quite a child, and he a very old man I lived in his house and he used often to tell the story of those events. I was most unwilling to listen and would often run away but in the end by sheer force he made me hear.'

Adalbert was evidently spiritual brother to Coleridge's Ancient Mariner and the dialogue between himself and the bored young boy, as recorded by the monk in his maturity, borders on slapstick. But posterity should be grateful to them both for theirs is the only full description of a robber's castle which held a loot so great that, when it was released, it seriously affected the economic balance of western Europe.

Now Adalbert used to explain the nature of the hiding place as follows: 'The land of the Huns,' he would say, 'was surrounded by nine rings.' I could not think of any rings except our ordinary wicker rings for sheepfolds and so I asked, 'What, in the name of wonder, do you mean, sire?' 'Well,' he said, 'it was fortified by nine hedges.' I could not think of any hedges except those that protect our cornfields, so again I asked and he answered, 'One ring was as wide – that is, it contained as much within it – as all the country between Tours and Constance. It was fashioned with logs of oak and ash and yew and was twenty feet wide and the same in height. All the space within [the logs] was filled with hard stones and binding clay; and the surface of these great ramparts was covered with sods and grass.'

So the rambling story goes on, the old man reaching back into his memory, back to the time when he, as a young Frankish warrior in his teens, stood with his comrades, awed in the midst of the vast Hungarian plain, looking at the smoking, reeking ruin they had accomplished, the dead goblin-like men lying thick on the plain in and around that vast structure which had been almost, but not quite, impregnable. It appears to have been a species of fortified camp (according to old Adalbert at least thirty miles across, though this doubtless was an exaggeration wrought by time). There was an inner core, defended by the nine famous Rings. Each of these rings would have consisted of a massive circumvallation of timber and earth, backed up by a tangled thorn hedge which would have been almost as efficient as modern barbed wire. Within each ring there were dwelling areas so arranged that the inhabitants could, if necessary, retreat towards the inner core. An attacker would have had to fight his way through nine successive defences, while being assailed by uncounted numbers of agile, ferocious men. No attacker had ever done so, until the coming of the Franks.

Although the Avars created nothing that we can now recognize as a civilization, they appear to have been highly organized under a ruler called the *Kagan* who worked through officials or ministers called *tuguns*. They were indeed so well organized that, allying themselves with the Persians, they nearly brought about the destruction of Constantinople. The emperor, the supposed lord of the world, was glad to buy them off, paying the astonishing sum of 80,000 gold *solidi* year after year for nearly a century, the gold pouring into that fortified camp and remaining there. Until the coming of the Franks. Destructive raids had been launched into western Europe during the reign of the Merovingians, and into northern Italy but, mindful perhaps of the nature of the monarch who now sat upon the throne of the Franks, the Avars had until recently avoided any military contacts. But, emboldened by Tassilo's foolish actions, they had begun to press in on Bavaria. Yet still they were reluctant to tangle with the might of the

Franks, actually sending envoys to Charlemagne in an attempt to smooth out their differences.

Charlemagne rejected the embassy. There is little doubt that he had, by now, matured a scheme of conquest that would remove, finally, the threat from the east. In 789 he had personally led an expedition against the Slavs. It was little more than a raiding excursion but it brought him to a point that even the Romans had never achieved – the Elbe. He refused to regard even this natural boundary between east and west as his own terminus but built two permanent bridges across it, protecting them with resident garrisons. Impressive though this was as a testimony to his determination to link east and west, even more impressive was his extraordinary feat in attempting to link the Rhine and the Danube via a canal. Although a land warrior through and through, he was alive to the value of water transport and had already begun to use the major rivers of Francia as highways. During the Avar wars it became obvious that if such a link could be made between the heartland of the state and its frontiers, the problem of transporting vast quantities of provisions would be immensely simplified. Thousands of workers – free soldiers as well as serfs and slaves – were transported to the Altmuhl River, a tributary of the Rhine, and some 2000 feet of the canal were actually dug before it became apparent that the swampy nature of the ground was beyond the Franks' primitive equipment. The weather, too, militated against the work, ceaseless rain turning the newly created banks into thick mud and the attempt was at last abandoned. But what little they had been able to achieve, the military engineers had achieved well, the fragment they had constructed surviving; in the eighteenth century Napoleon was to consider continuing the work, but abandoned the idea for much the same reason as the Frankish engineers, but the Karlsgrab, that mark of his determination which the king made upon nature itself, survives into the twentieth century as an ornamental lake.

The Assembly of 791 gave unanimous and enthusiastic approval to the Avar crusade – for so a military action against these fierce pagans could be shown to be. The campaign began in the summer of the same year and was to continue for eight years. Again the host was divided, this time into three sections. A northern contingent, including an impressive number of Saxons, was to march down the northern bank of the Danube, Charles would lead a Frankish army to the southern bank, while coming across from Italy was an Italian army, again commanded by his second son Pippin, now a boy of fourteen and gradually taking the reins into his own hands. The superb Lombard cavalry which formed the core of this army were to bear the brunt of the fighting; without them, it is doubtful if the lumbering Frankish host would ever have been able to come to grips with the Avars on their speedy mounts.

As though aware of the significance of this, the last major military campaign of his career in which he would personally take part, Charlemagne ordered a halt before crossing the Danube and for three days the entire army took part in a series of rigorous religious ceremonies. The first day was an absolute fast: the second porridge, bread and beans were permitted and a little thin beer added on the third day. Meanwhile, the priests were in complete control with an endless succession of prayers, masses and litanies to attract God's attention to the great work about to be undertaken. On the fourth day, the Danube was crossed, the two main forces united and the march begun into the heart of the Avar lands.

With the exception of the Lombard action, this first attack upon the most feared fighters in Europe was something of an anti-climax. Writing to his wife Fastrada, Charlemagne gives an account of young Pippin's success where the joy and pride of the father echoes even through the stilted report of the commander-in-chief. Fastrada is informed that the plan was for the Italians to attack across the southern borders of the Avars. 'Our beloved son tells us that the Lord God gave them overwhelming triumph: so great a number of men have never before been killed in battle.' The border fort had been taken, 150 prisoners captured together with great quantities of loot while the bulk of the enemy force had dispersed in panic. The army in concert now marched on to the Ring, fighting all the way, devastating the countryside, bringing the kind of terror to the Avars which they themselves were so skilful at bringing to others. But before the campaign could be brought to a successful conclusion, two disasters halted it in mid-stride. An epidemic wiped out most of the cavalry upon which the army was utterly dependent in this war against horsemen, and news came from Francia that Pippin, the hunchbacked, illegitimate, disinherited namesake and half-brother of the King Pippin who was basking now in military glory, Pippin the son of the long-forgotten mistress Himiltrude, had attempted a palace revolution.

Einhard, for one, was sure of the cause. Discussing the rebellion of Count Hardrad and Pippin's attempt apparently to seize the crown for himself he said: 'The cruelty of Queen Fastrada is believed to have been the cause and origin of these conspiracies. Both were caused by the belief that, upon the persuasion of his cruel wife he had swerved widely from his natural kindness and customary leniency.' The 4500 headless young Saxon men; the innumerable hostages automatically executed when their principals reneged on some treaty; Tassilo, Desiderius and their families now eating out their hearts in monasteries and nunneries; the Avars slaughtered whether or not they had surrendered – all these might perhaps call into question the reality of the king's 'natural kindness and customary leniency'. The man Einhard saw presiding with enormous bonhomie over the dinner table, who clambered around with him enthusiastically surveying a site for a new palace or church, was rather different from the man intent on carving out an empire. Charlemagne, unlike his son Louis, was perfectly capable of cruelty and violence – which was precisely why he was able to retain his throne whereas Louis, the gentle, thoughtful Louis, would lose control.

What is far more likely than that Fastrada altered his nature is that he allowed her far too much power. Unlike Hildegarde, who followed him everywhere even on his toughest campaigns, Fastrada preferred to stay comfortably at home. But she was not content to sit quietly in the women's quarters; although there was no provision for it within the structure of the state she had every intention of being her husband's deputy in his absence. To act, in effect, as regent. And though this was obviously a highly dangerous state of affairs to tolerate, there is equally obviously little doubt but that Charlemagne not only accepted this, but positively encouraged it. In his letter to her in which he was so touchingly proud of young Pippin's triumph, he ordered that thanksgiving services should be offered at home – and put the duty of organizing it upon her, although in fact it was something which should have been arranged by Angilbert, the arch-chaplain. Why? In that same letter is some indication as to why he gave in so much to Fastrada. She was young, and beautiful, and he was undoubtedly deeply in love with her as one would expect from so passionate and sensual a nature. But she was also in delicate health (her life was to be even shorter than Hildegarde's) and he implores her to take care of herself. Utterly ruthless though he might well be in affairs of state if the situation so demanded, in his personal relationships Carolus Magnus, King of the Franks, King of the Lombards, Patrician of the Romans was all too human. As a result Queen Fastrada found herself in a position likely to turn the head of many an older and wiser person than herself – the ability to exercise power without responsibility in her husband's absence.

There was, too, another and far more dangerous factor at work: the relationship between monarch and aristocracy in the Frankish state.

The spirit of the *comitatus* was at once a bulwark and a weakness to the throne: a bulwark, in that the king was assured of the loyalty of his paladins even unto death; a weakness in that they expected reciprocation. No longer could the tribal leader content them with a seat at the banquet and the gift of a sword. Land was now what was required. The early Merovingians were able to satisfy this hunger at the expense of the neighbouring peoples whom they defeated, but as the state expanded ever further, it became no longer possible to hand over vast tracts of 'enemy' lands to voracious nobles. It became necessary to carve gifts out of the very vitals of the state to keep them satisfied – and they gave very little in return. It was a vicious circle: the more the king gave, the more powerful the noble became, the less inclined he was to give service in exchange. The Carolingians checked the process by the system of vassalage, that pyramidal system which ensured that every man owed service to the one above him. Charlemagne, his father and his grandfather had all taken it in turn to tighten the screw. The tussle between baron and monarch, the one with a vested interest in anarchy, the other striving for autocracy, would be the central feature of European history for centuries to come. But in this formative period, there was an additional element of discord: the fact that the 'king' was removed by barely a generation from that heroic period when all Franks were equal, when the tribal leader was still merely *primus inter pares*, the first among equals. All these ingredients came together – the resentment against a crass young woman exercising power; the resentment against a curtailing of action and the more noble resentment of the loss of equality – all these came together to create a powder-keg while Charles was absent fighting the Avars.

Pippin the Hunchback provided the spark. Or, to be exact, was used as the spark as a man might strike flint against steel, for although the 'revolution' was in his name, from first to last he was merely the instrument of men who were both unscrupulous and skilful – certainly skilful enough to keep their names out of the limelight. All that Einhard was able to recall of the affair was that, 'This Pippin formed a conspiracy against his father with some of the leaders of the Franks who had seduced him by a vain promise of the kingdom.' The Monk of St Gall had a breathless, complicated tale to tell of how the plot was overheard by a Lombard loyal to the king, how he forced his way into the royal apartments in the middle of the night with the information and of how finally the wretched Pippin 'was cruelly scourged, tonsured and sent into a monastery, the poorest and it was judged the straitest in all the king's broad dominions.'

For the second time in barely five years the kingdom had been threatened from within. The annalists and the chroniclers alike give only the barest of outlines, but it was evident that there was some deep-seated malaise at work. Certainly the king felt it advisable to remain at the centre of affairs for the next two years, suspending the war against the Avars. But although the host remained at home, those undercover agents who were increasingly becoming an arm of state were busily at work in distant Pannonia. The shock of the Frankish attack had come as a deep and most unpleasant surprise to a people more accustomed to doing the slaughtering than to being slaughtered. They had nothing the equivalent of the *comitatus* to bind them together and Charlemagne was therefore unsurprised though gratified when the highest of the Avar *tuguns* – a man equivalent in office to his own chancellor – abruptly appeared in Aachen offering to accept baptism and to betray his *Kagan*. Did he, perhaps, hope to edge his leader aside and become a Frankish puppet king? If so, he was to be disappointed, for when the Franks had finished with the Avars there was no kingdom over which anybody could reign. The *tugun* brought not only evidence of disaffection among the Avars but, for the first time, Charlemagne heard from an unimpeachable source the story of the treasure of the Avars. A successful campaign would not only extend the Frankish arms eastward and remove a festering danger but would also replenish coffers that were now dangerously empty.

On this second expedition, the host was led not by the king but by a Lombard duke, Eric of Friuli, and by the king's eldest son Charles, a strapping young man of seventeen. Charlemagne was now approaching fifty, approximately the age at which his father, his uncle and his grandfather had died. He himself was as hale and hearty as ever – the only illness of his ever recorded was the last, fatal illness – but it was good now to share the burden of authority with the sons bred up to it. In the boys' education, he had steered a sensible course between allowing them to become parochial by staying too much at home, or by becoming 'foreign' by being away too long. Louis, King of Aquitaine, and Pippin, King of Italy, were brought home from time to time, sometimes to join the family gatherings of the great feasts of the Church, at other times for prolonged visits during which they were eased into the art of government at the centre. Charles, the eldest of the three, remained close to his father. Compared to the glittering titles that had been given his younger brothers, his office as ruler of the duchy of Maine in the 'Romanized' section of the State might seem meagre indeed. Yet he gave no indication of resenting it, nor did his father ever act towards him in any other manner than one of proud confidence. The two began to work together as a team, the one infusing youth and energy, the other experience and authority, the *comitatus* at its most potent. It is impossible now to guess just what provisions Charlemagne intended for his sons after his death for, as it happened, fate solved the problem of succession in his own lifetime. It seems extraordinary that a man of his wide-ranging vision, with his personal experience of the danger of dividing the state on equal terms between brothers, should have intended to perpetuate just this situation. The probability is that he envisaged the system of vassalage carried to its highest degree, with Louis and Pippin autonomous in their own lands yet subordinate to their brother Charles, the three of them in an indissoluble pyramidal bond.

Of the three boys, Louis alone aroused his misgivings for the future. He was a gentle little boy, deeply religious even as a child, fond of learning in a manner that could only win his father's approval, but also easily led and shrinking from the harsh world of battle. His father had taken him on the first Avar expedition but had had to send him home, despite such a disgrace to a Frankish lad of thirteen. Four years later, Charlemagne had had to send a special commission into Aquitaine to look into affairs there, for Louis had proved totally incapable of imposing his will – so much so that his personal treasury was empty and he was unable even to buy the New Year presents which it was customary to exchange among relatives and close friends. The commission had had a delicate task, that of restoring order without eroding what remained of the authority of the young king. They succeeded, but Aquitaine ever remained a nagging problem at the back of Charlemagne's mind.

The campaign against the Avars again gathered momentum. It would take two massive hammer-blows, two major musters of the host, drawing upon levies from every part of the now great kingdom, before the robbers' nest was exterminated. The army now was truly international: lithe dark men from Tuscany accustomed to fighting in great heat; square, solid Saxon infantry skilled at negotiating marshlands and finding cover on plains; axe-men from Brittany forgetting their racial grievance in the hope of plunder; bow-men from Aquitaine; Frankish swordsmen; river men from the Danube and the Rhine and the Meuse and the Scheldt to organize water transport and provide a rudimentary battle fleet on the Danube; and, spear-heading all, the cavalry of the Lombards, now recovered from the epidemic and their numbers replenished. Duke Eric was killed and the leadership fell to Prince Charles, the eldest son of the greatest of all Teutonic monarchs launching that *Drang nach Osten* which was to return again and again to haunt their Teutonic descendants. And at last, in the year 796, five years after the war began, the Avars cracked and lay utterly at the king's mercy. The survivors, offered the usual choice of death or baptism, accepted the latter and while the king was considering their ultimate fate, a letter arrived for him from his old friend and mentor, Alcuin, in Tours.

Alcuin had made no secret of his intense disapproval of the savage treatment meted out to the Saxons, in particular the rubbing of salt into the wound by forcing them to give tithes to a barely understood religion. Now he took up the theme again. He heartily congratulated the king on his signal victory over 'a nation formidable by their ancient savagery and courage,' but urged him not to repeat the mistake of Saxony.

> Let your Piety consider whether it is good to impose on a rude people like this the yoke of tithes exacted in full amount and from every house . . . We know that the tithing of property is a good thing: but it is better to forego it than to lose the faith. Even we, who were born bred and trained up to be Catholic, scarce consent to the full tithing of our substance: how much less with their tender faith, their childish intellects and their covetous dispositions consent to such large claims on their generosity.

The letter was opportune. Charlemagne was only too well aware that the savage Saxon capitulary had been counter-productive and was even then engaged in toning down its provisions. His attitude to the Avars was, in consequence, very much milder. But they were, it seems, less resilient than the Saxons, and they eventually disappeared, absorbed into the new peoples following them. Charlemagne departed from his usual custom and made no attempt to colonize the land he had conquered. It was as though he knew instinctively that he had come to the edge of the known world, that beyond the rolling plains of Hungary lay regions of night which even he could not explore. Instead, he sealed off what had been the land of the Avars as though it were a source of pestilence.

But the treasure of the Avars was brought into his kingdom.

Some time during the autumn of that year 796 fifteen massive wagons, each drawn by four oxen, rolled into Aachen. Travelling at a speed of around three miles an hour under good conditions, they had been weeks on the road, each one heaped high with precious metals in various forms, with gems and with pearls and priceless fabrics. There could be no better indication of the stability of the Frankish state than that this fabulous treasure, the ransom of several kings, passed unharmed through the wildest country of western Europe. They crossed the Elbe and the Danube and the Rhine, the latter crossing now very considerably eased by the handsome new bridge that spanned the river, and came at last into the new centre of the western world to the awe and wonderment of its citizens. Einhard, who was among those who witnessed the carts discharging their contents, was tempted into superlatives to try and describe the extent of the booty: 'The memory of man cannot recall any war waged by the Franks by which they were so much enriched and their wealth so increased. Up to this time, they were regarded almost as a poor people but now so much gold and silver were found in the [Avar] palace, such precious spoils were seized by them in their battles, that it might fairly be held that the Franks had righteously taken from the Huns what they had unrighteously taken from other nations.' The Avars had had little use for money: they erected no great buildings, built no roads, wrote no books, maintained no rich embassies in foreign parts. They seem to have collected like the magpie collects, attracted by anything that was shiny. The gold coinage from Byzantium alone must have weighed hundredweights but there was in addition plate looted from sacked towns, the personal ornaments from untold numbers of victims who had fallen into their hands, church treasures, garments or lengths of cloth-of-gold or silver . . . Europe would never again see such an influx of bullion until the Spanish conquest of the Americas flooded Spain with Aztec and Inca gold.

The treasure of the Avars had a similar effect upon the Frankish economy of the eighth century as the treasure of the Americas was to have upon the Spanish economy in the sixteenth century. In both cases, Europe had pumped dry its reservoir of gold, and the new flood contributed to a period of sudden expansion. Much of the glories of the Carolingian renaissance – its architecture, its manuscript illumination, its sculptures – all activities demanding specie – was the product of the goblin hoard. And certainly Charlemagne's kingdom, in these last decades of the eighth century, had need of bullion. The tens of thousands of Byzantine *solidi* which formed a substantial part of the Avar booty, were by way of being a museum piece, much as the Austrian silver thaler, or the British golden sovereign remained museum pieces beyond their period as currency in circulation, their intrinsic value surviving their extinction as currency. The *solidus* was the linear descendant of that *solidus aureus* which Julius Ceasar had established as the standard gold coin. After the fall of the Roman Empire the supply of gold gradually dried up – not an insignificant proportion of it diverted into the Ring of the *Kagans*. The process took a long time: the early Merovingians were able to pay their more important officials in currency and even make an annual contribution of 200 gold *solidi* to the royal abbey of St Denis, but by the time Charlemagne's grandfather had established himself as de facto ruler of the country, currency was only peripheral. Compared with the economy of the Roman Empire, that of the Carolingian state was based on barter, a brake on economic progress.

Charles's father, Pippin, began the task of reforming the currency, that lifeblood of a nation's economic life, by rigorously limiting the number of private mints. To the citizen of a modern state, accustomed to the idea that that state's currency is firmly controlled from the centre and that private enterprise minting is visited with the direst penalties, the casual, tangled state of Carolingian fiscal affairs comes as a surprise, an indication of its unsophisticated origins. Early in his reign, Charlemagne struck at the habit of private minting, in capitulary after capitulary emphasizing that the right of coinage belonged to him alone. But sheer convenience encouraged the survival of local mints: gold and silver plate held for economic as well as aesthetic purposes was turned into coinage not infrequently to pay the king's taxes. In 780 came the biggest change of all when, in modern terms, the state went off the gold standard; hereafter, the king decreed, the unit of currency would be the silver penny. A pound weight of silver was divided into 240 equal parts: each of these pennies, or *deniers* (from the latin *denarius*) was equal to one *sous* (the vernacular form of *solidus*). By a quirk of history, this monetary division was to cross the channel to Britain and there survived as £.s.d. with the same values relative to each other until Britain's currency reform in 1971. The state was able to provide its own silver for the coinage from the silver mines of Poitous and in the Harz mountains, but they were not equal to the demands of the economy and the silver penny grew lighter in weight, less intrinsically valuable, as well as scarcer.

In his treatment of the Avar treasure the king showed himself to be less shrewd than usual. Medieval vagueness regarding quantity makes it impossible to assess with any degree of accuracy the total value of the loot, except that it was immense. Husbanded in the royal treasury and discreetly released into the economy it would have had an immensely beneficial effect for years or decades. The king, however, chose to treat it like a windfall, making splendid gestures with it. Offa, King of Mercia, must have been surprised if delighted to receive a substantial part of the hoard; another handsome proportion was set aside for the pope and other European magnates received gifts as evidence of the power and wealth of the King of the Franks. Charlemagne possessed a species of dual vision: he was capable of taking an astonishingly long view, creating institutions which would have influence far into the future. But he was also a man of his own time, making judgements which hindsight dismisses as being almost primitive and parochial.

It was expected that a Frankish tribal leader should scatter largesse; and, conversely, much of the state's income was derived through means which later centuries would unhesitatingly define as banditry. Most of the wars undertaken were the result of the expansion of a vigorous new state, or the necessity of protecting its new frontiers. But it would be idle to deny that the prospect of booty was a powerful incentive. The Avar booty was outstanding, but there had been other massive intakes as a result of a successful campaign, notably the Saxon treasures discovered during the destruction of the Irminsul and a very handsome haul in Pavia after the conquest of the Lombards. The 'independent' Lombard duchy of Benevento paid for its freedom to the tune of 7000 gold *solidi* a year and there is little doubt that, if the Frankish treasury had kept full accounts, there would be recorded similar substantial sums flowing in from other conquered territories. A beneficial result of the increased flow of gold was that the king was no longer under such pressure to follow the dangerous practice of rewarding his nobles with gifts of land; they could be bought off with gold or silver.

The portion of the Avar hoard set aside for Pope Hadrian was intended as consolation or compensation for the fact that certain rich territories belonging to St Peter had not yet been returned to his successor, Pope Hadrian. Again and again Hadrian had written drawing this to the attention of the king: *when* would he honour that promise made by his father so long ago, and confirmed by himself in Rome? Charles temporized. Presumably he had become aware of the dangers inherent in turning the chair of St Peter into an earthly throne, the dangers inherent in turning the high priest of Christendom into a major temporal monarch with overwhelming influence in an area in which he himself was becoming ever more involved. So he went on temporizing, but evidently had a bad conscience about it, and chose from out of the hoard a generous selection of treasures and prepared to send them to Rome.

Hadrian never received them. He died on Christmas Day 795, still a comparatively young man and, according to Einhard, Charles wept because despite their many differences he had regarded the pope as a brother. For over twenty years, sometimes in alliance, sometimes in opposition, they had worked to establish a framework for a new Europe, a Europe free of Byzantine interference, working out its own destiny, ruled equally by a priest from the sacred city of Rome and a king in the royal city of Aachen. In all the long and bloody history of the relationship between the German emperors and the Roman popes, these two, for all their sparring, more nearly approached that ideal of the soldier ruling over all bodies, the priest over all souls, the two combining to make a true theocracy. But now Hadrian was dead and the man who succeeded him – who was elected with a remarkable lack of propriety on that very same day – had an unsavoury reputation in Rome itself.

The new pope took the name of Leo and fell over himself to ingratiate himself with the man who wielded the sword of St Paul. With the news of his election he sent rich symbolic gifts: the keys of the crypt in which lay the body of St Peter and the great gonfalon of the City of Rome. Leo must have been delighted to receive in reply not only a gracious acceptance of the gifts, but a promise that the treasures intended for his predecessor would be sent to him. But he must have been rendered exceedingly thoughtful by a lengthy paragraph in the letter which spelt out, without equivocation, the relative duties of monarch and pope:

> It is our duty, with the help of God, everywhere to defend the Church of Christ with our arms from the inroads of pagans and the devastation of infidels and internally to fortify it by our recognition of the Catholic Faith. It is yours, most Holy Father, with hands like the hands of Moses raised in prayer to God to help our warfare so that by your intercession, by the gift and guidance of God the Christian people may everywhere and always win the victory over the enemies of his holy Name.

Leo may well have reflected that the pope was being allocated a remarkably passive role in the scenario as sketched out by the monarch.

He had too much to lose to raise objections but shortly afterwards arranged for a permanent record that would put the matter in correct perspective. On the walls of the mother church, the Lateran, a mosaic was created in which St Peter – an immense figure against a gold background – is bestowing the symbols of power to two small men kneeling at his feet; Hadrian, as pope, is receiving the pallium, Charles as monarch, is receiving the banner of Rome – the same banner that Hadrian had sent him.

However, there was no doubt who, in real life, depended upon whom. In April 799 a pope made yet another journey over the Alps to plead for help from the mighty Frank. His plea was not, perhaps, very clear for a spirited attempt had been made to tear his tongue out, and it is probable that he could not see very clearly either, for at the same time an attempt had been made to gouge out his eyes. Who had conducted this outrage on the body of Christ's Vicar? Lombards? Saxons? Saracens? No, mumbled Pope Leo III, the people who had tried to tear out his eyes and tongue were fellow Romans, some of them fellow priests.

10 The Emperor

The story that Leo had to tell was startling in the extreme. On 25 April of that year he had been taking part in one of the great celebrations of the Church, the annual ceremony called the Greater Litany in which the pope, surrounded by his court, went in solemn procession through the city to the church of St Lawrence. Accompanying him in their proper place were two nephews of the late pope, Paschalis and Campulus, both high dignitaries of the Church, Paschalis being *primicerius* and Campulus Bishop of Gaeta. Paschalis had apologized for not wearing the heavy chasuble of his office, on the grounds of ill-health; Leo had forgiven him and the two men took their place near him.

Paschalis had divested himself of the heavy, clumsy garment because it would have impeded him in what he planned to do. Half-way along the street now known as the Corso, an armed band of conspirators burst upon the procession which broke up and scattered in alarm. Before the pope could escape, Paschalis and Campulus grasped him, dragged him off his mule and hurled him to the ground where he was held down while an attempt was made to cut out his tongue and gouge out his eyes. According to the official papal biographer, they actually succeeded but he was later miraculously healed. This is presumably the hyperbole one comes to expect of a papal biographer to enhance the sanctity of their subject, although the usually cautious Einhard too believed that the attackers had succeeded in their objective: 'The Romans had torn out his eyes and cut off his tongue,' he recorded. Later, however, Leo was able to resume his duties in the normal manner and the probability is that in the confusion of the attack with a number of men striving to wreak their hatred on the fallen man, only superficial injuries were inflicted.

After the attack Leo was imprisoned in a monastery but, with the help of a few loyal members of his court, he escaped and made his way to St Peter's. This, however, was only a respite: the men who had dared to lay hands on Christendom's high priest had already committed sacrilege and would not hesitate to invade the basilica in order to complete whatever work they had in mind. The pope, ironically, was saved from the Romans by a Lombard. Winichis, Duke of Spoleto, one of Charles's most loyal generals was in Rome in his capacity of *missus* sent by the king on an errand to the Lateran. Hearing of the outrage inflicted on the pope he hastened with a bodyguard to St Peter's, took Leo under his protection and removed him to Spoleto. He rested there while a messenger was sent hastening to Francia asking the king's will in the matter. Bring him here, was the response and, escorted by Winichis, Leo made his way to Paderborn where Charles was planning another campaign against the Saxons. Hard on the heels of Winichis there came another deputation sent by Paschalis and Campulus, accusing the pope of a remarkably wide variety of crimes, ranging from adultery to simony.

The murderous attack upon Leo by members of his own consecrated court was a harbinger of the shameful, degenerate period a century hence when the Golden City became a moral sewer; when popes gained the throne by murder and were themselves subject to the rule of courtesans in that period defined, by a cardinal historian, as the Pornocracy. The Donation of Constantine had turned a spiritual office into a highly lucrative earthly one. In the first months of his pontificate Leo had striven to correct a number of abuses which his predecessor Hadrian had tolerated. And Hadrian had tolerated them because they had been committed by relatives, his nephews. For the first time there appeared in the annals of the Church that phrase, which would be a bane to it for centuries: the 'papal nephew' who greedily sought to make as much hay as possible while the sun shone during his relative's reign. The cause of the outrage in the via Corso was a squabble over property rights, but because of the ecclesiastical nature of the people involved it could be wrapped up in high-sounding phrases. Leo could claim, reasonably enough, that the attack on his person was not only sacrilege but an outbreak of lawlessness and savagery intolerable in a civilized world. Paschalis and Campulus responded by reiterating their charges that Leo was unfit to be head of the Christian church in the west because of his moral failings. Both appealed to the king, tacitly recognizing in the most unequivocal manner that there was the only true source of law and order in Europe.

Charles was in a quandary. He was on the verge of launching what was intended to be the final, crushing campaign against the Saxons. Already his son Charles was in action as one arm of that pincer formation which had proved so successful in the past, advancing along the Elbe, calling in as reinforcements those new members of the Frankish state, the Slavs. In addition, there was about to be set in motion one of the largest forced migrations in history, with thousands of Saxons moved into the Rhineland and their places taken by an equal number of Franks. Was all this to be halted because of the endless internecine hatred among the wretched Romans?

Yes, was Alcuin's unequivocal advice. As soon as Charles had grasped the nature of the problem before him, he had called in his advisers of whom Alcuin, in this matter certainly, was chief. The old man pleaded ill-health to avoid the long, tiring journey from Tours to Paderborn and it is due to this fortunate accident that there survives documentary evidence of a moment of profound change in western Europe, the moment when a number of tributaries of thought began to merge into a main stream. For in his letter of advice to the king, discussing the nature of law and where its true source lay, Alcuin of York first used the words *Imperator Romanorum* in connection with the name of the King of the Franks.

Alcuin agreed that the Saxon campaign was important, but compared with what was happening in Rome it faded into insignificance. With his Anglo-Saxon love of analogy he argued, 'On no account must you forego the care of the head. It is a smaller matter that the feet, than that the head, should be in pain.' He then went on to outline the structure of legal authority in Europe: 'Hitherto, there have been three persons in the world higher than all others. One is the Apostolic Sublimity which is accustomed to rule by delegated power the see of St Peter, the Prince of the Apostles.' And we have just seen how his own people treat Peter's successor. 'The next is the imperial dignity and secular power of the Second Rome. How impiously the governor of that Empire has been treated not by strangers but by his own people universal fame has abundantly reported.' The third power was the 'royal dignity', that which Charlemagne wielded and which, Alcuin argued, whatever the theories, was the only one of the three able to exercise real authority. 'Lo, now upon you alone reposes the whole salvation of the Churches of Christ. You are the avenger of crime, the guide of the wanderers, the comforter of the mourners, the exaltation of the righteous.'

Charlemagne might well have pondered as to the nature of the road down which Alcuin was directing him. He, whose whole life had been shaped and formed by the spirit of the *comitatus*, that two-way relationship in which the many supported the one, the one protected the many, was invited to think the unthinkable. In the larger, as in the smaller *comitatus*, in the *comitatus* of the world itself, there could be but one head and he resided still in Constantinople. Yet Alcuin, that peerless guide through the jungle of morality, was suggesting that the Lord of the World might be found rather further to the west than was generally believed. 'These are the perilous times formerly predicted by the Truth itself because the love of many is waxing cold.'

From what happened later, it is probable that Leo, too, took up the refrain. For the king to assume the style of emperor would be simply the substituting of a de facto for a de jure situation, a repetition, if on an immensely wider scale, of the transformation of the Mayor of the Palace into the King of the Franks a generation earlier. Looking round, there was excellent grounds for such a transformation. Of the six capitals of the old Roman Empire four already recognized Charles as lord – Milan, Trier, Ravenna, and Rome – while only two – Constantinople and Nicomedia – recognized the so-called Roman Emperor. In the thirty years of his reign, he had doubled the extent of the kingdom, thrusting its frontiers out in each direction of the compass while, in that same period, the Byzantine empire had steadily contracted until the 'emperor' ruled over little more than a strip along the eastern Mediterranean.

Charles listened, but made no comment, certainly none of a nature to attract the attention of those eagerly waiting for a sign. This was a path, alluring though it might be, down which he was not willing, at the moment, to tread. Immediately, there was the need to re-establish Leo. Charles seems to have had no real doubt that the charges against the pope were trumped up. During his lengthy sojourn in Paderborn, Leo consecrated a new church, proof enough that the king continued to regard him as authentic priest and pontiff. Nevertheless, the bodyguard and guard of honour which accompanied him back to Rome in the autumn of that same year included a number of the royal *missi* charged to conduct what was, in effect, a trial of the pope in Rome itself. It was an unprecedented situation. In the Byzantine court the Patriarch was simply another palace official, but in the west the pope had long been a virtually autonomous figure. The fact that Leo had not simply assented to his trial, but had actually brought it about, was one more brick in that growing structure to which no man had yet given a name. The trial took place in December, found the pope innocent of the charges levied against him and, by extension, condemned his attackers and accusers, Paschalis and Campulus – but their fate was postponed until the king could come to Rome in his capacity of Patrician.

It was an inescapable journey but Charles, it seems, was in no hurry to undertake it. His reluctance to become further embroiled in Rome might have been sparked off by the visit of yet another Byzantine embassy to the Frankish court. The ambassador brought interesting news: indeed, within the context of its day, bizarre news. The young emperor, Constantine VI, had been virtually deposed, and his mother Irene ruled in his stead. She was evidently anxious to have as friend the man who was de facto ruler of the major part of the western world. The marriage between Hrotrud and the titular emperor was still on the cards – but it was not out of the question for there to be another and even more dazzling marriage between Franks and Byzantines, for Charles was again a widower. Throughout that year of 799 and into the first spring of the ninth century, the king seems to have been pondering a number of related problems, unable or unwilling to come to a decision. But in spring 800 he began a very leisurely move southwards. Leaving Aachen, he sailed down the Rhine into what would be the North Sea, and turned south on an inspection of the coast. Viking attacks were becoming ever more common and though, at this stage, they were little more than pinpricks in the enormous body of the kingdom, still it behoved a good general to look to his defences.

He had a particular and personal reason for coming to this part of the country for his 'son-in-law', the poet Angilbert, was Abbot of the monastery of St Riquier, about thirty miles from modern Amiens. The fact that the abbot had given the king's daughter two bastards seems, if anything, to have influenced the king in his favour for the young man had been put in charge of a very important project indeed, the building and running of the largest monastery in Europe, and the 'sacred city' of Centula attached to it. Charles was personally paying for the building, probably out of the Avar treasure, and work had begun some two years earlier. On completion in 799 it housed some 300 monks – but even this was surpassed by the city on its doorstep, conceived as an integral part of the project. Today, St Riquier's population is a little over 1000; in Charlemagne's time the town housed at least 7000 people – and housed them not in the haphazard manner of a later medieval town but as planned as a Roman city. A census taken in 831 disclosed that it had 2500 houses and five churches arranged in wards, each ward being allocated to a particular class or profession. Thus in the 'military ward' there were 110 knights, their houses clustered round their own church. Most of the inhabitants paid for accommodation by service to the monastery.

Surrounding this 'holy city' was a complex of suburbs and seven villages, all taking part in the ceremonial of the monastery. These details were recorded and their survival gives a remarkably clear picture of the order, virtually amounting to a military discipline, which prevailed in and around a Carolingian monastery. Here one sees, momentarily but vividly, the forces at work turning barbarism into civilization, the monastery processing the raw materials of rural life into polished form. Centula, like so much else, was swallowed up by the wave of barbarism that swept across Europe after the collapse of the Carolingian empire, for it was burned by the Norsemen in 881. But the seed so carefully sown flourished again to create a resurrected if smaller community, the present town of St Riquier whose parish church is the chapel of the original monastery.

The next stage of the King's journey was up the Seine to Rouen, thence by land to the monastery of St Martin's where he planned a lengthy stay with Alcuin. He had already warmly invited the Englishman to accompany him to Rome but again Alcuin pleaded old age and ill-health and, in so doing, gave a picture of the conditions in the Golden City which had come to his ears.

> You chide me that I prefer the smoke-grimed roofs of Tours to the gilded citadels of the Romans but remember the saying of Solomon, 'It is better to dwell in a corner of the house-top than with a brawling woman in a wide house'. Tours, thanks to your bounty, rests in peace. But Rome, which has once been touched by the discord of brethren, still keeps the poison which has been instilled into her veins and thus compels your venerable Dignity to hasten from your sweet abodes in Germany in order to repress the fury of this pestilence.

Charles arrived in Rome on 24 November. Leo had come to meet him some fourteen miles outside the city and, in response to the pope's urgent request, for the second time only in his life he abandoned the traditional dress of the Franks and dressed himself in the simple, dignified costume of a Patrician of Rome. On 2 December he presided over a great synod in the basilica in St Peter's where Leo formally declared his innocence of the charges levied against him. This was indeed a show trial for it was now that Paschalis and Campulus were brought forward before the assembled dignitaries of the Church, including those of their own family who deemed it safer now to disassociate themselves. Each sought to blame the other, Campulus screaming at his companion in disaster, 'In an evil hour did I behold your face. It is you who have brought me to this peril.' They were condemned to death on a charge not of sacrilege but of treason, Charlemagne tacitly allowing this recognition of the pope as sovereign in his own city. At Leo's request, the death sentence was reduced to life imprisonment.

On 25 December, the king attended mass in St Peter's, dressed in Roman costume and, while kneeling in prayer, was startled to see the pope approaching him with a glittering, golden object in his hand. With a rehearsed gesture Leo raised the imperial crown high and placed it on the silvering head of the Frank. Simultaneously, and again obviously rehearsed, the entire congregation burst out: 'To Carolus Augustus, crowned by God, mighty and pacific emperor, be life and victory.' Disconcerted, the new emperor rose, towering above the pope and his court as they sank in the ritual obeisance. Later he was to tell Einhard forcefully that 'he would not have entered the church on that day, though it was the chief festival of the Church, if he could have foreseen the design of the pope'. But the act had been accomplished, a completely illegal act which created an emperor in the west as mirror and parody of him who ruled in the east. So said the Byzantine lawyers and they were right, for there could be only one Lord of the World, only one *Imperator Romanorum*.

In the year 747, shortly before the birth of the newly created emperor, one of the terrifying plagues of the Middle East carried off probably half the population of Constantinople. A high proportion of the dead were the descendants of the original Latin founders of the city, those who had come over with Constantine in the fourth century to turn the city of Byzantium into the city of Constantinople and so make it the new capital of the still undivided Roman Empire. Greeks began to occupy the places once occupied by Latins, irrevocably altering the racial structure of the city and contributing to the drift away from the west. In the eighth century, a few years before Charlemagne's birth, the drift was accelerated into rift by religion when the iconoclastic controversy hammered in the final wedge.

As with so much regarding the religious beliefs of these earlier centuries it is again essential for the twentieth century to practise a virtual suspension of belief – of the kind which accepts the Ghost in *Hamlet* as an essential part of the plot – fully to understand the effect of the impact of religion on society. From the distance of a millennium it is scarcely possible to believe that the civilized world could be sundered into two, that Christians should rend Christians in one of the bloodiest of wars and that the two rulers of the world should devote endless hours and skill all occasioned by a consideration as to whether graphic or sculptured representations of the human form should be permitted in sacred buildings. But so it was.

The Christian emperor in Constantinople had inherited the dual role of priest and king that the pagan emperors in Rome had enjoyed. When the seat of the empire moved to the east, the bishop of Rome naturally enjoyed rather more freedom than his opposite number, the patriarch of Constantinople, but both, in the eyes of the emperor, were subordinate to him in spiritual as well as temporal matters. Constantinople developed into the true theological centre of Christianity, to the accompaniment of endless intrigues and ferocious palace revolutions as religion and politics interacted upon each other.

Nevertheless, there was no major clash between emperor and bishop on a purely religious issue until the year 726 when the reigning emperor Leo issued an edict forbidding the erection of images in churches. The edict spelt the doom of his empire in the west: the peoples of Italy and those influenced by them were touched, for the first time, on a universally personal matter.

The primitive Christians had attacked image-worship as the work of the devil and there had been wholesale destruction of idols when Christianity had at last triumphed. But over the succeeding centuries the images crept back, appearing under new names but, to the critical eye, with a role identical to that of the old idols. It was the Christians of the east who first began to feel that much of the pagan religion that their forefathers had destroyed, at so great a cost of martyrs' blood, was imperceptibly being restored. Disturbed by the mockery of their iconoclastic Muslim neighbours, their devotion to images was subject to a strain of which their western brethren were free. In a decade the infidel Muslims had overcome city after Christian city, each of which had been under the protection of some holy image. In vain, monks made the standard defence of supernatural prophylactics – that it was the lack of faith of the possessor, not the lack of virtue in the image, which rendered it useless. The religious disputation became political, bringing with it riot and the ever-present threat of civil war. The emperor Leo then solved the problem, as he thought, by coming down on the side of the iconoclasts and issued his edict in 726 commanding the breaking of all images in the empire, in the west as well as the east.

The reigning pope, Gregory II, was the first Roman-born pope to occupy the Chair of St Peter after a long succession of Greeks, a man as unsubtle as the emperor. He defied the edict, returning again and again to the theme that he and his followers did not worship, but only reverenced images. But in referring to a threat of an attack upon the great statue of St Peter in Rome, he slipped into a curious and ambiguous phraseology. He himself had no fear of the emperor's rage, he said. 'I have but to retire twenty-four miles into the Campania and you might as well follow the wind. But for the statue of Peter himself, which all the kingdoms of the West esteem as a god on earth, the whole West would take a terrible revenge.' Whether he intended it to be understood that it was the statue, or St Peter himself, whom the west held as a god on earth, the statement could have helped little to repudiate the charge that Europe was fast falling into idolatry.

The westerners were indifferent to the theological niceties. The bishop of Rome had spoken for them clearly and definitively, and his Italian subjects supported him even at cost of their own blood. It was in defence of the gods of the hearth, the little familiar objects that rendered local and personal the vast impersonality of Christian theology, that they broke the cord that bound them to the east.

Imperial edict was followed by imperial action, and troops who could not be found to defend a province from barbarian invaders were swiftly available to enforce a theological point. A fierce and bloody war was fought around the Byzantine exarchate of Ravenna in 726. The Byzantines retreated northward and the scenes of carnage were so frightful and bloody that for six years thereafter the inhabitants of the Po valley were urged by their priests to abstain from eating fish from the river for fear of involuntary cannibalism. After the violence of open warfare had abated there remained still a nominal allegiance to the emperor. Gregory himself had no intention of usurping temporal power but he had charted a path that others could not fail to follow. Just nine months after his death in 731, the effective severance from the east was made when a synod in Rome pronounced: excommunicate all those who would attack the images of the saints. It was a discreet enough pronouncement, for the emperor was not mentioned by name and there was some doubt, too, as to exactly who had the power to excommunicate whom, but the implications were clear. The emperor and his theologians alike were rejected by the west.

All this had happened some twenty years before Charlemagne's birth, but like a hidden fire in a peat bog it continued to burn, now smouldering invisibly, now bursting into open flame, gradually absorbing more and more of his attention. And affairs took a bizarre twist when, in 769, the young heir to the Byzantine throne married a beautiful Athenian girl called Irene. As it happened, the year before, Charlemagne had himself inherited the Frankish crown from his father: he and Irene were destined never to meet but the lives of the beautiful, devious Athenian and the outwardly bluff but inwardly equally subtle Frank were to be curiously intertwined.

At the heart of Constantinople was the imperial palace, with its beautiful gardens swooping down to the Bosphorus, flanked by the great building still called the Roman Senate House and, nearby, the forum which still bore the name of Augusteum. In the heart of the palace, like a golden spider at the centre of an intricate web, was the vice-regent of God, Basileus, the very apex and distillation of Byzantine society, the emperor. In his costume and the ceremonial attending him he was an extraordinary amalgam of east and west, of Roman and Greek, of Pagan and Christian. He was still acclaimed by the army as the Caesars had been acclaimed, emphasizing still that *imperator* was an army rank. He was crowned still with the *torque* of a centurion, and the general's cloak, the *paludamentum* placed over his shoulders. But beneath the cloak was the *chlamys* of a Macedonian soldier and he no longer held in his hand the terrestrial orb of Constantine but, instead, the *akakia* or parchment scroll signifying his orthodox belief and a pouch of earth signifying mortality. For, though the patriarch might be subordinate to the emperor, the priest had firm control of the ruler, influencing every aspect of society.

Irene's father-in-law was Constantine V, nicknamed Copronymus. The insulting nature of the nickname (he was supposed to have defiled the font when lowered into it for baptism) was part of the campaign of vilification which has helped to obscure his many real qualities. It was he who gave that organ to Charlemagne's father which so impressed the Frankish chroniclers and had no little effect upon Charlemagne's own cultural development. But Constantine V was a passionate iconoclast, continuing the stern policy of his father Leo; not content with simply breaking or forbidding images but torturing and executing those suspected of their worship. He welcomed the Athenian girl into his house, greeting her with a splendid naval pageant when she arrived off the Golden Horn for her wedding to the young Leo IV. But what Constantine did not know was that he had introduced a species of Trojan horse into the kingdom. During his lifetime, when deviation from the pure practice of iconoclasm was visited with instant and most severe punishment, she conformed perforce to the prevailing code. But it was scarcely possible for Irene, daughter of a city that was the very well-spring of European art, to embrace the austere cult of iconoclasm, and with the death of Constantine she discreetly began to revert. But not discreetly enough. Her husband was a nonentity with only one real interest in life, the maintenance of his father's policy, and he was enraged and outraged when some of the demonic images were actually found in his wife's bed. His father would have solved the problem of such treachery in a simple, direct manner; Leo lacked the courage, limiting himself to banishing her from the palace. And it would be unwise, too, to overlook the part that sexual love can play in the affairs of kingdoms, for his wooing of the Athenian girl had undoubtedly been at his personal desire and not simply a dynastic negotiation. He loved his wife, unfortunately for himself, unfortunately for his empire and, most unfortunately of all, for his son. He died soon after at the age of twenty-five and his widow, still a young woman in the full flush of her beauty, stepped into the foreground as regent of her ten-year-old son Constantine VI.

The Byzantine constitution placed the Empress Irene in an unusually powerful position. She had been regarded as Augusta on marriage to her husband and that role was now transmitted to her in her capacity of regent – in effect, co-emperor with her son. She therefore had dual control of the levers of power, as empress and as co-ruler, together with the influence a mother could wield over a son – particularly a weak little boy like Constantine. Nevertheless, secure though she might be consti-tutionally, her position was unenviable both as a woman in a male-dominated society, and as the holder of an unpopular religious belief. She cautiously set about restoring image-worship, a move which would at least gain her the tacit backing of the pope and his co-religionists. It was largely through her influence that the Second Nicene Council came up with those tortuous definitions, attempting to draw distinctions between the honour paid to saints and the worship paid only to God, which brought the idols flooding back into the Byzantine Church. And to secure her position she made that marriage overture to Charlemagne, the proposal to unite his little daughter Hrotrud with the eleven-year-old Constantine.

Charlemagne accepted in principle, a Greek entourage was provided for the little princess to give her a tincture of Byzantine culture in what Irene privately thought was the barbarism of Francia, and one of the great Ifs of history came into being. Would the marriage of these two children have served to mend the split between east and west, creating eventually one great empire from Asia Minor to the Baltic? It seems improbable, and yet the seemingly frail bond of a matrimonial alliance was to produce remarkably strong structures over the ensuing centuries. Charlemagne, who already had strong reservations about the wisdom of accepting an imperial crown, would certainly have rejected it outright if his daughter was reigning as empress. The Holy Roman Empire, with all its endless ramifications down the centuries to the Habsburgs, would have been stillborn.

The marriage never came into being. For six years, from its first proposal in 781 to the final rupture in 787, Charles temporized while the Greeks at first continued to press the matter and then, too, changed their minds. The cause of the breakdown was a tangle of personal and political motivations, with the personal probably predominating. It is impossible to overlook Charles's ambiguous attitude towards his daughters, his deep reluctance to have them leave his side – a reluctance so deep that he was perfectly prepared to see them bear bastards. This was, in fact, to be Hrotrud's destiny: she died, a beautiful spinster at the age of thirty-eight, leaving a son who eventually became abbot of St Denis, creating one more confusion in the endlessly confused Carolingian genealogy. But the personal reluctance may not have been all the king's. It is probable that Fastrada, too, had a hand in the marriage breakdown, reluctant to see her step-daughter elevated to a position far above her own. And such an attitude, though for different reasons, may well have influenced Irene. By the time she became aware that the Franks were dragging their feet she had come to certain conclusions as to how the Byzantine empire might best be governed, and they emphatically did not include her son, with or without a Frankish empress by his side. There was one further element that contributed to the breakdown: Adelchis, the son of the conquered and deposed Lombard king Desiderius, was in Constantinople and, through him, the Byzantines hoped to re-establish themselves in Italy, regaining control of what they still regarded merely as a rebellious province. What they had overlooked was summed up in a proverb by the Italians – who had considerable experience of this type of situation – 'He who is thrown out by the door rarely returns through the window.'

The Byzantine attempt to use Adelchis as a catspaw by placing him on the throne of his father was a total and utter disaster, demonstrating once and for all that not only was the east now completely sundered from the west, but that the west had found its identity through the king of the Franks. A large Byzantine army landed at Brindisi and marched towards the still independent Lombard duchy of Benevento, naturally expecting the Beneventans to rise and join them in their fight for 'freedom'. The Byzantine intelligence system, so effective in palace intrigues, proved woefully inadequate for military purposes. Franks were actually in a minority of the army opposing them, the bulk being made up of Lombards. The commanders of the army were Lombards: Winichis – the same man who would later save Pope Leo – actually commanded the Frankish detachment while the Duke of Spoleto, and Adelchis's own uncle the Duke of Benevento, commanded the Lombard cavalry. The Byzantines were smashed, over 4000 of them killed and only 1000 captured. Adelchis managed to escape and returned to Constantinople with the news that there were no longer 'Franks' and 'Lombards' and 'Italians', only members of one great state, an international *comitatus*.

Meanwhile, in the warren of the imperial palace on the shores of the Bosphorus, an even deadlier and far more unnatural struggle was in process: the battle for dominance between Empress Irene and her twenty-year-old son, the titular *Imperator Romanorum*. The battle was to continue for seven murderous years, seven years during which now the one, now the other would emerge briefly as victor in one of those palace feuds of the Byzantines which would give the world a synonym for all that was complex, treacherous and lethal. During those seven years, while the king of the Franks steadily, competently, extended his hegemony over western Europe, the Byzantine empire inflicted grievous wounds upon itself. In August 797 Irene gained a temporary advantage and decided to make it permanent. Her son Constantine, now twenty-seven years of age, was betrayed to his mother by his supposed supporters when he attempted to flee the country. He was brought back to the palace and there, in the same Purple Chamber where he had been born, his eyes were torn out on the orders of his mother. Blinding, and amputation of tongue, were common Byzantine methods of disabling an opponent short of death, but even the Byzantines, inured to almost every cruelty of a palace feud, were brought up sharp by the monstrous act. 'The sun was darkened for seventeen days and did not give forth his rays so that ships wandered about and drifted hither and thither and all men said and confessed that on account of the blinding of the Emperor the sun withheld his beams. And thus did Irene his mother acquire the sovereignty'. So recorded the chronicler Theophanes.

For acquire it she had. At the sacred season of Easter the following year, that same Easter of 799 when in distant Rome Pope Leo was attacked by his own people and a train of events was set in motion, 'the Greek woman' went in state through the streets of Constantinople to her crowning. She travelled, in the imperial manner, in a golden chariot drawn by white horses; patricians of the empire, in the imperial manner, walked humbly beside her; she threw, in the imperial manner, handfuls of money into the crowd who were only too happy to cry out, in response, 'Long life to the Augusta Irene'. But among the more thoughtful members of the Byzantine court there began to be whispered the belief that 'a wonderful and horrible thing had been done in the polity of the Romans'. Far to the west, the king of the Franks heard of the affair and shook his head and gave it of his opinion that it was sacrilege for a woman to pick up the sceptre and the *akakia* and so rule, for God had decreed that 'woman, as the weaker vessel and the one most easily deceived, ought to be in subjection and repressed by the authority of the man'. And, pondering, he perhaps came to certain conclusions regarding the nature of imperial power and who best should wield it.

There is no reason to doubt Charlemagne's word when he told Einhard that, if he had known what the pope intended to do on that Christmas Day of 800 in the basilica of St Peter, he would never have entered the church even on such a day. What he was objecting to was either the timing or, more likely, that the pope had stolen a march on him by performing the actual act of coronation, for the inescapable implication was that he who could bestow a crown had the right to take it away again. Eleven years later, when he arranged the coronation of his surviving son Louis as co-emperor, he took very great care to ensure that the crown was bestowed by himself, and not by any representative of the Church – a precedent Napoleon Bonaparte was to observe and to follow.

But though Charlemagne may well have been surprised and, indeed, disconcerted by the timing of Leo's act, he must have been perfectly well aware that something of this nature was in the wind. Every action of the pope's since his accession three years earlier had been directed towards the concept of a dual ruler of Christendom, general and priest, emperor and pope. Alcuin had spelled out the fact that there was a vacuum at the summit of power and that it was his duty, not simply his privilege, to fill it and so provide protection for God's church. His favourite theological work, St Augustine's *City of God*, gave substance and authority for the idea. This was the book which, during the quiet periods of his meals, the king had had read aloud to him until he must have known every chapter by heart, familiar with its great ideal of a society in which the faith of Christ was strengthened by the discipline of the Caesars.

At a purely practical level, it was unthinkable that Alcuin who was in regular contact with correspondents in Rome, in regular contact with his friend and master in Aachen, would not have been aware of, and would not have passed on, the information that the Romans were prepared to grant him the greatest of all titles, that of *Imperator Romanorum*. Whoever stage-managed the event in St Peter's on that Christmas Day had done his work well by arranging that 'acclamation' by the Roman people and clergy as the crown was put on the King's head. Even in the most dictatorial and tyrannical days of the classical empire the concept that the emperor was chosen – was acclaimed – by the army and the people, that despite outward appearances the great structure of the Roman Empire was a *res publica* (that which belonged to all the people), was never abandoned even though it became a formality. Whatever his private thoughts might have been on that day, the new emperor not only acquiesced in the ceremonies that followed but quite evidently had been prepared for some aspect of them. He was anointed, and afterwards presided over the anointing of his son Charles, thereby making clear to the world who was his natural successor. Later, on that visit to Rome, he gave great gifts to the shrine of St Peter, gifts quite distinct from that treasure of the Avars already promised and which, in their ostentatiousness, argues that their intention was to commemorate an occasion far more important than that of the visit of the Patrician to his city. There seems to have been a certain sly, not unamiable malice in his gift of an enormous golden chalice to the pope. Made out of solid metal and decorated with precious stones, it weighed an astonishing fifty pounds, its golden pattern adding a further twenty-five pounds. Every time the unfortunate pontiff hoisted it in the act of consecration he must have been forcibly reminded of the occasion on which it was donated. His successors prudently turned it into specie.

With that act of coronation the arguments started, arguments regarding the legitimacy of the act, begun by the Byzantines and continuing on century after century into our own time. The Byzantines were simultaneously indignant and contemptuous. The Empress Irene at *her* coronation the year before had specifically taken the title *basileus* (emperor) and not the neutral *basilissa* (empress), and though the Byzantines might deplore her character and her sex and the manner in which she had gained power, that power had been legitimately granted her by all the ancient due customs and ceremonies. In their eyes, Charlemagne was but the latest of a long line of rebellious generals who had got above themselves. Theophanes, the same chronicler who had recorded how the sun had hid its face on Irene's hideous crime, also mockingly reported how the ignorant Romans had anointed their upstart 'emperor' from head to toe in oil, stripping him for the purpose in the cold of a Roman December. At intervals, down the centuries, other critics would follow suit, particularly during those periods when the new race of Germanic emperors was seeking to impose order upon the turbulent city whence they took their name. Thus a chronicler of Salerno two centuries later was bitterly recording, 'The men about the court of Charles the Great called him Emperor because he wore a precious crown upon his head. But in truth, no one should be called Emperor save the man who presides over the Roman – that is, the Constantinopolitan kingdom. The kings of the Gauls have now usurped to themselves that name, but in ancient times they were never so called.' And, standing neutral over them all, in the nineteenth century the great British historian James Bryce who first analysed and dissected then rebuilt the enigmatic structure called the Holy Roman Empire, remarked, 'Charles did not conquer, nor the pope give, nor the people elect. As the act was unprecedented, so it was illegal.' But it was justified, Bryce concluded, in effect echoing Alcuin a thousand years later: 'It was the revolt of the ancient Western capital against a daughter who had become a mistress: an exercise of the sacred right of insurrection, justified by the weakness and wickedness of the Byzantine princes, hallowed to the eyes of the world by the sanction of Christ's representative'.

Some feeble apologists sought to argue that the new emperor was the emperor of the west only, taking up the crown that had been laid down by the pathetic little Romulus Augustulus, the last 'western' emperor in 476. The Romans themselves, the actual citizens of the city on the banks of the Tiber which had given birth to the stupendous concept eight centuries before, would have nothing of this hesitant, diffident, dubious approach – at least, during the honeymoon period. As far as they were concerned it was they who had created the *Imperator Romanorum*, they who could withdraw the title from one and give it to another. The enormous silver-haired Frank, dressed in the tunic of a Patrician and wearing the imperial crown as he descended the great flight of steps of St Peter's on that winter's afternoon was, as far as they were concerned, Lord of the World, *Imperator Romanorum*.

Charles himself was not so sure. He was fully prepared to regard himself as the ultimate lawful authority in the world but he had no wish to be known as 'Emperor of the Romans'. Over the years, he and his constitutional advisers had worked out a system in which all nations in his immense state would be equal, a kind of federation. He was King of the Franks, King of the Saxons, King of the Lombards; if, now, he were to accept that title 'Emperor of the Romans' it would put these arrogant men in a position of honour they had done nothing to earn. The Romans, and by extension the Italians, were no more, even if they were no less, than other citizens of the reborn empire. For the first few months after his coronation he therefore studiously used his old, purely royal titles. But passing through Ravenna, the old Byzantine exarchate, on his way back to Aachen, the scholars on his staff, delving in the extensive archives, came across a title which exactly stated what he wanted to state, *Romanum gubernans Imperium* ('Governing the Roman Empire'), and this he took so that ever afterwards the resounding title of the first of the Western Emperors was 'Charles, Most Serene Augustus, crowned by God, great and peaceful Emperor, governing the Roman Empire and, by the mercy of God, king of the Lombards and the Franks'. But the new Roman Emperor carried away from Ravenna something in addition to an idea and a phrase. Without troubling to obtain the formal permission of Pope Leo, nominal overlord of the city, Charles gave orders that the great statue of Theodoric, that other Teuton who had so nearly refounded the Roman Empire four centuries before, should be removed from his palace and carried to the palace of Aachen, the New Rome.

11   Aachen: The Rome
of the North

Out of the great wreck of empire only one building remains which can be associated, beyond doubt, with Charlemagne, the chapel of the palace of Aachen. But it has survived in such a perfect form, its interior so intensely evocative, that it acts as a distillation of all that the man created. Indeed, the fact that it has not only survived, but is unscathed, in earlier centuries would have been defined quite simply as a miracle. For the relatively small city of Aachen, with a population of under 200,000, was mercilessly bombarded by the Allies during their advance to the Rhine in 1944 and, when captured, was as mercilessly bombarded by the retreating Wehrmacht.

Charlemagne built his palace on the slope of a hill. At the top is the palace proper. The Carolingian remains consist of the massive tower known as the *Granusturm*, and the undercroft of brick whose pink cement is evidence of Roman precursors for it is made of crushed Roman bricks. In the early fourteenth century the burghers of Aachen took over the decaying palace and transformed it into their *Rathaus* (town hall) and, if the existence of the undercroft and the *Granusturm*, still integral parts of the building, be taken as continuity, the building represents probably the oldest example, in Europe certainly, of a municipal building in continual use. It is in the massive fourteenth-century Coronation Hall, with its murals of the exploits of Charlemagne, that each year on Ascension Day the Karlpreis is presented to the statesman who has contributed most to the cause of European unity. Their portraits hang on the stars, one for every year, beginning with that of Winston Churchill.

The chapel stands lower down the slope, connected to the palace by a low line of buildings on one side of a great open square, the *Katschof*. The first and oldest chapel in the world, taking its name from the fact that the capella of St Martin was housed in it, it is curiously reticent. The visitor approaching it from the lower town and passing through the tangle of medieval streets that also survived the bombardment will all but stumble upon it before being aware of its identity. The original polygon within which is the sacred octagon is plain to see, the later additions of building huddling protectively round it without masking its shape. The entrance is also low-key, through a little Baroque porch in which hang the great original bronze doors. The chapel is rigorously controlled by its custodians, the central area under Barbarossa's great chandelier being always reserved for prayer. But standing near the golden high altar and looking up towards the gallery one becomes aware of a glimmer, a subdued light. Charlemagne's throne is made of a light-coloured marble which glimmers in the rich gloom so that it is as though a presence were brooding over the chapel. At the gallery level are the thirty-two exquisite marble columns which were brought from Ravenna and which, perhaps, are as great an indication of the power and stability of the Carolingian state as was the transportation of the Avar treasure. Charlemagne was still only king of the Franks when the pope eagerly replied to his request 'that we should grant you the mosaics and marbles of the palace in the city of Ravenna, as well as other specimens to be found both on the pavement and on the walls. We willingly grant your request because, by your royal struggles, the church of your patron St Peter enjoys many benefits for which great will be your reward in heaven.' Each of the great columns must have required its own ox-cart, drawn by at least two oxen, each with its driver, forming a remarkable convoy of some thirty-two carts and men and at least sixty-four oxen, travelling at a snail's pace from Ravenna, through the passes of the Alps and so at last into the heart of the kingdom of the Franks. A thousand years later, Napoleon stole them during his great looting operation but they were returned after the collapse of his own empire.

The access to the gallery and the throne is remarkable only for its lack of anything remarkable. It would be natural to expect here, the approach to the ultimate majesty of empire, some grandiloquent stair-case. Instead there is a simple flight of steps that could belong to a country church. In keeping with the all-pervading symbolism of the chapel the rough stone steps that lead up directly to the throne itself are six in number, the same as those leading to Solomon's throne. The throne of the first Emperor of the Western Empire consists of a few, simple marble slabs with no decoration whatsoever. In deference to the origins of his people, Charlemagne placed a symbolic wooden seat in the centre of the Mediterranean marble, but that is all. Between 962, when Otto the Great chose Aachen for his coronation, and 1531, thirty emperors have been crowned on this marble chair. All resisted the temptation, endemic among powerful men, to add their own impress, to 'improve' or embellish the plain, simple structure or to add their own monograms and slogans.

In Aachen, as in so many other ancient cities of Europe, the murderous bombardment of World War II destroyed much, but also involuntarily revealed much, in this case tearing away the architectural accretions of intervening centuries to reveal the Roman origins of the city. The Romans knew it as Aquisgranum, from the Gallo-Roman god of healing, Apollo/Granus, for the pungently sulphurous hot springs, still flowing abundantly, were supposed to have the power of healing as well as providing ready-made hot baths. It was these baths which first attracted Pippin, and later his son Charlemagne, together with the vast forests which made the perfect hunting ground. There was a modest villa or hunting lodge here, but the place was unknown to history until 765 when Charles, still simply the heir to the throne, made his first recorded visit. Over the years the visits grew ever more frequent for he came to love the spot and in 789 began the building of the palace. The architect was Einhard and, following the models of the Roman architect Vitruvius, he created a building which, from the sparse descriptions of it, deliberately set out to create an impression of magnificence. The imperial crown was still ten years away but this palace was intended to rival the other palace 1500 miles away at Constantinople and the sudden avalanche of Avar gold made it possible. The great hall was a long, massive building two storeys high – essentially the same proportions as the existing *Rathaus*. The ground floor housed the service quarters, while the upper contained the great reception hall and the throne room. Marble, imported from Italy, was used lavishly throughout while tapestries and murals contributed to the rich effect. Regrettably, none of the murals survived: here, of all places, would have been preserved authentic portraits of the king and his court together with at least the official view of military campaigns. Einhard linked the palace to Aachen's hot springs, providing the luxury of heating throughout the building.

The palace/chapel complex was orientated east–west whereas the street system of the Roman city had been north–south. The great building therefore permanently affected the topography of Aachen, turning the innumerable Roman squares into triangles. A line of domestic buildings on the western side of the Katschof connects the great hall with the chapel. The architect here was not Einhard but a man called Odo of Metz – not because Charlemagne had any doubts about his friend's ability but because he wanted the work to be finished as soon as possible, construction of palace and chapel probably proceeding simultaneously. Significantly, Odo, on the emperor's instructions, looked towards Byzantium, not Rome, for inspiration, for the design of the chapel closely followed that of the great Byzantine church of San Vitale in Ravenna. It was a deliberate decision but mysterious in its implications, particularly if it is considered that work began long before there was any speculation as to obtaining the imperial crown. It may have been simply a personal choice, the Frank instinctively preferring the richness and colour of Byzantine architecture compared with the austerity of Rome. But it may have been, too, a recognition that Constantinople, for all its faults, was a powerhouse of Christian thought. Symbolism pervades the whole structure for its proportions are based on the heavenly city which St John described as descending to earth in the Apocalypse. And here it is impossible to mistake the symbolism. Aachen was to be the sacred city of the north, its role summed up in that exquisite little building. Over a thousand years after its completion, the interior of the octagon probably looks exactly as it did when the emperor seated himself in the simple marble throne, for his successors, with an extraordinary sense of piety, refrained from putting their impress upon it, just as they had left the throne itself unadorned. The Emperor Henry II presented the golden altar some time before 1024 and Barbarossa gave the great chandelier, with its crown of eight lights, to mark the occasion of Charlemagne's canonization in 1165. But these are ornaments, rather than structural alterations.

From the time that the palace was ready for occupation, Charlemagne spent ever longer periods at Aachen until eventually it became his permanent base. It was never the formal, administrative centre of an empire, in the sense that Rome had been. In one sense, its establishment as his permanent base may have somewhat loosened the already exiguous bonds which linked the parts of the sprawling state, for his restless perambulations with relatively brief sojourns in widely separated towns or villas in themselves acted as a prime channel of communication. There is some substance in the gibe that the empire was never truly an empire precisely because it lacked good channels of communication. The lack of anything resembling a literate civil service meant that no matter how well-meaning or how forceful was an edict emanating from the centre, by the time it had passed through non-literate hands its subject could not but be modified, at times beyond recognition.

Nevertheless, there was one clear, constant centre to the state, the mind of the emperor, a mind wrestling not only with an unprecedented task, that of creating a blueprint for a new society, but also striving to transmit those ideals not to the handful of enlightened people around him, but to the hundreds of thousands of men, speaking a dozen different languages, who composed the empire. This comes out very clearly in the great capitulary of March 802 whose ostensible purpose was to arrange for all his subjects to take a new oath of fidelity to him as emperor. But it went far beyond that limited intention. In the words of the French historian Robert Folz, not a writer given to superlatives: 'It is impossible to overstress the nobility and originality of this language.' The capitulary begins with the technical instructions, 'I order that every man in my whole kingdom whether ecclesiastic or layman, each one according to his prayer and his purpose, who may have before promised fidelity to me in the king's name, shall now repeat that promise to me in the name of Caesar.' The order applied to everybody over the age of twelve, and the swearing was to be done in public, *missi* being despatched throughout the empire to supervise the operation. But then the capitulary goes on to emphasize that, in taking the oath, the subject was not simply binding himself to the emperor, but was binding himself to a whole new way of life. That the subject should abstain from fraud and perjury; that he should promise not to steal the emperor's goods, nor give shelter to his enemies was to be expected. But, in addition, were the exhortations to aid the poor, the sick, the helpless of all kinds, to follow the rule of the Christian Church in all things. The phrase 'Holy' Roman Empire had not yet been coined but, quite clearly, within months of that ceremony in St Peter's on Christmas Day 800, this was what Charlemagne envisaged for the future. The capitulary was only the first of a number streaming out from Aachen, couched in language that has been compared to that of sermons, striving to turn the vision into reality. The clergy were his shock troops and again and again they are threatened, encouraged, exhorted. Aware that to few men was it given to be fluent in language, to be able to express in speech the sentiments of the heart, he commissioned Paul the Deacon to compile a volume of sermons and ordered that these be used throughout the Frankish Church.

The new emperor had no hesitation in laying down theological law, consciously or unconsciously assuming that dual function of priest-king that the Caesars had possessed. It is never, in fact, wholly clear, in all those religious controversies throughout his reign upon which he pronounced as king, and later as emperor, what was his personal opinion expressed directly, what was received opinion formulated by his advisers and expressed under his seal, and what was his opinion but expressed through the medium of one or other of his advisers. At the height of the iconoclastic controversy there appeared under his authority a treatise, now known as the *Libri Carolini*, which in effect sharply rapped the knuckles of both contending parties, in particular openly and specifically criticizing the pope for his immoderate defence of iconology which came perilously near image-worship – but condemning, too, the extremists who would strip churches bare. It was not only a display of common sense remarkable for its time, but in its strong criticism of Rome made very clear that the Italian city by no means had a monopoly of religious or moral truth. (One wonders what this monarch might have made of the doctrine of papal infallibility, propounded a millennium later.) Alcuin has been credited with the authorship of the supposed *Libri Carolini*, but though Charlemagne would doubtless have consulted him, the vigour of the language, its opinions indifferently bruising the *amour propre* of Constantinople and Rome alike, make it manifestly his work. The gentle, courteous Alcuin would never have used such a phrase as 'those who with their infamous and silly synods strive to bring into the Church practices which neither the Saviour nor his Apostles ever taught'. After Charles became emperor there came another occasion, even more bizarre, in which again that essential common sense modified the instinctive desire for miracles. A report had come to him that some of the precious blood of Christ had been found in Mantua. So startling a claim needed to be checked out at the highest level and a request was sent to Rome asking Pope Leo to investigate personally. And Leo, obviously grasping at the opportunity to ingratiate himself still further with the Roman emperor, not only initiated such an investigation, but undertook it himself, making a personal journey beyond the Alps to report to the king in Aachen. The fact that he had undertaken such a journey implies very strongly that he, personally, believed in the 'miracle'. The fact that nothing further was heard of the 'miracle' implies, even more strongly, that the common-sense factor had again come uppermost.

It was at about this time that the champion of common sense

contemplated a measure that seemed rooted in the deepest and most lurid romanticism. Shortly after that imperial acclamation, he sent a marriage proposal to Irene in Constantinople. Fastrada, the arrogant, unsubtle, dangerous Fastrada, had died in 794, after ten years of marriage, probably in her mid-twenties. She had been succeeded almost immediately by Liutgard, a girl of whom virtually nothing is known except that she seemed to have shared the qualities of the gentle Hildegarde. She survived long enough to know the heady delight of being proclaimed empress, but within months of the coronation she too was dead. The usual succession of mistresses and concubines would have found their way to the imperial bed but none was ever able to call herself empress. And considering that, in the past, wife had followed wife in a matter of months, Charlemagne's restraint on this occasion has some significance whose import became clear when his ambassadors, Jesse, Bishop of Amiens, and a certain Helmgaud, set sail for Constantinople bearing a marriage proposal. Charles's envoys were accompanied by papal legates bearing the pope's blessing on the proposed match, for now that Irene had emerged as a good orthodox empress, countenancing the all-important display of images in the churches of her land, here would seem to be an ideal opportunity to heal the breach between two halves of the same church. And Charles? Despite his immense self-confidence he could not eradicate the impression placed upon him by his upbringing. Throughout his life he had been conditioned to think of 'the' emperor as he who resided in Constantinople, no matter how weak or corrupt. Byzantine canon lawyers mocked his claim to an imperial crown, and that mockery must have pierced even his self-confidence. By marrying Irene, those mouths would be closed for ever.

Irene accepted the proposal – but it had come too late. In her long-drawn-out, murderous struggles with her son, she had been obliged to rely more and more upon officials opposed to him. And, as she should have known and doubtless did but sheer weariness blinded her, those who supported her did so for their own devious purposes. The knowledge that she was prepared to hand over the state to a barbarian, a barbarian who had had the temerity to take the sacred name of 'emperor', strengthened their hand and in yet another contorted Byzantine palace revolution, she was overthrown. Theophanes, the chronicler who recorded her last tragic days, a decline and fall which she endured with surprising dignity, remarked maliciously that her downfall was actually witnessed by the Frankish envoys who had come to claim her hand for their master, but they had done nothing about it. But there was nothing they, or their master, could do about it – or wished to do about it. This last attempt to unite the eastern and western halves of Christian civilization seems to have been done in an almost absent-minded manner, as a matter of form and little more. There might have been some chance of such a union succeeding if it had been built on the earlier matrimonial alliance between two children whose every move would have been monitored and directed. A union between the Empress Irene and the Emperor Charles could never have been more than formal, quite apart from the fact the eastern and western empires had now polarized, the split becoming hardened, permanent.

The new emperor, Nicephorus, was essentially a bureaucrat, a skilled survivor of Byzantine intrigues and a man who made much of his plebeian origins. He had troubles enough at home and so made some haste to make overtures to the Franks. Charlemagne received his embassy courteously and a treaty was actually drafted, but as he apparently insisted that it contained some formula which recognized his own imperial status, Nicephorus refused to sign it. Diplomatic contact was broken off; the next contact between east and west was on the battlefield south of the Alps, fighting for possession of a number of islets on the Adriatic coast known collectively as Venice.

Some time during the fifth century, when the rule of law was collapsing throughout Italy, a group of people fleeing the barbarian invaders found refuge of a sort on a group of mud- and sand-banks in the north-west corner of the Adriatic. The firstcomers established themselves on the northernmost of these strips, known as Lido, but gradually moved inward to settle upon the other islands – Murano, Torcello, Burano and the closely connected group known as Rialto. Over the following decades other refugees followed. There was nothing on these drab little islands in their grey lagoon to tempt the cupidity of greedy, armed men. The jewelled cities of Italy lay defenceless before them: why bother about a handful of islands inhabited by poor but remarkably pugnacious fishermen? So, over the years, the refugees turned into a community. They hammered down stakes into the mud and sand and began to build upon them; they drew upon two local products, fish and salt, to begin a trade that would develop into an empire in its own right.

By the time of Charlemagne's coronation, the Venetians had emerged finally into corporate identity. But they were torn then, as they would be torn for centuries, by two conflicting attractions – the 'kingdom of the sea' or that of 'terra firma'. The party that favoured the kingdom of the sea automatically became partisans of the Byzantine empire; the party that saw the land as the city's natural sphere of expansion became, with some reservations, allies of the Franks. In 806, the Frankish party having the upper hand, ambassadors came to the emperor at Christmas and formally ceded the city of the lagoon to him. But this was more than Nicephorus could take: a passive acceptance of spheres of influence was one thing, but for the Byzantine empire to lose one more foothold on the Italian mainland was another. In the autumn of that year, a Byzantine fleet left Constantinople bound for the Adriatic. At the same time the King of Italy, Pippin, Charlemagne's son now aged thirty-three, left Pavia for the Adriatic coast.

The Franks were a land power: the fact that now they were not only challenging, but actually held their own against one of the greatest of all sea powers was honour enough to them. The emperor, anticipating some such development, aware too of the pressing threat of those other consummate seamen, the Norsemen, had put in motion an ambitious programme of ship-building and King Pippin had an impressive naval force at his command. It is possible that, had he only the Byzantines with which to contend, Frankish arms might well have prevailed even in this unfamiliar warfare. But the balance had shifted yet again in Venice. According to an account later written by the Byzantine emperor Constantine Porphyrogenitus, Pippin reminded them that they had taken the oath to his father: 'You are under my hand and my sovereignty since you belong to my country and sphere of rule.' But the Venetians answered, 'We are servants of the Emperor of the Romans and not of thee,' the Venetians, too, sharing the Byzantine view of that coronation in Rome. Consummate seamen, knowing the waters of their treacherous sea coast as they knew the streets of their own towns, they checked the ponderous Frankish fleet. Later Venetian propaganda was to expand this into a resounding victory. Certainly, the events of that year 810 were to have a profound effect upon subsequent Venetian history for, while they had undoubtedly thrown off what they saw as the Frankish yolk and were therefore spared the disasters that occurred after the end of the Frankish empire, neither had they delivered themselves over totally to the Byzantine emperor. Byzantine influence would remain and most fruitfully affect the development of Venetian culture. But they remained their own men.

Nevertheless, despite the fact that Venetian artists would later be instructed to portray the Frankish withdrawal as a famous victory it was, in fact, a species of truce or even stalemate, for the Venetians agreed to pay a massive tribute in silver and would continue to do so for nearly a century. Pippin withdrew to his capital at Pavia, probably to regroup and consider a new attack, for it would have been inconceivable to leave Venice as a hostile enclave on his very doorstep. But on 8 July 810, Pippin, King of Italy, the second son of Charlemagne, a vigorous man at the very height of his powers, died suddenly, probably of the plague. And that was the first of the domestic tragedies that would cloud the closing years of Charlemagne.

The Byzantines, too, had had enough, for a new and most formidable enemy, the man the west would know as Haroun al Raschid, had risen on their flanks. By a quirk of history the great caliph of Islam became a brother-in-arms to the ageing but still vigorous Emperor of the West. In one of his great set pieces Edward Gibbon describes the opening of hostilities between Nicephorus and Haroun. The Byzantine emperor sent an insulting embassy to Baghdad bearing a letter referring to the game of chess which had already spread from the Persians to the Greeks.

> 'The Queen [Irene] considered you as a rook and herself as a pawn. That pusillanimous female submitted to pay a tribute, the double of which she ought to have exacted from the Barbarians. Restore therefore the fruits of your injustice or abide the determination of the sword.'
> At these words the ambassadors cast a bundle of swords before the foot of the throne. The caliph smiled at the menace, and drawing his scimitar, *samsamah*, a weapon of historic or fabulous renown, he cut asunder the feeble arms of the Greeks, without turning the edge, or endangering the temper of his blade. He then dictated an epistle of tremendous brevity: 'In the name of the most merciful God, Harun al Raschid, commander of the faithful, to Nicephorus the Roman dog. I have read thy letter, O son of an unbelieving mother. Thou shalt not hear, though shalt behold my reply.' It was written in characters of blood and fire on the plains of Phrygia.

With that terrifying menace at his back, Nicephorus had no stomach for adventures in Europe. A peace mission was sent, not to the emperor but to King Pippin, unaware that already he lay in his grave. Grieving, Charlemagne accepted, on his dead son's behalf, the olive branch so offered, but by the time the manifold details were agreed – each change in the draft necessitating a week's long journey from northern Europe to the Middle East – Nicephorus's head was rotting on a spike and it was a briefly reigning successor, Michael, who signed a document in 812 in which Charlemagne was formally saluted as *basileus*. In that almost casual manner the Roman Empire ceased to be a single entity: there was an empire now of the east and an empire of the west. In that manner, too, the awesome title *Imperator* which, by definition, was uniquely applied to the one Lord of the World, began its long slow degradation until at last there was an 'emperor' of France, an 'emperor' of Mexico and, ultimate contradictory absurdity, the British-style 'King-Emperor' of India.

The friendship of Haroun al Raschid was based on that most sincere of foundations, the possession of common enemies, the Byzantines and the Ommayyad dynasty of Spain. But though caliph and emperor were never to meet, they seem to have been able to establish some relationship through the medium of their envoys and their letters which transcended the purely pragmatic. Charlemagne undoubtedly brought off something of a coup when, in effect, he stood in for the Byzantine protectors of the Holy Places in Palestine during the bitter wars between the Baghdad caliphate and the Byzantine empire. It says much for Haroun's own innate nobility, as well as Charlemagne's eloquence, that Islam drew a distinction between infidels and, in response to the Frankish request, Haroun personally ordered an easing on the restrictions and harassments that had been the lot of the Christian communities in Palestine. In addition, the Franks were allowed to distribute much-needed alms. On their return to Europe, the Frankish envoys were accompanied by two Palestinian monks bringing from the grateful patriarch of Jerusalem the keys of the Holy Sepulchre as well as of Jerusalem itself. It was out of this that there arose the later legend that the emperor had anticipated the crusades by two centuries and had led a great army into the Holy Land.

Einhard knew Haroun al Raschid, Caliph of Baghdad, as 'Aron, king of the Persians' who ruled all over the east with the exception of India and claimed that the caliph allowed the Holy Places 'to be reckoned as part of the possessions of the Frankish king', a somewhat over-optimistic interpretation of the admittedly very generous licence that Haroun had granted. All the Frankish chroniclers recorded the extraordinary richness of the gifts which Haroun sent his brother monarch some time after the imperial coronation – gifts whose richness must have rendered their recipient very thoughtful indeed, evidence as they were of a fabulous civilization just beyond his reach. The priceless perfumes and ointments of the orient in great jars; bale upon bale of silks and brocades; an enormous tent with numerous curtained apartments, so high that an archer could not hit its roof with an arrow. There was an extraordinary clock which must have drawn the emperor's fascinated attention, interested as he was in all things mechanical. It was a water-clock made of brass, with brass balls that would drop on the hour, signalling the movement of a little army of twelve knights on horseback – the kind of intricate toy that would not appear in Europe for another five centuries or more. But literally overshadowing and dwarfing all these was the fabulous creature from the fabulous continent: an immense African elephant, bearing the dignified name of Abul Ahaz. He came to Aachen in the year 802, at about the time that the great palace and chapel were completed, and he must have seemed a fitting complement and comment. He appeared in all the great outdoor ceremonies of the emperor, drawing gasps of admiration from the crowd, adding something that was at once solid and exotic to the processions. He had a prominent role in the last campaigns of the emperor, although the role was exclusively decorative; so unique a possession could not be risked in humdrum battle. He was expected to live for at least 300 years, for such was the life-span confidently stated in the bestiaries. He died, suddenly, after a bare eight years, prosaically a victim of the damp northern climate.

Yet, externally, these last years of Charlemagne's rule appear only that of a mellow fruition – not even of triumph, for triumph implies the dramatic, victorious cessation of long-drawn-out struggle, whereas the threats from the outer enemies of the state fell away like autumn leaves. Widukind, that stubborn core of opposition in the Saxon state, had long since accepted Christianity with that deep and genuine piety of which his ferocious nation was capable, while the Saxon war itself, that war which had been all but co-terminous with the reign, had come to an end in 804. Again, there had been nothing dramatic about that ending, no topless towers of Ilium falling in flaming ruin, simply an exhausted collapse of a courageous people who had fought on to the end because it was unthinkable not to do so. Thousands upon thousands of them, men, women and children, had been transported out of their country, breaking at last the backbone of resistance. Bishops now resided in the newborn cities of Paderborn and Bremen and Munster on sites where a few years earlier the last pagans of Europe had held those rites whose very meaning was already being forgotten. The destruction of the Saxons had led inevitably to lethal contact with the next in line, the Danes. For a while it seemed as though they had inherited the Saxon mantle, the shirt of Nessus which would condemn them to be the last effective enemy of the Frankish state until they too were destroyed and absorbed. But the Danes, perhaps scenting easier pickings on the other side of the North Sea, murdered their too defiant King Godefride and made a truce with the Franks which lasted Charlemagne's lifetime. In Italy, the last flicker of Lombard independence died away when the prince of Benevento agreed to that annual tribute of 7000 *solidi*. The Caliph of Baghdad was Charlemagne's admiring friend and ally; the eastern Roman Emperor (whoever transiently sat on that throne) was the grateful partner of the western Roman Emperor: Slavs and Avars, Saxons, Bretons, Aquitanians, Bavarians acknowledged him as overlord . . . Regarding these broad dominions with their Babel of languages, revolving in his mind those schemes of his for a true City of God, in 806 he had summoned a general Assembly specifically to settle the problem of succession once for all so that the great work could go forward without hiatus. The provisions, minutely detailed, were published in a capitulary of February of that year and it was here that the emperor gave way to the tribal leader, here that the Frank took over from the international statesman, here that the empire was divided up between his three legitimate sons as though it had been a family estate. The eldest son, Charles, was to be given the heartland of the state – the old original Frankish lands of Neustria and Austrasia with the neighbouring, conquered lands; Pippin was to have all Italy as well as Bavaria and the lands of the Avars; while Louis was to rule in Aquitaine those areas that had been wrested from the Saracen in Spain and parts of Burgundy. Charles evidently relied upon the power of family love to make the system workable: thus both Charles and Louis were to have access through each other's domains in order that they could go to the aid of Pippin, who would otherwise be cut off in the south.

Of all the many enigmatic acts of Charlemagne, this *divisio regnorum* is the most mysterious. Generations of lawyers were to pore over its provisions, trying to reconcile its apparent continuation of the disastrous tribal policy of division between sons, with the known fact of the emperor's personal experience of the effect of such a measure, his political acumen, and that breadth of vision which had persuaded him, perhaps reluctantly, to take up the title and burden of an imperial crown. The three divisions did not follow any specific ethnic or geographic boundaries: indeed, it seemed as though Charlemagne was deliberately blurring the edges so that one would melt into the other, forming a unity composed of a trinity – a religious interpretation which he actually used in his preamble. Yet of all people he must have known that good fences make good neighbours. He must have known that the provision of a 'corridor' across the lands of Charles and Pippin could be grounds for future dissension. There was already bad feeling between these two, more combative brothers, a fact he recognized by exhorting upon all three the sacred duty of working with each other. He still retained his long-distance vision. Only one of his sons, Pippin, as yet had an heir but the emperor looked forward to the possible time when the ruler of one of these three 'kingdoms' might die, leaving an heir. He enjoined upon the two survivors the responsibility of seeing that their dead brother's heir should succeed him and resist the temptation to take over his realm. No brother should give asylum to any man who should flee to him from the territory of either of the others. Each brother should recognize as freemen, the freemen of the others. All citizens of the empire could acquire property in any part of that empire and, similarly, all should have the right to marry across the supposed divisions. So the capitulary goes on in minute detail, taking account of every eventuality but one – the human desire to dominate, the fact that one brother would certainly, sooner or later, attempt to exercise power over the other two.

The matter was never put to the test, for death resolved it.

Death beat its wings around the emperor's head throughout these opening years of the ninth century as though following some divine plan of balance, rounding off a too-fortunate life with a corrective. Alcuin died in 804 and though his departure was a grievous loss to Charlemagne, both as ruler and as man, it was not unexpected for his old friend had been nearly seventy. But eighteen months afterwards Pippin had died, aged thirty-three, Pippin's elder brother Charles died suddenly and mysteriously at the age of thirty-nine. In a matter of months the two tough, competent, loyal young men who were gradually taking the weight of empire from their father were taken off in the full flush of vigorous manhood. With them went their sister, the Dove, Hrotrud, who should have worn the crown of the Byzantine empress but instead spent her life in her father's palace, nursing her two illegitimate children. In that same sweep of the scythe, death took off the tragic, humpbacked first-born Pippin, half-brother to these glamorous siblings who, through that ill-planned, ill-timed act of his was lucky to escape with his life – if luck could be said to apply to how he spent the remainder of that life under rigorous control in a monastery. And as though this sweeping clearance of his immediate family were not bad enough, in that same period Charlemagne lost the last person who was in a position adequately to measure the degree of his progress, adequately to assess the pressures that had been placed upon him, adequately thence to offer forgiveness. His sister, the Abbess Gisila, the last surviving link with the heroic past, took her quizzical support and love to the grave. In Italy, too, the game little Lombard Paul Warnefried took the last long journey of all, from the monastery crowning Monte Cassino to the graveyard at its side.

The emperor's public life reflected his inner melancholy. At times the tone of the capitularies promulgated at this period is almost one of despair: despite his exhortations the poor are still oppressed – and that frequently by their natural protectors, the clergy; the counts are failing in their duty not simply in ensuring that men answer the *ban* but in diverting to their own use men whose energies should be devoted to the state: 'They say that if a poor man will not give up his property, these great men make some excuse for getting him into trouble with the courts or else are continually ordering him on military service till the wretched man, quite ruined, has to surrender or sell his property.' One capitulary, that regulating the means of supplying soldiers to the national militia and published in 811, foreshadows the break-up of the empire with its apparently impotent complaint that the counts are building up private armies instead of ensuring warriors for the host.

At one stage the emperor seems to have contemplated the easy way out, following the example of his long-dead great-uncle Carloman by taking the tonsure and ending his days in a monastery. But the old habits of discipline, of responsibility, drove him on. He hoisted his ageing body on to horseback, riding out yet again on campaign to attend a matter on the Danish frontier. One morning, on leaving the camp at sunrise, his horse was startled by what appears to have been a meteor and threw him heavily, 'so violently,' Einhard records, 'that the girdle of his cloak was broken and his sword slipped from it. His javelin, too, which he had been holding in his hand at the time of his fall, fell twenty paces and more away from him.' Einhard classed this, in hindsight, with those prodigies which always appear towards the end of a great man's life. Other signs and portents 'during the last three years of his life were the constant eclipses of sun and moon. The gallery which he had built between the palace and the church at Aachen fell in ruins down even to the foundations.' Lightning struck the chapel. The inscription which Alcuin had composed for the interior, saying by whom it was built, lost the word '*princeps*' in the line '*Carolus princeps*' – all infallible indications that the end was near. The fall from the horse must certainly have badly shaken him, a heavy man approaching his seventieth year. But he had one more task to perform for the thing that he had created and, in performing it, he makes even more enigmatic that earlier *divisio regnorum* and at the same time disposes emphatically of the theory that the imperial crown was, for him, simply a useful political device to be discarded if circumstances warranted. He summoned his son Louis, King of Aquitaine, to Aachen and there began grooming him for the burden of empire.

There was no lack of opponents of the idea. The soubriquets attached to Louis, now thirty-three years of age, are indication enough of his character: the Pious, the Debonair, the Gentle, the Monk. His biographer, Thegan, who came to know him as well as any man says, 'he was apt to give undue heed to the advice of his counsellors while he gave himself up to psalmody and diligent reading'. It is doubtful if Louis would even have made a good abbot, as has been claimed for him; his gentleness and piety would have been appropriate but even in a monastery its ruler needs consistency of aim whereas Louis could be turned aside by the most recent argument, switching backward and forward according to the proximity of his interlocutor, or the persuasiveness of the argument. His kingdom of Aquitaine had, in fact, been run by remote control by Charlemagne's counsellors during most of Louis's supposed reign. There was a strong body of opinion which held that the dead Pippin's young son Bernard was a far more suitable candidate, although only a boy. Charlemagne must have pondered long on this bitter dilemma and come to the understandable decision that to pass over his son in favour of his immature grandson would only create problems in the future. It was a reasonable decision, but it condemned Bernard to a hideous death at the hands of the uncle who had sworn to protect him.

Throughout the spring and summer of 813 Louis was at his father's side as though his father, by a process of osmosis, hoped to infuse in him, even at this late date the precepts of command. On Saturday 10 September he called a great Assembly – the last Assembly of his long reign and there he asked, formally, if it were the will of his people that his son Louis, King of Aquitaine, should be crowned co-emperor with him. The Annales attributed to Einhard make much of the fact that the question was addressed to individual representatives, from the highest to the lowest, thus ensuring the unanimous consent of his Franks to this act without precedent among Franks. The reply was unanimous and the coronation took place, in the emperor's beloved chapel of the palace of

Aachen, on the following day. He departed from his usual custom, donning the glittering finery of a Roman emperor: cloth-of-gold covered his still upright, massive body; a golden girdle around his waist, jewelled boots, a glittering diadem of jewels set in gold. Kneeling, Louis was subjected to a lengthy sermon from his father and his emperor: to protect the weak; to give honour to the clergy; to choose God-fearing ministers. Then came the formal question, 'Wilt thou obey all these my precepts?' and Louis answered, 'Most willingly, with the help of God'. Charlemagne then turned to the altar, picked up from it a replica of the diadem that crowned his own head and hobbling forward – for he was now afflicted by gout – stood in front of his kneeling son. There is some slight contradiction about what happened next. Einhard says that Charles himself placed the crown upon Louis's head whereas Louis's biographer, Thegan, claims that it was Louis who performed this last, seemingly slight, but vital act. But whatever happened at that moment was according to Charlemagne's decision and whether it was he, or his son, who made that all-important gesture, the Church was firmly excluded from it. By eliminating the intervention of the clergy at this point he had emphasized, at a period when symbolism was merely the reverse side of reality, that the empire was self-perpetuating, that its head again played the dual role of priest-king as it had in the days of the Caesars – and that its seat was no longer Rome, but beyond the Alps.

Leaning heavily upon the arm of his son, Charlemagne led the procession back to the palace, inaugurating some days of spectacular celebration, after which Louis returned to his own kingdom of Aquitaine. Father and son were never to meet again. What doubts the old man may have had about the future of the empire in such feeble hands, he kept to himself. He had already made his will, an immensely complicated document to which Einhard gives a curiously dispro-portionate amount of space. But it was an essentially private document, disposing of his personal treasure. Three items of that treasure were to enter European legend. As Einhard describes them factually they were three tables made of silver and gold. 'One of them, square in shape, containing a map of the city of Constantinople shall be sent to Rome for the cathedral of the holy Apostle Peter: the second, round in shape, inscribed with a picture of the city of Rome, shall be given to the bishopric of the Church of Ravenna. The third . . . which is made of three circles and contains a map of the whole world . . . shall go to alms.' Over the centuries that followed, as time worked its alchemy upon reality and the ageing, ill and worried man became all but supernatural in legend, so those three tables became magical devices, mirrors in which he was able to discern whatever was happening everywhere in his vast realm.

The end was sudden. Autumn was spent in the customary pleasures of the chase but in January the emperor contracted what Einhard called 'a sharp fever complicated by a pain in the side which the Greeks call pleurisy'. Like many a powerful man, he had little faith in doctors and, instead of following the sensible regime suggested to him, subjected his body to a rigorous fast. Weakened by lack of food in addition to that 'fever' and, perhaps, still shaken by the heavy fall from his horse, he sank rapidly. A week after he had taken to his bed he received Holy Communion in anticipation of the end but lingered on for another twenty-four hours, feeble but still in control of himself. At dawn on 29 January 814 he made the sign of the Cross, intoned 'Into thy hands, Lord, I commend my spirit' and died. He was probably not quite seventy-two years old.

Immediately upon his death the mysteries begin, mysteries which developed into legend. According to the unimpeachable witness of Einhard he was buried in the chapel of the palace of Aachen on the same day he died. Einhard gives no reason for this hurried interment, made necessary neither by the nature of the last illness nor by the climate, for it was a cold winter's day. The firm, if casual, statement, however, disposes beyond doubt of the extraordinarily circumstantial story told of the supposed opening of the tomb by the young emperor Otto III in the apocalyptic year 1000. Otto, son of a German father and a Greek mother, was one of the romantic Germans who succumbed to the lure of Rome, the lure which Charlemagne had resisted to the last. Otto intended fully, exactly, literally, to 'restore' the Roman Empire; to restore the ancient rituals of the Caesars; to set his seat again in the mother city of Europe. And the mother city destroyed him as she destroyed all northerners who sought to possess her.

In that year 1000, that year of the millennium when, many believed, Christ would again come in judgement, Otto came to Aachen on his way to Rome and was welcomed by the then Count of the Palace, a man called Otho of Lomello. What happened next is related by the contemporary chronicler of Novalese, claiming to record the words of Otho himself:

> We went in unto Charles and found him not lying as is the manner of other dead bodies, but sitting on a chair as if alive. He was crowned with a golden

crown, and he held a sceptre in his hands. These were covered with gloves, through which the growing nails had forced their way. Above him was an alcove, wonderfully built of marbles and mortar into which we made a hole before we came to the Emperor. As soon as we entered we perceived a very strong smell. We at once fell on our knees and did him reverence, and made good all that was lacking round him. But none of his limbs had fallen away through decay: only there was a little piece gone from the tip of his nose which the emperor caused to be replaced with gold. Then having taken one tooth out of his mouth and rebuilt the alcove, so we departed.

The precise, circumstantial detail of Otho's story makes it hard to dismiss: the strong smell of decay as the alcove was broached; the macabre detail of the nails growing through the gloves; the fact that the tip of the nose was missing – all this has an unimpeachable air of verisimilitude. Certainly it entered history as well as legend: the nineteenth-century mural on the walls of the Coronation Hall in the present *Rathaus* of Aachen commemorates this eerie obeisance to the great emperor. Its details were to be repeated again and again, each repetition adding a little more colour. One of the illuminated Gospels that still survive was supposed to have been resting on his knee and was reverently removed by Otto; a member of the party was supposed to have tried on the crown and measured his own leg against that of the seated corpse – both inherently improbable actions when it is considered that the living emperor Otto was present. But the whole story is contradicted by Einhard's statement that Charlemagne was buried the same day that he died and that he had made no particular arrangements for his burial place. There would have been no time to embalm the body, and certainly no time to have created an elaborate vault for it.

In 1165, the Emperor Frederick Barbarossa arranged for the canonization of the man whose personal morals had disturbed his closest friends and counsellors, the king who had ordered the beheading of 4500 young men, the emperor who had disdainfully excluded the Church from the coronation ceremony. The canonization was, essentially, a political act, the means whereby Barbarossa glorified his own origins, emphasizing the Germanic origins of the new Roman Empire to counterbalance the French claims that Charlemagne was a Frenchman. But the pope, Paschal III, who agreed to the act was not being merely submissive. Over the years there had developed a number of cults centred round the emperor and the canonization drew together the spontaneous growths and made them official. Barbarossa's next act totally disposes of the story of Otho of Lomello for he ordered that the bones of the emperor should be placed in a specially made golden shrine. They found the remains in an immense Roman sarcophagus buried beneath the chapel floor.

Why had Otho of Lomello told his incredible story? It is impossible at this distance in time to arrive at any certain explanation of his personal motivation. One can only reflect that it belonged to the same process that turned a shameful defeat at Roncesvalles into a story of epic valour; the same process that turned an all-too-human man into a saint; that transformed three beautiful but not otherwise remarkable artefacts into magical mirrors; that turned a company of ruthless soldiers, the *comitatus*, into the paladins, stainless warriors of Christ; that turned a Teutonic war-band leader into an epic hero of Christian Europe. It was the result of the alchemy, time, working upon memory, turning an ad hoc, experimental, somewhat ramshackle political system that yet gave hope of order, into a Golden Age, becoming ever more richly glowing as the night grew ever darker over Europe.

For within a generation of Charlemagne's death the great experiment was ended, shattered as it fell from the hands of those incapable of supporting it. There was a brief, false dawn. Charlemagne's successor, his son Louis, appeared actually to be improving on the work of his father, shaping up and firming the concept of empire by his *Ordinatio Imperii* of 817 which ended the kind of speculation that had so long been directed at him and unequivocally recognized his son Lothair as emperor and binding Lothair's brothers to recognize him as such. The seeds of education that Alcuin and Charlemagne had sown with such love and care, now began to bear fruit. The capitularies are clearer, far more precise, no longer rambling personal disquisitions but blueprints of empire. The illuminated books glow with a luminous beauty.

But it was a dying glow. Louis, the gentle, pious, vacillating 'emperor' was incapable of holding together a state whose parts had not had time to become homogenized. He was forced into abdication by his three ferocious sons who then repeated the Frankish tragedy, though repeated it now on a European scale, fighting for dominance among themselves until, at Fontenoy on 25 June 841, they tore the empire apart:

> When the dawn at early morning drove the sullen night away
> Treachery of Saturn was it, not the holy Sabbath day
> Over peace of brothers broken, joys the Fiend in devilry.

So said Angilbert, who was there.

The Holy Roman Empire

On 2 February 962, 162 years after Charlemagne had received his crown and 148 years after his death, the Holy Roman Empire of the German Nation came into being. During those 148 years the crown of the Carolingian empire had become the debased pretext for faction war, a hollow title for which bandit families in Italy and across the Alps could aim. Yet still there lingered the memory of the high compact made on that distant Christmas Day in Rome when the warring nations of western Europe had again been united under a single head. And the knowledge remained, despite Charlemagne's determined attempt at auto-coronation, that the bishop of Rome could create a supreme Lord of Europe who could bring back law and, with it, peace.

When, therefore, a truly great king, Otto of Saxony, arose in Germany it was as though he stepped upon a stage that had been waiting for its protagonist for over a hundred years. He found Germany divided into five great dukedoms. He welded them into one and placed himself at its head.

Otto could not claim descent from Charlemagne for he was not even of the same race, being a member of that Saxon race which had given the first Carolingian emperor so much trouble. But, like his great predecessor, personal might overcame the arguments of lawyers and to emphasize his goal – the re-establishment of the Carolingian empire – he re-enacted Charlemagne's coronation. He received the German crown in Charlemagne's chapel at Aachen, and was given, successively, the Frankish monarch's great sword, sceptre and the priceless Sacred Lance – the very spear that had pierced Christ on the Cross – that had been the most precious possession of the emperor. The court he established was modelled upon Charlemagne's and though it could not compare in intellectual qualities, yet it rose above its time as the powerful young king attracted to himself the most diverse peoples from distant corners of Europe.

But it was not his intellectual and imperial pretensions that made Otto great in the eyes of people far beyond his German forests. Imperial pretenders were commonplace and intellectual pursuits were best left to clerks. What he had done was to smash the terrifying Hun threat that had loomed over Europe for a generation and more. In the eyes of Europeans, the Huns had appeared like goblins from some diabolical mythology as, hundreds of thousands strong, they had swept in from the east. The little men with their deeply sunken eyes and partially shaved heads were totally unlike anything Europe had known. They habitually fed upon raw flesh, giving rise to the belief that they devoured the corpses of the slain. Incredibly hardy and superb horsemen, they terrified even those who had experienced the bloodlust of the Norsemen and the refined cruelty of Greeks and Saracens.

Germany was in the front line of this new wave of migrants and, in combating it, the Germans found a national hero and a national identity. The Huns poured across the frontiers in a horde so numerous that they boasted their horses would drink the rivers dry and pound the cities to dust with their hooves. Otto met them outside Augsburg on 10 August 955. The dead on the German side alone climbed into the tens of thousands but the Hun dead were uncountable. It was the end of the menace. Western Europe had shown it could protect its re-born civilization and the Huns ebbed back to the east.

With the prestige of Augsburg added to his demonstrated skill as statesman, Otto towered in Europe without equal, his influence stretching from England to Spain, with even the Danes acknowledging him as overlord. But still there was the memory of that Christmas Day compact to haunt him, as it would haunt so many Germans to their nation's cost. He was clothed in Charlemagne's mantle; he ruled as de facto lord over much of Charlemagne's empire; after Augsburg his troops had spontaneously hailed him as 'Imperator'. But still he had not been anointed by the successor of the priest who had anointed Charlemagne. And until he received the sacred oil he was a pretender, a barbarian king who happened to have the military might to dominate Europe. So, at least, he thought and, with him, most Europeans.

Meanwhile, in Rome, a dissolute, twenty-year-old Pope called John XII had become embroiled in one of the endless Roman civic battles and appealed to Otto for help, promising the imperial crown in return. Otto accepted with alacrity and marched to Rome, entering the city on

2 February. But these were no longer the Romans of Charlemagne's day, a people still with pride in their past and prepared to bestow their name upon a Frank who could maintain the rule of law. In a century the city had degenerated beyond belief, its citizens endlessly fighting among themselves, uniting only against the outsider. In spite of Otto's pretensions to culture, in the eyes of the Romans his army was barely preferable in appearance to the Huns it had destroyed. 'Terrible in appearance' were these Germans – huge, bearded, shaggy men from the northern forests, wolves barely leashed in by their king, as contemptuous of the effete Romans as the Romans despised them as barbarians.

Otto left the bulk of his army outside the city, entering it in formal procession but accompanied by a strong bodyguard. The crowds were sullen but passive and the Germans marched without hindrance to the base of the marble steps up which Charlemagne had marched to the great open court before St Peter's. There the bodyguard fell away, but Otto had already taken his sword-bearer Ansfried to one side and warned him to be prepared for anything, even within the sacred precincts of the basilica. 'When I kneel today at the grave of the Apostle, stand behind me with the sword. I know only too well what my ancestors have experienced from these faithless Romans.' Ansfried accompanied his master up the steps to where young John, gorgeously robed, powdered and simpering, awaited him. The procession, now augmented by priests, moved across the courtyard and into the vast, dim basilica. There was no incident and above the shrine of St Peter – a shrine stripped of its treasures and with the shaft leading down to the tomb blocked with rubbish – Otto knelt and received the crown whose weight eventually crushed the crown of the German kingdom.

Over the following nine centuries there would be some great men who wore that crown: Frederick Hohenstaufen, Stupor Mundi, the Wonder of the World, ruling equally from Germany and Sicily; Frederick Barbarossa who was to die on Crusade rescuing a page boy from a river; Charles V who by genetic chance inherited the Low Countries, Burgundy, Austria, Spain and much of Italy and stood in judgement over Luther; men from the houses of Hohenstaufen, Wittlesbach, Habsburg, many of them great men, but none great enough to transcend their time and overcome the centrifugal forces that were tearing Europe apart. Meanwhile French propaganda successfully transformed the Frank, Karl der Grosse, into the Frenchman Charlemagne so that the Corsican Napoleon Bonaparte could eventually array himself in stolen robes and complacently announce, '*Je n'ai pas succédé à Louis Quatorze, mais à Charlemagne'*. Two years later, on 6 August 1806, Francis II, the true emperor, abdicated under pressure, releasing all states from their oath of allegiance. So ended the empire, 1006 years after Charlemagne had received its crown.

But throughout those long centuries, in inverse proportion to the political significance of the empire, the legends surrounding its founder grew. It was in the western section of his homeland, the part now known as France, that the legends were planted and nurtured. The Germans were creating their own apocalyptic literature around the Nibelungs; the English, though saluting 'the holy battles of bold Charlemaine' and turning them into rollicking folk-tales, used their incomparable language to enshrine their own national hero Arthur. It was the French, ever seeking to honour *'la douce France'*, who took the raw materials of the Charlemagne legend and turned them into literature, the *chansons de geste*.

A commonplace of all the Charlemagne legends is their gradual replacement of all his enemies, whatever their ethnic origin, with the Saracen, simultaneously identifying Charlemagne and his empire with Christendom and reflecting the increasing preoccupation with the Crusades. Even as the French *Chanson de Roland* turned Basque hillmen into *'paynims'* so, in the English folk-tale *The Sowdone of Babylone*, the Lombards who, in fact, attacked Rome become Saracens led by the Sultan. The English, too, borrow the *Chanson de Roland* and add their own twist to it, sending Charlemagne to Constantinople: Constantitius, the emperor, oppressed by the Saracens has been advised by an angel to call in Charlemagne. He refuses costly gifts for his aid, asking instead only for relics of the Passion and receiving the Crown of Thorns, part of the Cross, our Lady's smock, the rod of Aaron, Longinus's spear and one of the nails – all evidently an embroidered version of the actual gift of the Holy Spear. In the extraordinary Latin forgery known to scholarship as the Pseudo Turpin, Roland engages in single combat with a Saracen giant called Ferragutus during which they frequently break to engage in lengthy theological debate about which is the true religion. The forgery was the work of twelfth-century French Cluniac monks anxious to advertise their shrine of Compostela with which they were associated. Their audacious approach is reminiscent of the forger of the Donation of Constantine, for they too fastened their work upon a real person, Turpin, Archbishop of Rheims, a contemporary of Charlemagne's and a battle-companion as well. The story of Roncesvalles is told, but at no great length, while in contrast there is a wealth of miracles and magical stories which will enter folklore. The French put spears in the ground before a great battle; the spears of those destined to die put forth leaves, at which the potential martyrs rejoice. Charlemagne encounters and overcomes all the idols of the Saracens in Spain – except the Great Idol of Cadiz, made by Muhammad himself and shut up with a legion of demons to defend it.

But all these stories are auxiliaries and handmaidens to the one great epic, the *Chanson de Roland*. This is not a 'manufactured' poem, an *Aeneid* or a *Paradise Lost* created by some great poet consciously adding to the stock of his country's literature. There *was* a poet behind it, a great poet, but he is totally unknown and what he did was to bring together two shorter, lesser *chansons* combining and elaborating them in this epic. He was working some time between the Norman Conquest of England and the first Crusade some thirty years later in 1096. It immediately became enormously popular, the principal stock-in-trade of scores of wandering minstrels or *jongleurs*. It is, in fact, from a minstrel's pocket copy – battered, stained, torn – that the only complete manuscript of the poem survived. For at least 500 years the song of Roland would be chanted in market-places, in castles, in great houses, beginning, as abruptly as the *Iliad* begins, with a conference of Saracens debating how to drive Charlemagne from Spain, and ending equally abruptly with the ageing, weary Emperor being summoned by an angel to go yet again to the aid of Christians:

'Ah, God,' he crieth, 'how burdened is my life with travail and pain'
His hoary beard he teareth, from his eyes the hot tears rain.

And so it ends.

For 500 years the French kept the *Chanson de Roland* alive and then, abruptly, with the Renaissance it fell out of fashion among the sophisti-cated, its place taken by the classics. So totally was it forgotten that, when search began for it in the early nineteenth century, only two copies were discovered. In 1837 Francisque Michel found the *jongleurs'* copy in the Bodleian Library in Oxford and laboriously copied out its 40,002 lines. There were errors and omissions and excisions but another copy turned up in the Library of San Marco in Venice and this, though physically far inferior, allowed corrections to be made. 'So near did the great epic of France come to extinction,' as its translator, Arthur Way, remarked.

Nineteenth-century historians could confidently dismiss all that came before the fifteenth century in Europe as one long preparation. Their view is well summed up by the British historian J. A. Symonds. 'The arts and inventions, the knowledge and the books which suddenly became vital at the time of the Renaissance had long since lain neglected on the shores of that Dead Sea we call the Middle Ages.' To describe as a Dead Sea those long centuries which, among other achievements, produced the cathedrals, the logical system of Aquinas, the literature of Dante and Chaucer, the illuminators of the *Très Riches Heures* and, finally, the empire of Charlemagne is, to put it mildly, short-sighted. And even this blinkered view was further narrowed when the opprobrious term 'Dark Ages' was applied to that period of time which saw the Carolingian renaissance coming to its full flowering. In our own time there has been a much-needed reappraisal, yet it has been curiously patchy. Adolf Hitler, with that eye of his to history, code-named the attack on Russia – that great *Drang nach Osten* which Charlemagne had begun – after Barbarossa, reserving the greater name for a battalion of French renegades, the Charlemagne Division, who wore German uniform in World War II. But on Christmas Day 1949 the citizens of Charlemagne's own beloved city of Aachen restored a great name to honour. On that day, this city which had been almost battered to death by fellow Europeans raised itself from the ashes to proclaim the unity of all Europeans, establishing 'In remembrance of the great founder of western civilization' a prize to be called 'Karlspreis der Stadt Aachen'. And this Charlemagne Prize of the City of Aachen was to be awarded to any statesman of whatever race or nationality who forwarded the ideal of the first Carolingian emperor.

Chronology

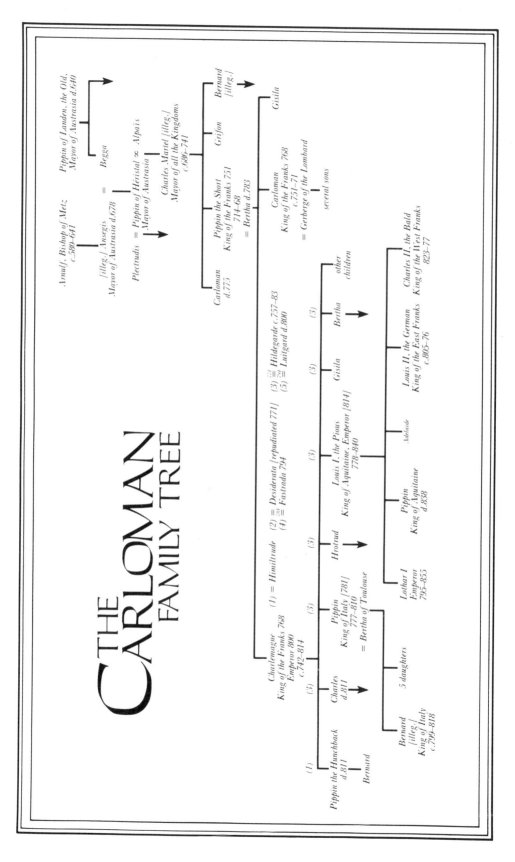

THE CARLOMAN FAMILY TREE

Arnulf, Bishop of Metz
c.580–641

[illeg.] Ansegis
Mayor of Austrasia d.678
=

Pippin of Landen, the Old.
Mayor of Austrasia d.640

Begga

Plectrudis = Pippin of Héristal ∞ Alpaïs
Mayor of Austrasia

Charles Martel [illeg.]
Mayor of all the Kingdoms
c.686–741

Carloman
d.775

Pippin the Short
King of the Franks 751
714–68
= Bertha d.783

Grifon

Bernard
[illeg.]

Carloman
King of the Franks 768
c.751–71
= Gerberge of the Lombard

Gisila

several sons

Charlemagne
King of the Franks 768
Emperor 800
c.742–814

(1) = Himiltrude   (2) = Desiderata [repudiated 771]   (3) ²ᵈ = Hildegarde c.757–83
                    (4) = Fastrada 794   (5) ⁵ᵗʰ = Luitgard d.800

(1)   (3)   (3)   (3)   (3)   (3)   (3)   (3)

Pippin the Hunchback
d.811

Charles
d.811

Pippin King of Italy [781]
777–810
= Bertha of Toulouse

Lothar I
Emperor
795–855

Hrotrud

Louis I. the Pious
King of Aquitaine, Emperor [814]
778–840

Gisila

Bertha

other
children

Bernard
[illeg.]
King of Italy
c.799–818

5 daughters

Pippin
King of Aquitaine
d.838

Adelaide

Louis II. the German
King of the East Franks
c.805–76

Charles II, the Bald
King of the West Franks
823–77

Bernard

APPENDIX II
The 'Oath of Strasbourg'

On 14 February 842, the grandsons of Charlemagne, Louis and Charles, pledged common support to each other against the third brother, Lothair. The followers of each swore not to support their leader should he break the oath. East Franks and West Franks had by now so far diverged that it was necessary to swear in each other's language for common understanding. The Oath of Strasbourg records the oldest form of the French language and is itself the earliest documentary indication of the fragmentation of the empire.

The occasion, and the oath, is recorded by Nithard, another grandson of Charlemagne's, though illegitimate. His mother was Bertha, his father Angilbert:

> The oath which the people swore, each in their own tongue, was in the Roman (i.e. 'French') tongue as follows:
>
> 'Si Lodhuuigs sagrement que son fradre Karlo jurat conservat et Karlus, meos sendra, de suo part non l'ostabit, si io returnar no l'int pois, ne io ne neuls cui eo returnar int pois, in nulla aiudha contra Lodhuuig nun li iu er'
> And in the German tongue:
> 'Oba Karl then eid then er sinemo bruodher Ludhuuuige gesuor geleistit, indi Ludhuuuig, min herro, then er imo gesuor forbrihchit, ob ih inan es iruuenden ne mag, noh ih no thero nohein then ih es iruuenden mag, uuidhar Karle imo ce follusti ne uuirdhit'
>
> (Modern translation: If Louis/Charles observes the oath which he has sworn to his brother Charles/Louis, and if Charles/Louis my lord for his part does not keep it and I am unable to prevail upon him to do so, then neither I myself nor anyone upon whom I can prevail shall give him any assistance against Louis/Charles.)

The Karlspreis
of Aachen

If the Oath of Strasbourg marks the beginning of the break-up of the ideal of European unity, then the Karlspreis proclaimed by the City of Aachen on Christmas Day 1949, 1149 years after Charlemagne's crowning in Rome, marks the beginning of at least the desire to restore the ideal.

The following is taken from the *Proklamation*:

The City of Aachen, once a focus of cultural life and political activity in the entire western world, has in the course of time become a border town . . . The two World Wars proved that the sincere endeavours of several generations to overcome imagined national antagonisms seemed impossible. The fact that Aachen is situated in a frontier area then worked much to our disadvantage . . . Having suffered dreadful experience, our citizens are ready to urge European Unity . . . a number of Aachen's citizens, devoted to their town by birth and profession, or by the exercise of their offices, have therefore agreed upon establishing an INTERNATIONAL PRIZE OF THE CITY OF AACHEN. In remembrance of the great founder of western civilization, this prize shall be called Charlemagne Prize of the City of Aachen. It is to be awarded annually to personages of merit who have promoted the idea of western unity by their political, economic and literary endeavours.

The Prize, consisting of a medallion embossed with the city's seal, an illuminated document and a money prize of DM5000 is presented on each Ascension Day in the Rathaus. The first winner of the award, in 1950, was Graf Richard Coudenhove-Kalergi, founder of the Pan-European Movement. Successive winners have included the Italian premier, Alcide Gasperi, the German Chancellor Konrad Adenauer, three British statesmen – Winston Churchill, Edward Heath and Roy Jenkins, Simone Weil, President of the European Parliament and the

American Secretary of State, George C. Marshall. On this occasion the award was made in Washington as Mr Marshall was prevented by ill-health from travelling to Aachen.

Select Bibliography

CONTEMPORARY SOURCES (Modern translations)
The main general source for Charlemagne's reign is the record known as the Royal Annales (*Annales Regni Francorum*). A recent English translation of these is by B. W. Scholz (with Barbara Rogers) published under the title of *Carolingian Chronicles* (Ann Arbor, Michigan, 1970). For the Capitularies see F. L. Ganshof's *Recherches sur les Capitulaires* (Paris, 1958) and his *Frankish Institutions under Charlemagne* translated by S. Bruce and Mary Lyon (Providence, Rhode Island, 1968). The biographies by Einhard and the Monk of St Gall have recently (1969) been translated by Lewis Thorpe under the title *Two Lives of Charlemagne* in addition to that cited below. Thegan's life of Charlemagne's son and successor Louis the Pious has been partially translated by Hodgkin (see below) and Loyn & Percival, *The Reign of Charlemagne* (1975). This latter is an anthology of translations which gives an excellent bird's-eye view of the man and his times seen contemporaneously. Hodgkin (op.cit.) also gives substantial translations of papal utterances taken from the *Liber Pontificalis*, of which the standard edition is that of L. Duchesne (Paris, 1886–92).

In 1965, the 800th anniversary of Charlemagne's canonization, the city of Aachen put on an immense art-historical exhibition which, in the words of the British scholar D. A. Bullough, 'provided a unique opportunity for taking stock, for asking scholars of many nations to provide a considered account of the man, the reign, the achievement'. Their work is embodied in four massive, handsome volumes, edited by Wolfgang Braunfels under the title of *Karl der Grosse: Lebenswerk und Nachleben* which is now, and is likely to remain for the foreseeable future, the standard work.

OTHER WORKS
Augustine, St, *The City of God*, trans. John Healey
Baker, G. P., *Charlemagne and the United States of Europe*, 1933
Bibliotheca Rerum Germanicarum, *Monumenta Carolina*, ed. P. Jaffe, 1867
Billings, Anna Hunt, *A Guide to the Middle English Metrical Romances*, 1901
Bloch, Marc, *Feudal Society*, trans. L. A. Manquin, 1961
Boissonade, P., *Life and Work in Medieval Europe*, trans. Eileen Power, 1927
Bryce, James, *The Holy Roman Empire*, 1897

Buckler, F. W., *Harun'l Rashid and Charles the Great*, 1931

Bullough, D. A., *Age of Charlemagne*, 1965

Clapham, J. H. and Power, Eileen, *The Agrarian Life of the Middle Ages* (Cambridge Economic History, V, 1, 1941)

Duckett, Eleanor, *Alcuin, Friend of Charlemagne*, 1951

Dupuy, A., *Alcuin et l'Ecole de St Martin de Tours*, 1876

Early English Text Society, Vols 40, 41, 43, 50, *English Charlemagne Romances*, 1882–7

Einhard/Eginhard, *see* Grant, A. J.

Falkenstein, Ludwig, *Der 'Lateran' der Karolingischen Pfalz zu Aachen*, 1966

Fichtenau, Heinrich, *The Carolingian Empire*, trans. Peter Munz, 1957

Folz, Robert, *The Coronation of Charlemagne*, trans. J. E. Anderson, 1974

Gaskoin, C. J. B., *Alcuin*, 1904

Grant, A. J. (ed.), *Early Lives of Charlemagne* (including *The Life of Charlemagne* by Eginhard and *The Life of Charlemagne* by the Monk of St Gall), 1905

Gregorovius, Ferdinand, *History of the City of Rome in the Middle Ages*, trans. Annie Hamilton, Vols I and II, 1909–11

Gregory of Tours, *History of the Franks*, trans. O. M. Dalton, 1927

Halphen, Louis, *Charlemagne et l'Empire Carolingien*, 1947

Haussig, H. W., *A History of Byzantine Civilization*, trans. J. M. Hussey, 1966

Heer, Friedrich, *The Holy Roman Empire*, trans. Janet Sonderheimer, 1967

——*Charlemagne and His World*, 1975

Hodgkin, Thomas, *Italy and Her Invaders*. Vol. VII: *The Frankish Invasions*, 1899; Vol. VIII: *The Frankish Empire*, 1899

Howell, Wilbur Samuel, *The Rhetoric of Alcuin and Charlemagne*, 1941

Hubert, J. and others, *Carolingian Art*, 1970

Ker, W. P., *The Dark Ages*, 1904

Laistner, M. L. W., *Thought and Letters in Western Europe AD 500 to 900*, 1931

Lasko, Peter, *The Kingdom of the Franks: North-West Europe before Charlemagne*, 1971

Llewellyn, Peter, *Rome in the Dark Ages*, 1970

Mullinger, J. B., *The Schools of Charles the Great*, 1887

Munz, Peter, *Frederick Barbarossa*, 1969

Oman, Charles, *A History of the Art of War in the Middle Ages*, 1921

Paris, Gaston, *Histoire poétique de Charlemagne*, 1865

Pseudo Turpin, The, edited from Bibliothèque Nationale, Fonds MS 17656 by H. M. Smyser, 1937

Sawyer, P. H. and Wood, I. N., *Kings, Kingdoms and Consent in Early Medieval Kingship*, 1977

Song of Roland, The, trans. into English verse by Arthur S. Way, 1913

Taylor, Henry Osborn, *The Medieval Mind*, 1911

Waddell, Helen (trans.), *Medieval Latin Lyrics*, 1933

—— *The Wandering Scholars*, 1954

Wallace-Hadrill, J. M., *The Long-haired Kings*, 1962

Wallach, L., *Alcuin and Charlemagne*, 1959

White, Lyn, *Medieval Technology and Social Change*, 1963

Index